AF538965

Empowerment of Women : New Dimensions

Empowerment of Women : New Dimensions

Edited by
P. Kumar

GLOBAL PUBLICATIONS
NEW DELHI-110 002 (INDIA)

GLOBAL PUBLICATIONS
4378/4B, G-4 JMD House
Murari Lal Street, Ansari Road
Daryaganj, New Delhi - 110 002
Phone : 23278062 (Off.)
e-mail : omega_publications@yahoo.com

Head Office :
79/23, Laxmi Garden
Near Satya Jyoti School,
Gurgaon (Haryana)
Mob : 9213562438

Empowerment of Women : New Dimensions

First Published : 2011

ISBN : 978–93–80833–45–3

PRINTED IN INDIA

Published by Ishwari Prasad Garg for Global Publications, New Delhi-110 002 and Printed at Suman Printers, Delhi

Preface

The change in the status of women in India is a slow, steady and continuing process. It began a century and half ago when Rammohan Roy and his successors and followers focussed attention on the social evils which victimised women and thereby hampered progress. The founding of the Brahmo Samaj in 1828 started the movement for the emancipation of Indian women from the clutches of ignorance and evil social customs. Two developmental trends run through the movement for reform and change, which are interesting. The reform movement led by the Brahmo Samaj and continued by a host of others wanted to eliminate evils, which not only hampered progress but also enslaved women to harsh customs.

It was a humanitarian and rational movement and led to the abolition of suttee and the validation of widow remarriage by legislation. The initiative came from the people and it was supported by enlightened administrators like Lord William Bentinick who responded to the call for action promptly. The revivalist group like the Arya Samaj also initiated reform and encouraged girl's education. But they found their raison d'etre in the ancient past when women were free and not bound down by the existing evils, and these later were regarded as a violation of the true traditions of India. The efforts of these two groups were supplemented by the attempts of the foreign Christian missionaries to open schools for girls. All these agencies played a significant role in changing the status of women in India.

The major topics dealt in this book are : *Hindu Ideology and Women; Woman of Ancient Meghaduta; Developmental Issues; Entrepreneurship Approach; Theory of Women Development; Social Causation of Love; Women Welfare Policies; Humanists and Traditinalists; Technical Development Scenerio; Psychological Gender Differences; Ordination of Women; Women Status in Society;* etc.

No doubt, these will serve the purpose of trainees and trainers, professionals and policy planners in the field. Since the sources of information are all secondary, we express our gratitude to the scholars whose works are cited or substantially made use of. We are thankful to all those who rendered ready help and cooperation while working on this project.

We express our gratitude to various scholars, teachers and friends for their assistance and guidance. Finally, we thank our publishers for bringing out this book in very limited time.

P. Kumar

Contents

1

Hindu Ideology and Women

The concept of the female in Hinduism presents an important duality: on the one hand, the woman is fertile, benevolent—the bestower; on the other, she is aggressive, malevolent—the destroyer. A popular statement characterizes the goddess in all her manifestations thus: 'in times of prosperity she indeed is Lakshmi, who bestows prosperity in the homes of men; and in times of misfortune, she herself becomes the goddess of misfortune and brings about ruin'. In a similar vein, Brenda Bech discusses the name of the South Indian goddess, Mariyamman, noted for her dual character using Sanskrit and Tamil etymologies, mari means death or rain while the folk etymology has mari meaning 'to change', while amman means 'lady' or 'mother', so that the goddess is in fact recognized as the 'changing lady'—a clear acknowledgement of her dual character. Both goddesses and women for there is no differentiation of super-human and human in Hindu belief reflect these characteristics of the female as both benevolent, fertile bestower and malevolent, aggressive destroyer.

Two facets of femaleness relate to this duality, and perhaps provide a cultural logic for it. The female is first of all sakti (energy power), the energizing principle of the universe. The female is also prakriti (Nature)—the un-differentiated Matter of the universe. I shall examine each of these in turn, elaborating their role in illuminating the dual character of the Hindu female.

In Hindu cosmology, the universal substratum from which all being arises is known as brahman: 'Invisible, inactive, beyond grasp, without qualifications, inconceivable, indescribable... ever aloof from manifestation' (Mandukya Upanishad quoted by Danielou, 1964). From this unmanifest substance, beings are made manifest through the tension created by the opposition of cohesion (Visnu) and disintegration (Siva). This tension defines sakti—the manifesting power, the creative principle. The Hindu notion of divinity rests upon that of sakti (power); Danielou, 1964): greater power is what distinguishes gods from men. So, sakti underlies both creation and divinity; and sakti is female. Therefore, all creation and all power in the Hindu world is based on femaleness—there would be no being without energy/power.

Although without the female there would be no energy in the universe, in fact all beings contain their share of sakti, their share of power and energy, with which they are endowed by birth along with their defining qualities (guna) and actions (kanna). Furthermore, the sakti that is part of an individual at birth can be increased or decreased through later actions. For example, a woman by being a true and devoted wife (pativrat, literally 'one who fasts for her husband'), increases her sakti. Various austerities, particularly sexual abstinence, also increase a person's sakti. But even though both men and women have sakti as a personal attribute, the woman embodies sakti, the original energy of the universe.

A common metaphor is that woman is the field or earth into which man puts his seed. By the sacred tradition the woman is declared to be the soil, the man is declared to be the seed; the production of all corporeal beings (takes place) through the union of the soil with the seed's. The image of field or earth also symbolizes a second facet of femaleness: woman is prakriti (Nature). Nature is the active female counterpart of the Cosmic Person, purusa, the inactive for male aspect. Moreover, Nature is Matter; the Cosmic Person is Spirit. But whereas prakriti represents the undiffer-entiated matter of Nature, purusa provides the Spirit, which is a structured code. Thus, purusa (Cosmic Person) is code (differentiated Spirit), as opposed to prakriti, which is Nature (undifferentiated Matter). The union of Spirit and Matter, code and noncode, inactive and active, leads to the creation of the world with all of its differentiated life forms. No life exists without both Matter and Spirit; prakriti and purusa are in all beings. The relationship can be represented diagrammatically (Fig. 1).

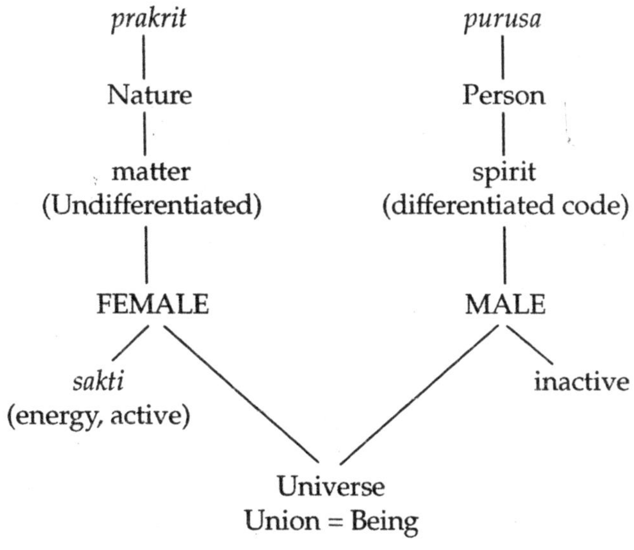

Fig. 1

The unity of purusa-prakriti underlies the beliefs regarding biological conception. Here we find that the male contributes the hard substances: the bones, nerves and structuring elements of a child. The woman contributes the soft substances: the flesh, skin, blood, and unstructured parts of a child. Whichever partner dominated at the time or conception, determines the sex of the child. The Laws of

Manu speak on this point: 'On comparing the seed and the receptacle, the seed is declared to be more important: for, the offspring of all created beings is marked by the charateristics of the seed' (Buhler, 1964). The hard substance (seed) is structure (culture?) as opposed to the soft substance which is non-structure (Nature?). Women, then, are automatically more Nature than men. The nature and nonstructure in the dominates over codes Spirit and structure.

Uniting these two facets of femaleness, women are both energy/power and Nature; and nature is uncultured. In fact, the Aryan vernacular languages of ancient India are called Prakrit ('Uncultured' or 'Natural'), as opposed to the priestly religious langauge Sanskrit (literally, 'Cultured'). Uncultured Power is dangerous. The equation, Woman = Power = Nature = Danger, represents the essence of femaleness as it underlies Hindu religious belief and action about women. The equation summaarizes a conception of the world order that explains the woman/goddess as the malevolent, aggressive destroyer.

As we saw above, however, the Hindu view of woman is not only one of danger—woman is also the benevolent, fertile bestower. Fertility is easily comprehended, for woman is the necessary receptor of man's seed: she, like the closely conjoined images of cow and earth, represents growth, prosperity and fertility. Benevolence and goodness, however, are more complex. One possible explanation of female benevolence is that woman is capricious, therefore she sometiems uses her Uncultured Power for human benefit. Recent studies have provided a sharper insight; 'good females—goddess or human—are controlled by males; that is, Culture controls Nature'.

A popular myth presents the male controlling dangerous female Power, thus rendering that Power positive and benevolent. Kali, the Black One, one of the many wives of Siva, was sent by the gods to oppose a demon and his army when the gods could not control him themselves. Kali defeated the demons. Delighted with her victory she performed a savage killing dance so furiously that the earth trembled beneath her weight and its destruction appeared imminent. The gods, frightened and unable to stop her, sent Siva to induce her to desist. Entranced in her bloody rampage and not noticing him, Kali continued killing and dancing. So Siva lay down at her feet. When eventually Kali was about to step on hi, she realized that it was her husband upon whom she was placing her feet—an inexcusable act for the Hindu wife. She stopped her rampage and the earth was saved—because her husband had regained control over her.

The benevolent goddesses in the Hindu pantheon are those ho are properly married and who have transferred control of their sexuality (Power/Nature) to their husbands. Symbolically, a woman is 'a part' of her husband his 'half-body'. Rules for proper conduct mandate that she transfer her powers, as they accumulate, to her husband for his use. Mythology is replete with stories of the properly chaste wife who aIds her husband in winning his battle by virtue of her proper behaviour and ensuing transfer of power (it is probable that females, in the last analysis, win all battles). In the following two myths of gods' triumph depends on the control of female power.

> There was once a continuous twelve-year war between the gods and the de!Jlons. The gods were losing badly and Indra felt that there was no way except for losing his life. At this time, Indrani said to her husband: 'Don't be afraid. I am a faithful wife. I will tell you one way by which you can win and protect yourself.' After saying this much, Indrani bound the *rakhi* (a bracelet, literally 'protection') on the wrist of her husband. After she bound the *rakhi*, Indra again went to war and defeated all the demons.

> There was a demon named Jalandhar. He had a very beautiful and faithful wife named Branda. Because of the power accruing to him from the faithfulness of his wife, the demon conquered the whole world. The gods were in trouble and arrived at this solution: changing a dead body into the shape of Jalandhar, Visnu threw it into the courtyard of Branda's family. Then Visnu gave life to the body and, in this way, Branda embraced another man and marred her faithfulness. Owing to her loss of faithfulness, Jalandhar's power was weakened and Visnu killed him in a big war.

According to Hindu cosmology, if a female controls her own sexuality, she is changeable; she represents both death and fertility; she is both malevolent and benevolent. It however, she loses control of her sexuality (Power/Nature) by transferring it to a man, she is portrayed as consistently benevolent. There are two images, then, of the woman in Hinduism, linked by the basic conceptions of the nature of femaleness: the fact that the female is both *sakti* (Power/ Energy), and *prakriti* (Nature).

As Power and nature, and controlling her own sexuality, the female is potentially destructive and malevolent:

> Kali (the Black One): Bearing the strange skull topped staft decorated with a garland of skulls, clad in a tiger's skin, very appalling owing to her emaciated flesh, with gaping mouth, fearful with her tongue lolling out, having deep-sunk reddish eyes and filling the regions of the sky with her roars... (Jagdisvarananda, 1953), quoted in Babb, 1970.

With the control of her sexuality transferred to men, the female is fertile and benevolent:

> *Lakshmi* (the Goddess of Fortune): "She who springs forth from the body of all the gods has a thousand

indeed countless, arms, although her images are shown with out eighteen. Her face is white, made from the light streaming from the lord of sleep (Siva), her arms made of the substance of Visnu are deep blue: her round breasts made of soma, the sacrificial ambrosia, are white ... She wears a gaily coloured lower garment, brilliant garlands, and a veil.... He who worships the Transcendent Divinity of Fortune becomes the lord of all the worlds' (Karapatri, 'Sri Bhagavati Tattva', quoted in Danielou, 1964).

The Ideal Hindu Woman

Understanding the dual character of the Hindu female's essential nature (her *sakti* and *prakriti*), provides a backdrop for understanding the rules and role models for women in Hindu South Asia. A central theme of the norms and guidelines for proper female behaviour, especially in the male-dominated classical literature, is that men must control women and their power. But whether in classical texts or folk traditions, the dual character of the Hindu female emerges definitely, and is seen most clearly in the roles of wife (good, benevolent, dutifut controlled) and mother (fertile, but dangerous, uncontrolled).

I draw on a variety of materials to explicate these roles. Rules for proper conduct are explicitly laid down in Hindu law books, collectively known as the Dharmasastras (the Rules of Right Conduct). Mythology, written and oral, in Sanskrit and in the vernaculars, provides many examples of female behaviour and its consequences, thus setting up explict role models for the Hindu woman. Folklore yields yet other beliefs about female behaviour. Finally, social organisation and structure mesh with, allow for, and reinforce these beliefs about the proper conduct of women.

The dominant norms for the Hindu woman concern her role as wife. Classifical Hindu laws focus almost exclusively on this aspect of the woman. Role models and norms for mothers, daughters, sisters, etc., are less prominent and are more apt to appear in folklore and vernacular traditions. In addition, in most written traditions, the emphasis is on women's behaviour in relationship to men: wife/husband; mother/son; daughter/father; sister/brother. Role models for female behaviour concerning other females (mother/daughter; sister/sister) are almost nonexistent in any of the literature. In contrast, two female/female relationships-mother-in-law/daughter-in-law and husband's sister/wife—are common themes in folklore and oral traditions but not in the more authoritative religious literature. These two relationships are vital to the well-being of women, but of little concern to men. That they do not occur as important themes in the maleoriented and written literature of the Sanskrit tradition is not surprising. Rather, they surface in the popular oral traditions of women themselves. The male orientation in classifical literature is also apparent in differing depictions of the husband/wife and brother/sister relationships. With these factors in mind, let us examine norms for female behaviour in Hindu South Asia.

The basic rules for women's behaviour are expressed in the following passages from the Laws of Manu, written early in the Christian era. These passages stress the need to control women because of the evils of the female character. The first set is experted from a section dealing with the duties of women:

(i) By a young girl, by a young woman, or even by an aged one, nothing must be done independently, even in her own house.

(ii) In childhood a female must be subject to her father, in youth to her husband, when her lord is dead, to her sons; a woman must never be independent ...

(iii) Though destitute of virtue, or seeking pleasure (elsewhere), or devoid of good qualities, (yet) a husband must be constantly worshipped as a god by a faithful wife ...

(iv) By violating her duty towards her husband, a wife is disgraced in this world; (after death) she enters the womb of a jackal, and is tormented by diseases (the punishment) of her sin.

(v) She who controlling her thoughts, words, and deeds, never slights her lord, resides (after death) with her husband (in heaven), and is called a virtuous (wife).

The following set is excerpted from the section regarding the duties of wife and husband:

(i) Day and night, women must be kept in dependency by the males (of) their (families), and if they attach themselves to sensual enjoyment, they must be kept under one's control ...

(ii) Considering that the highest duty to all castes, even weak husbands (must) strive to guard their wives ....

(iii) Women do not care for beauty, nor is their attention fixed on age: (thinking) '(it is enough that) he is a man', they give themselves to the handsome and the ugly.

(iv) Through their passion for men, through their mutable temper, through their natural heartlessness, they become disloyal towards their husbands, however carefully they are guarded in this (world).

(v) Knowing their disposition, which the Lord of creatures laid in them at the creation, to be such, (every) man should most strenuously exert himself to guard them.

Thus, women, because of their evil inclinations and birth, are to be kept under the control of men at all stages of their lives. The ideal women are those who do not strive to break these bonds of control. Moreover, the salvation and happiness of women revolve around their virtue and chastity as daughters, wives and widows.

These themes are not relegated merely to laws in ancient Sanskrit texts. The continually reap per in later Sanskrit and vernacular writings as well as in oral traditions. One of the most popular religious texts in India is the Ramayana, found in Sanskrit and in most vernaculars. This text tells the story of Rama, an incarnation of Visnu, sent to earth to destroy the menacing demon Ravana as he was on the verge of upsetting the right moral order of the earth. In the Ramayana, Rama's wife Sita exemplifies the behaviour of the proper Hindu wife, devotedly following her husband into forest exile for fourteen years, and eventually, after being kidnapped for a time by the evil Ravana whom Rama finally destroys, proving her wifely virtue by placing herself on a lighted pyre. When she remains unscatched by the flames, the gods above pour flowers down upon her. In a happy ending her husband accepts her back into his household.

The story of Rama and Sita is well known to most Hindus and is enacted yearly, with greater or lesser splendour, in villages and cities all over India. Pictures of Sita following her husband to the forest, of Sita being kidnapped by Ravana, of Sita on the pyre, are found in a great many homes, on the walls of shops and even in government offices. Famous cinema stars portray Rama and Sita in gargantuan film epics. The message of the *Ramayana* is clear, and remarkably similar to that of the more esoteric and inaccessible lawbook written years before.

Sita is to most Hindu women the epitome of the proper wife. She represents the ideal towards which all should strive. Other wives in the Hindu tradition also provide popular role models. Women who have committed *sati* (burning themselves on their husbands' funeral pyres), are acclaimed as godesses and are honoured with shrines and rituals. The theme of the devoted wife also recurs in connection with calendrical rites. Throughout North India, women yearly worship the goddess Savitri. Her renown emanates from her extreme devotion to her husband, through which she saves him from the god of death. The story of Savitri is held up as a prime example of the lengths to which a wife should go in aiding her husband. The good wife saves her husband from death, follows him anywhere, proves her virtue, remains under his control and gives him her power.

These aspects of wifely behaviour and norms are also found in oral traditions, with one crucial addition: the wife's side for her husband and her dismay at his absence. The theme of love between husband and wife is minor in the classical written literature, whether Sanskrit or vernacular; rather, devotion and dutifulness dominate.

However, the traditions of women, those created and perpetuated by women alone, continuously reiterate the longing for a husband's return and their mutual love as these examples illustrate:

> One seer of wheat I will eat for one year, eat for one year,
>
> (But) I will not allow my husband to go. I will keep him before my eyes, (and) I will not allow my husband to go.
>
> I will not allow you to go for the whole night,
>
> O beautiful wife, I will not allow you to go for the whole night.

The above discussion emphasizes, as does the literature, the wife's regard for and duties to her husband, not his towards her, though this theme does emerge partially in the oral traditions. The textual traditions contain few injunctions for husbandly behaviour beyond stating that a man must marry to procure sons who are needed for his salvation. One passage from Manu is critical, however, stipulating that men should treat their women well or women will destroy them:

> Women must be honoured and adorned by their fathers, brothers, husbands, and brothers-in-law who desire (their own welfare) .... The houses on which female relations, not being duly honoured, pronounce a curse, perish completely, as if destroyed by magic. Hence, men who seek (their own) welfare, should always honour women on holidays and festivals with (gifts of) ornaments, clothes and (dainty) food.

Thus, women ideally have some recourse when illtreated—using their power, they can destroy. But, as we saw above, the best of wives (Sita) will worship their husbands even when abused.

The wifely role is pre-eminent in Hinduism. There are other roles but they are not generally considered normative patterns. Rather, they provide expectations for possible behaviour. The woman as mother is the most critical of the other female roles.

The norms for mothers are less explicit than those for wives. Whereas mythology and lawboooks provide endless examples of the good wife, there are no prime examples of the good mother. However, it is the goddesses as mothers rather than as wives who are village guardians, who are worshipped regularly for their protection and aid, and who are feared. A common name for many goddesses is 'Mother'; a goddess is never called 'Wife'. The wifely role is one of subordination, of devotion in any circumstances, of dutifulness. It is the mother who gives, who must be obeyed, who loves, and who sometimes rejects. Although there are no popular and well-known role models of the mother treating her children well, the mother as a giving, loving individual, although sometimes cruel and rejecting, is present at a sub-conscious but critical level in Hindu thought.

It is the mother, transformed into the mother goddess whose devotees are her 'children', who is both the bestower and destroyer. Mothers and mother goddesses represent clearly the dual character of Hindu females. They can give and take away, whether from children or devotees. As such, the mother role is not acclaimed as proper or ideal behaviour; rather, her danger is accepted because she is necessary. The mother, also, more than the wife, represents the polluting aspects of the Hindu female as well as representing the purifying milk. In her very biology—a biology necessary for motherhood but not for wifehood—the mother is a contradictiony. Last, mothers and the mother goddesses are in control of their sexuality; wives are not. Again, we find the opposition of Lakshmi, the wife and Kali, the mother.

Hinduism also includes women who are totally malevolent, who never change from an evil maliciousness. These figures, primarily ghosts of women who died in childbirth or in other inauspicious ways, but also witches, are the antithesis of the wife. Beck has suggested that they themselves have lost control of their sexuality and cannot channel their actions towards any positive end (Beck, 1971). If this interpretation is correct, we obtain the following model of women's roles in Hinduism :

Wife	*Mother*	*Ghost*
Culture *via* male control	Nature but in self control	Nature but out of control
Good	Good/Bad	Bad
Subordinated	Worshipped	Appeased

Expectations for other female behaviour can be summarized briefly. The daughter obeys her father and the sister is under the protection of her brother (and fervently desires his protection as he is her primary link with her natal home, especially in North India). The husband's mother is threatening and the husband's sister is an unreliable alloy in the husband's home. The expectations for these latter three come mostly from women's oral traditions and reflect women's concern for their day-to-welfare.

Norms for women in Hinduism derive for two separate, though related, sources. First, the male-dominated literature prescribes control and subordination of the woman. Second, folki and oral traditions, often created and propagated by women, yield norms that are concerned with women's welfare and emphasize the behaviour of crucial male kin (the husband as lover, the brother as protector, the son as security) as well as female kin (the mother-in-law, the husband's sister). In both these realms we find the mother-not merely as the bearer of children, but also as the mother of the devotee given extreme importance. The wife is the woman under male control; the mother is the woman in control of herself and her 'children'. These two figures dominate Hindu thought about women.

Women in Hindu Religious Practice

Women are active religious practitioners, but they have little religious authority-legitimate, actually sanctioned religious power-which is limited to a small group of men. Paradoxically, however, at the popular level, women are prominent religious participants, both as specialists and non-specialists.

To comprehend the place of women in Hindu religious practice, a brief summary of Hindu social organisation is necessary. As is well known, India is a society based on hierarchies, including not only that of caste but also that of kinship and others. The many thousands of castes in India are grouped into five broader social classes: the four varna that originated in ancient times (Brahman, priest; Ksatriya, warrior; vaisya, tradesman' Sudra, worker) and the untouchable One's membership (via a specific caste) in a particular verna is of little importance most of the time. However, religious activity is sometimes based on varna membership. Specifically only male members of the first three varna have access to the sacred texts of the Vedas, the earliest and most authoritative of the Hindu scriptures. Women, Sudras and Untouchables are not allowed to know, or sometimes even to hear, the Vedas. Further restrictions dictate that only Brahman men are to use the Vedas in approaching the gods, *i.e.*, in rituals. Thus, men of the top three varnas are 'twice born' (*i.e.*, can wear the sacred thread after a ritual second birth and can know the scriptures). And only Brahman men can perform Vedic rituals. Women, therefore, are no worse off than a great many men in terms of access to the principal authoritative sources of religious power.

Women's access to the Vedas and other authoritative texts apparently underwent revision sometime around 600 BC Previously, women had been able to undertake fasts for themselves, to hear and learn the Vedas, etc. By the time of Manu, women were no longer allowed to hear the Vedas or to be major participants in rituals. During this time, perceptions of women as dangerous were developing among the Aryan population. Most probably, these redefinitions of the nature of femaleness affected women's positions in ritual activities.

Fortunately, Hindu religious activity is not based solely on Vedic rituals. The dominant form of ritual activity today is that of bhakti, or devotion to a deity. Stemming from the Bhagavad Gita and gaining strength from an anti-Brahman, anti-Vedic movement which started in about AD 700, bhakti (devotion) and associated ritual forms do not require the services of a priest to approach one's chosen deity. One result is that women have direct access to the gods, and thus to salvation. Today, puja (devotional ritual) is the principal form of ritual activity in India. Vedic rituals are reserved for life-cycle rites and other male-dominated occasions, such as the opening of a new temple.

Although women may approach the deities directly through bhakti rituals, men continue to be recognized as legitimate religious specialists. Males are temple priests; males conduct life-cycle rites; males are the leaders of most public rituals. To understand the female as religious specialist, we must first understand the varying roles of male specialists. Table 1 summarizes the discussion of Hindu religious specialists and their social characteristics.

Table 1

Religious Specialization in Hinduism

Specialist	*Male*	*Female*	*Textually Sanctioned*
Priest:			
Pandit	x (B)	(wife)	x (not wife)
Purohit	x (B)	—	x
Pujari	x	—	—
Actor as God	x (B)	—	?
Shaman	x	x	—
Exorcist	x	—	—
Client in jajmani system	x	(wife)	—
Yogi/Sadhu	x	seldom	x
Personality cult-leader	x	x	—
Devadasi	—	x	x (South India only)

Explnation: x (B) means, must be Brahman.
(wife) indicates 'plays role by virtue of wifehood'.

The best-known Indian religious specialists are the priests-the care-takers of temples and the family priests who conduct life-cycle rites. Priests are called by various terms: in North India, two (pandit, purohit) refer only to Brahmans; the third (pujari) often refers to a lower-caste priest/caretaker of a temple. Normally, pandits are temple priest. Purohits-family priests-serve their patrons whenever called, sometiems daily, sometimes only for major life-cycle rites. Both must be Brahman males. Pujaris are often lower-caste males who function as priests at the temples of local die ties who lack scriptural sanction. In addition, the wives of Brahman priests often act as specialists for life-cycle rites or on other ritual occasions. Generally, they are experts in oral tradition, knowing the sons or stories associated with a particular rite or the unwritten rules for women's correct ritual behaviour. Their husband's role has scriptural sanction; theirs does not.

A related specialist, often also called pandit, is the astrologer. He is the expert who provides essential information and advice at the time of marriages and births and fixes auspicious dates for journeys and other understakings. The astrologer is also a Brahman male.

Brahman men dominate still other forms of public ritual. For example, various forms of religious folk operas and plays are found throughout India: in these, the actors portraying a deity are all male—whether the deity by male or female. In fact, the actor as the deity, is worshipped as a manifestation of the diety, and because worship of the actor as diety is required, the actor must usually be a Brahman.

Less legitimate participants in public rituals, are more likely to be non-Brahman males. Possession rituals, which are not textually sanctioned, appear to be male-dooinated; many exorcists and shamans are non-Brahman. Occasionally, a shaman will be female. Shamans and exorcists are religious power figures who lack textual sanction; their power comes from oral traditions and societal recognition. As such, they provide access to religious power for those normally forbidden such access; non-Brahman males and all females.

Other rituals specialists must also be considered, particularly those who are specialists by virtue of their position in the jajrnani system, a system of inherited parton-client ties found throughout most of south Asia. Several of the clients (workers who provide services in return for payment) have primarily ritual connections with their patrons. One such client is the barber and his wife, who are necessary figures in most life-cycle rites. In addition to providing services (hair cutting, bathing the new infant, bathing the groom, etc.), they instruct and guide their patrons through the proper rituals forms. The midwife is another such ritual guide. None of these have textual rituals forms. The midwife is another such ritual guide. None of these have textual sanction for their roles as religious specialists *per se*, and the instruction they provide is usually based on local traditions.

Other specialists are the sadhus and yogis many play no vital role in Hindu religious practice beyond that of a 'presence', while others are important lecturers and teachers. Occasionally, a woman will be a yogini. Both male and female yogis are sanctioned by various textual traditions. However, the yogi is considered to be outside the case system and removed from family ties; he/she is outside society and its structures. All members of society can thus opt for being non-members. Thes non-members lacking caste and sexual distinctions, are sanctioned by the classical texts.

Popular, non-classical religious specialists in hinduism can be either male or female—the 'personality cult' leader such as Guru Maharajji or The Mother. Women are less often the figureheads of such movements than men; nevertheless, female leaders do recur regularly and are sanctioned by society if not by textual tradition.

Traditionally, only one religious specialist so far as I know was always female—the devadasi (votary of God). Found in South India, the devadasis were nominally married to the god of the temple but allowed mates. Their offspring were legitimate: the girls were often, in turn, dedicated to the temple; the boys might become professional musicians. The devadasi was always felt to be distinct from the 'dancer'; her role was definitely religious. Outlawed by the British, the institution of the Devadasi fell into disrepute, although its traditions of dance still exist with some descendants and as 'dance' are having a revival in both East and West. Traditionally, the devadasi was a religious specialist who had textual sanction only in South India.

These facets of religious specialization are summarized in Table 1. Textually recognized specialists are, with one exception, Brahman men. Women and non-Brahman men are religious specialists, but are only rarely sanctioned by authoritative traditions. Thus, women, like low caste men, have religious power in Hinduism, but non-legitimate, non-authoritative power. Clearly, then, Hindu women have considerable religious involvement. Women as non-specialists are 'invisible religious practitioners, since most of their observances are performed non-publicly (in the home or 'domestic' sphere) and their role is not textually sanctioned; indeed the Laws of Manu forbid a woman to fast or participate in rituals without her husband. Yet, if we look at folk religious practices rather than the Hinduism of the texts, women, along with low caste men, are the primary actors.

Women alone perform a large number of the yearly calendrical rituals in both rural and urban India and are essential to most others. In Karimpur, a village in North India, women are the instigators and prime participants in twenty-one of the thirty-three annual rites Wadley. Women also dominate nine of the twenty-one annual rites in the village Mohana near Lucknow and are apparently the sole participants in nine of the twenty two festivals in the annual cycle of Rampur, a village north of Delhi. The exact 'great tradition' status of the rites of women—which are all based on puja (devotional ritual) rather than on Vedic fire sacrifices—has yet to be determined. However, most festivals which can be easily identified as having no 'great tradition' ties are women's festivals. I suspect that if the rituals of women do have textual sanction, their performance varies widely and reflects manifold local differences. Women's participation in life-cycle rites is definitely part of the 'little tradition'. Women surround these rituals, in which they are mere accessories, with local folk practices. During actual ceremonial time, women's practices clearly dominate: taking a marriage or a birth ceremony as a whole, men's rites take very little time, although the men's rites are a crucial subsidiary (to women).

Much of India is a society with strict sexual segregation. Purdah is generally associated with sexual division of labour and existence in separate worlds. As a corollary, women's concerns are very different from those of men. This separation is found also in religion: the many folk practices of women focus on the prosperity and well—being of the family. Women's rites seek the protection and well being of crucial kinsmen (especially husband, brother and son), the general prosperity and health of family members, and 'good' husbands. This emphasis is found in both calendrical and life-cycle rits. Men's rites do not seek 'good' wives or ones who will have a long life; rather, they are concerned with a good wheat crop, ridding the village of disease, etc. It is not surprising to find this religious division of labour in the sexually-segregated purdah society of traditional India.

Women's religious practices are influenced in part by conceptions of the female: her danger provides a justification for her not being an active participant in the most authoritative rites; yet within the domestic sphere women are vital religious practitioners who have developed a subsidiary religious realm of largely folk, or local, non-textual traditions. The sexual segregation of Hindu society also articulates with the role that religion plays in drawing women together: female solidarity is continuously reinforced through religious practices. Moreover, many women's rites relate to their dual roles as wives and mothers but females, such as the mother goddesses, who protect most villages in India are, nevertheless, frequent objects of worship by both men and women.

●●

2

Woman of Ancient Meghaduta

Much as the modern critic endeavours to pick his way through the vast domain of Sanskrit literature for a peep at the actual conditions of life and thought of the people who produced it, he is confronted with types in the place of individuals, opinions for statement of facts, theories instead of description of practices. The great masters of Indian art aimed at the creation of ideals, which would not be bound by the limitations of particular ages and peoples, but would be true for all time and all climes. There must be a Homeric touch in the commonest of themes, a shadow of the divine over the humblest of heroes. This inevitable idealistic outlook of the greatest Indians of antiquity affects their treatment of even such admittedly secular departments of human inquiry as politics or military science. The astute Kautilya sits down to write a political manual for the guidance of his sovereign or his officials; he leaves for his posterity a masterly treatise setting forth his own ideals of an autocratic, socialistic state, which existed nowhere in his time and was never approximated to at any time in India.

The truth of the foregoing proposition can be established by many examples; but it is not implied that we never meet a familiar face in the dreamland of our classical inheritance. The greatest of the Indian poets, indeed, gives us the best information on many a point about which our curiosity is roused. If Kalidasa excels his compeers in the loftiness of his fancy and the nobility of his ideals, he is also 'truest to the kindred points of heaven and home.' Indian poetry had not yet had the burden of symbols, conventions and conceits, which clogged its weary steps in a later age; and the heroes and heroines of Kalidasa's poetry are real men and women and not nayakas and nayikas for whom literary convention has dictated rigid rules of speech and action in a number of prescribed moods and situations. Again, if in the human he perceived the divine, his divine is also what is best in the human.

If Kalidasa is thus a great poet of humanity, he is also a child of the age in which he lived. There are good reasons for believing that in his works generally and in the Meghaduta in particular he has reflected in a great measure the habit, tastes and opinions of his contemporaries in the words and actions of his heroes and heroines. Whether the Meghaduta was composed in his early youth or it is the "In Memoriam" of a widower written in his ripe old age, it unquestionably is the composition of a versatile observer, who has been a 'part' of many lands besides his own. The world of the Meghaduta is very much the same as that of the golden age of the Imperial Guptas. It is a vivid sketch of the life of a people who were in the enjoyment of such peace, prosperity and the amenities of a highly developed, artificial civilisation as, we know, were witnessed in India during the rule of the great Guptas, when, it is believed, the great poet lived. The bustling, vigorous life of the city of Ujjayini as recorded in the Meghaduta undoubtedly represents its actual condition after Candragupta II's conquest of Guzerat, which made it the great emporium for western trade.

A very important role in this lyrical masterpiece of India is played by the women. As a matter of fact, the very charm of the poem lies mainly in its description of the fair objects of nature and the fair sex. In the eye of the poet, indeed, there was not a difference of kind but only of form between woman and nature. He certainly perceived one great consciousness pervading both. It was part of his creed to think that nature was sentient and that it participated in the joys and sorrows of man. Even while describing beauty of form, Kalidasa frequently calls in nature to bring out his conception of womanly grace and dignity, and vice versa. If for the dark iris and white ball of a full black eye, he finds no fitter object of comparison than a large black bee sitting right on the centre of the cup of the white Kunda flower, if for the lovely heroine rendered pale and wan on account of separation from her beloved, his ready simile is the moon kerchieft in a dark, comely cloud, or the lotus blighted by winter or again the Sthala-kamalini flower on a cloudy day when it is neither open nor shut, he similarly invokes the comely grace of the woman's body and her various moods in order to describe nature. He compares the Narmada lying in a thin stream at the foot of the Vindhya hill to the woman's lovely locks tied in a single braid, the Vertravati with her dancing waves to the face of a woman broken into a frown, the tumultuous Nirvindhya river with rows of birds flying aloft to the girdlestring which graces a lady's waist, and the water of the reededged Gambhira to a blue garment slipping down and being held up by the hand.

A striking point about Kalidasa's treatment of women in the Meghaduta is that he has always placed them in a natural setting, Natural scenery, likewise, is generally described with some tair one as its enjoyer. Thus, the Ramagiri groves are mentioned along with the fact that the daughter of Janaka loved to bathe in its limpid lakes; the Nicaih hills are the haunts of young courtesans; lovely flower-girls are busy culling flowers in gardens adjacent to swift-flowing rivulets. In fact, so great was the harmony between woman and nature that the one is almost the other in his poetry. The exquisite lines in which the Yaksa sums up his message to his beloved wife gives us the clue to Kalidasa's creed of nature (Meghaduta, II, 45):

Syamasv angam cakitaharinipreksane drstipatam

Vaktracchayam sasini sikhinam barhabharesu kesån

Utapasyami pratanusu nadivicisu bhruvilasan

Hantaikasmin kvacid api na te candi sadrsyam asti

I shall now proceed to an examination of the types of woman described in the Meghaduta. A few preliminary observations on the attitude which Kalidasa seems to take towards woman in this poem are, however, necessary. In the first place, it rather forces itself on our attention that the principal, if not the only, objects of interest for Kalidasa are the young women alone and that he may be said to have neglected altogether girls of a tender age. Again, it is rather strange that what seems to interest him in the character of these women is their sensuousness and passionateness; he represents youth as a disquieting, distracting element, which finds its expression and satisfaction in the pleasures of the senses. We fail to know from Kalidasa what part our ladies played in the serious concerns of life. When the great poet introduces us to a young housewife, we find her busy at her toilet, or, we are informed, she is still on her bed, the morning breeze which should have called her to her household duties making her sleep all the more soundly. Another very striking thing in the Meghaduta is the prominence given to courtesans of various classes. It would be no exaggeration, in fact, to say that an unblushing, candid and realistic picture of the charms of these women is a special theme of this poem.

Mr. Havell has observed that Indian art takes cognisance of women primarily as matrons and not as objects of physical beauty. It is spiritual beauty, says he, that Indian art insists upon. One would wish that these observations, which are true of Indian art as a whole, were also true of this great artistic production of Kalidasa as well. But, if they are not applicable in this case, we need not deplore the fact or condemn the poet. To a great extent Kalidasa was bound down by the choice of his subject. The mental state of his hero, destined to live away from his beloved the wretched life of an exile, necessarily colours his whole outlook upon life. And I have already stated that Kalidasa's art is never so idealistic that it leaves actualities behind or that it fails to reflect real human elements or passions. It seems to me that the description of women in the Meghaduta is a substantially accurate representation of their actual condition in the age in which he lived, and that there are omissions but not mistakes. He does not, it is true, touch on every possible side of woman's activity in his time-the subject-matter does not allow it-but he describes a variety of types, and his descriptions are vivid and faithful.

The types of women described or noticed in this poem are:

1. The women of Non-Aryan primitive races of India (vanacaravadhu). They live in the forest to the south of the Narmada. The poet throws out a dark hint at their character by the expression 'bhuktakunje'.

2. The women of the Siddhas (siddhangana). According to Mallinatha the Siddhas were a class of devas (holy men). They lived with their wives on hill-tops and worshipped the god Siva for attaining heaven after death. They led simple and abstemious lives and played upon the lute, perhaps as a devotional exercise. The Siddha wives were so simple-minded that when during the rains the clouds were driven by wind, they would wonder with faces upturned whether it was the crest of the hill blown away by the storm.

3. The village maiden (janapadavadhu). Kalidasa devotes only one stanza to a description of the most common type of the women-folk of India, who are numerically the strongest and form really the backbone of the nation, *viz.*, the peasant women. We meet the peasant girl on the field where the day's task has just been finished and the air is thick with the aroma of the freshly tilled soil. Kalidasa praises the pleasant, affectionate look of her eyes, full of simplicity and purity of heart and draws a comparison with the looks of the eyes of the city damsel.

4. Wives whose husbands are travelling in foreign lands (pathikavanita or virahini). In the days of Kalidasa such women were numerous enough, both in towns and villages, to form a class by themselves. Travelling, both for pleasure and business, was, it seems, a usual thing in those days of brisk trade and stirring events. The customs of society in early times required that the wife should put on a sign of mourning for her absent lord: she should neither dress herself gaily, nor toilet her hair, which should hang in a single braid over her back to signify her sorrow and anxiety for her husband. It was certainly in the fitness of things in a Hindu home with our notions of chastity that the wife should behave so in the absence of her husband, and in many cases undoubtedly his neglect of proper toileting was a genuine expression of the feelings of the girl. But there is not doubt that it gradually became a mere pose, a mere affection; and there were certainly some frisky girls who had their eye on heightening their charms and improving their looks by an 'agreeable negligence.' In a class of Sanskrit literature, therefore, we find the virahini or pathikavanita as a regular conventional nayika, whom poets represent as they like.

The Meghaduta is full of references to the virahint, and, because the wife of the Yaksa is in the same predicament, the poet approaches the subject with the tender respect that the condition of the woman demands. As the events described in the Meghaduta happen in the rainy season, when the men return from foreign lands, the poet describes the anxious wives as getting consolation at the sight of the first cloud of the month of Asadha.

5. Unmarried girls (kanya). The poet describes the girls of his dream-city of Alaka as playing the 'Guptamani' game under the shade of the Mandara trees, being refreshed by the breeze, cooled by contact with the water of the divine Mandakini river. These would-be brides of the gods resemble their human sisters so much that we would not be wrong if we take them as representing the average Hindu girl of a good family of the poet's time.

6. The flower-girls (puspalavi). As flowers were in great demand in cities, gardens in the suburbs where the jasmine plants naturally grew were frequented by young flower-girls busy plucking the flowers. The poet describes them as hard at their work, perspiring freely, their cheeks flushed and their floral ear-pendants withered and drooping. If they are girls of tender age, they are, I think, the only ones noticed in this poem, with possibly one exception which I will presently mention.

7. The city damsels (paurangana). The poet describes the damsels of the great cities of Ujjayini and Dasapura (modern Mandasor), as well as those of his dream-city of Alaka and brings into sharp relief their highly artificial, luxurious ways of life. The prominent objects of interest in Ujjayini, according to the poet, are the women; and he says that those who have not looked at their beautiful eyes are as good as blind. The women of Dasapura are adept in sending speechless messages through their eyes, and when they lift the dark lashes of their charming eyes, it seems that black-bees are chasing the white Kunda flowers. The poet describes the lalita-vanita (fair women) of Ujjayini as living in gorgeous palaces, scented with flowers and dyed red with lac-marks left by their feet.

8. The courtesans. The same reasons which gave rise to the class of the hetaiera in Athens were also responsible for the growth of the free women in the cities of ancient India. They played an important part in the public and private life of our country, and undoubtedly contained many women of the type of Theodote and Aspasia, Our poet seems to have collected a good deal of information about them and does not hesitate to describe them as objects of beauty. He notices three classes of these women, which are as follows:

(i) ***Panyastri.*** The expression is clear enough to need any explanation.

(ii) ***Vesya.*** These are the same as the Devadasis of modern Hindu temples. We find them dancing before the god Mahakala at Ujjain, their girdles jingling beautifully at the rhythmic movement of their feet and their hands wearied with waving the jewelled camara. But the poet does not fail to notice the long side-glances thrown by the play of their dark eye-lashes, resembling bees in flight, at young visitors of the temple.

(iii) ***Abhisarika.*** They would go out to meet their lovers under cover of a dark night in the trysts. They seem to have been married women or in any case not free to carryon their love affairs, as the poet says that they were extremely timid. These women sometimes came from rich families; for we learn that while passing through the streets at night they would drop, through trepidation, some of their golden ear-rings, pearl necklaces, etc.

The foregoing survey of the various types of women described in the Meghaduta prepares us for our next object of inquiry, *viz.*, the poet's ideal of a beautiful woman. Let us find out the features on which the poet lays stress in describing the various types of womanhood. That a chief element of woman's glory lay in dark and shining locks may be proved by the fact that the poet refers to it more than once and uses it as a simile. The ladies of Kalidasa's time used to dress their hair in various ways as they do now, and flowers as well as strings of pearls were used for the hair to heighten the beauty of the face. Dark eye-lashes resembling a line of bees are described more than once by Kalidasa and the looks in the eyes more than the eyes themselves were to him the main objects of interest. He contrasts the gentle, affectionate looks of the village maids with the artful glances of the city damsels, and at Alaka, says he, cupid would do his work by the graceful play of the creeper-like eye-brows alone. The lips of a fair woman the poet usually compares to the ripe bimba fruit, and in one stanza the word bimbadhara is used almost as a synonym for a beautiful woman. It is rather surprising that the breast and the waist, which are such prominent objects of interest for Sanskrit poets, are never elaborately described in the Meghaduta: they generally come in as similes or in connection with the ornaments used for them. For the feet Kalidasa uses the lotus as a simile, and it seems that his ear is sooner captivated by the jingling of the anklets than his eye by the beauty of the foot. The various traces of loveliness we find combined in the wife of the Yaksa, who, of course, is the most perfect woman. She is thus described by the poet:—"young and slim, with pointed teeth, and lips like ripe bimba fruit, thin-waisted, with eyes like those of a timid fawn; her gait sedate on account of the heaviness of her hips and her form slightly bent on account of her full-grown orbs." This type of beauty was, unquestionably, the poet's ideal, for we find other heroines, such as Urpa, Sakuntala, etc., similarly described. (d., for example, 'avarjita kincid iva stanabhyam' etc., in the Kumarasambhava.) We find also similar expressions in contemporary works of art, and this certainly was the standard of beauty in the poet's time.

I shall now endeavour to find out and discuss the light which the Meghaduta throws on the life of the women described above. I have already observed that the city dames had an extremely artificial and luxurious way of living. What Miss Olive Schreiner calls the 'parasitic' stage in the life of the woman may indeed be discerned in the palaces of the rich at Ujjyaini and Dasapura, as described by the poet. Nevertheless, even a superficial perusal of the poem does not fail to impress us with the fact that our ladies in that age were in constant touch with nature. There is certainly an amount of poetical exaggeration in the poet's account, but all deductions and eliminations notwithstanding, the fact remains that in the life of the women of ancient India, nature played a very important and altogether wholesome part. We would, of course, call it a superstition, but there was undoubtedly more than that in the custom which required the woman to put her left foot on the Asoka tree that it might blossom. The deep sympathy between nature and woman is a very important feature of the life described in the Meghaduta.

The repeated mention of floral ornaments in the Meghaduta indicates the extensive use of them by the ladies of all classes. We find the lotus being used by the puspalavi as an ear-pendant, the Sirisa flower used for the ear by the fair women of Alaka. Parvati sought to heighten her celestial charms by using the lotus leaf as an ear-pendant. We learn that the flower counted as an important article for the toilet of the hair. It was not only inlaid with Kunda buds, but fresh Kuruvaka flowers were stuck to the braided hair, and the Kadamba was flung from up the parting of the hair. The Mandara flower was used for the same purpose by the abhisarikas of the place. We learn further from the poet that the ladies of the time would apply to their face the pollen of the Lodhra blossom in order to make it look yellowish white.

The young ladies, it seems, spent a good deal of time over their toilet. The ladies of Ujjain perfumed their locks with scented fumes, and the use of lacks for reddening the foot was a universal custom. The fair ones would also use scents of various sorts (*e.g.*, sandal paste etc.) so that when they were engaged in water sports, the air would become thick with their smell. Among the ornaments worn by ladies we find the following mentioned:—a net of pearls for the tresses, the jingling girdle for the waist, bangles, both plain and with diamond points, bangles, which would make a pleasing, jingling sound (worn by the wife of the Yaksa), golden lilies for the hair, and various sorts of necklaces,—a variety particularly mentioned being a string of pearls with an Indranila gem as pendant. The poet informs us that an important object of attraction for sight-seers at Ujjain were the pearls, corals, diamonds, etc., with the shoots of their rays jetting forth. They were exposed for sale in the marketstalls. He also mentions various sorts of silken garments as being worn by the ladies and himself shows a partiality for the blue colour when put on by the fair ladies.

The women of the time lived a gay, robust life. They certainly enjoyed light and air, the two blessings of god, more freely than their less fortunate sisters of the cities of modern India, and we have already seen that life was then not devoid of romance. Their intimate touch with nature lifted life out of the dull routine of household duties. The wife of the Yaks a found some consolation in her grief by rearing up a young Mandara plant as her son. Another diversion for her was talking with the caged parrot or making the pea-fowl dance by clapping her beautiful hands.

Many of the fine arts of ancient India were diligently cultivated by the ladies. The wife of the Yaksa was a good musician. She could not only play upon the lute, but could herself compose songs in which her husband's name would occur again and again. She was skilled in painting too, and could draw from her imagination the likeness of her husband emaciated by separation. The poet tells us that the walls of the palaces of Ujjain were adorned by numerous paintings, and it is possible that some of them were drawn by the ladies of the house.

It is not easy always to separate the real from the ideal in the works of the poets. In the foregoing discussion on the condition of the women described in the Meghaduta, I have proceeded on the assumption that the poem reflects their actual condition in the age of the poet. The picture that he gives a happy and bright one. In the works of this immortal in a country, which for centuries had been the site of a mighty civilisation, and which, as yet, was on the whole undisturbed by foreign conquest.

●●

3

Developmental Issues

The current situation in developing countries in agriculture, food production and rural development derives from a historical pattern of development in which investment has been skewed in favour of industrialisation and urban areas with the result that in the majority of countries rural areas have lagged behind in their development. In Africa, Latin America, the Middle East and certain parts of Asia the development paradigms pursued so far have created food shortages and a structural cleavage in rural society.

The resultant rural transformation has led to a cleavage between commercial or large-scale agriculture, which has been rapidly modernised through application of scientific and technological innovations, higher capital investment with higher returns, and small scale subsistence agriculture with little or no capital investment and a low level of technology, requiring high labour inputs with low and even declining returns. Such developments in agriculture have sometimes been due to the need to earn foreign currency. Furthermore, this cleavage has taken the form of a gender differentiation in which men predominate in the decision-making and management of commercial or large-scale agriculture, while women continue to predominate in the food and subsistence sector in which they expend large amounts of labour—as evidenced by the long hours of work with low levels of technology and low returns. Moreover, within commercial agriculture the gender division is also reflected by the high demand for female labour in those cycle of production requiring hoe and hand methods (*e.g.*, weeding or paddy transplanting) with low remuneration. This cleavage has meant that many developing countries have not been able to attain the goal self-reliance in the areas of food, agriculture and rural development. A substantial number of countries continue to experience a severe decline in food production, leading to food shortages and even outright hunger and famine. Moreover, even in countries, which have been able to expand their food sectors, the system of distribution is inadequate and poverty, hunger and malnutrition still afflict large masses of the people.

According to the FAO, malnutrition and hunger increased by 15 percent during the seventies, affecting 450 million people in Asia, Africa and Latin America. In developing market economies as a whole, daily per capita calorie consumption has remained at 2 percent below the minimum requirement. The gap is largest in Africa, followed by South and South-East Asia. In Sub-Saharan Africa, the growth rate of agricultural production fell to 1.3 percent annum while population growth remained at 27 percent over the second development decade.

Women in developing countries are a major resource in agriculture, food production and rural development, as evidenced by their numerical proportions, their share of labour in agriculture and food production and the division of labour by sex in this sector. Their share of labour is particularly significant in view of the fact that in many cases they perform their agricultural work in addition to long and arduous work in child-care household maintenance, cooking and fuel wood collection, as well as food preparation and processing. Despite women's crucial role in agriculture and food production their potential for accelerating rural development has not often been well understood or appreciated. Inherited biases in the agrarian development approaches have led 'to an inadequate perception of women's economic role, undercounting or devaluation of their work and thus to a perpetuation of the dependency of developing countries on external factors of production.

The undercounting of women's work in rural economics results from:

(a) The use of industrialised countries definitions of work, employment, jobs, primary activity etc.

(b) The invisibility of many types of work in the subsistence mode of production, and

(c) The association of women's non-work with the family's social status in Asian and Latin American Countries.

In practice, women have not benefited from adequate policy support. First of all the accumulated evidence suggests that agrarian and land tenure policies have restricted women's access to land and other factors of agricultural production, such as technology, credit subsidy and inputs (*e.g.* fertilisers and seeds). Secondly, women have not had equal access to support services and incentive system for expanding agriculture, food production and rural development, for instance, extension and training services and information. Thirdly, lack of an integrated approach to development at the national level has consistently perpetuated a fragmentary approach to women's position in the society and their role in development, thereby perpetuating the promotion of women's programmes through social welfare, humanitarian and demographic approaches only, without provisions for long term integration.

In traditional societies women's role in agriculture and food production was recognised by customary rights of access to land, forests, and to support from family labour. Structural changes under colonialism and in the postcolonial phases have eroded many of these rights, but the responsibility of feeding the family still rests primarily with the women in many rural communities of Africa and in the economically least affluent sections of many Asian and Latin American societies. The privatisation of land and the introduction of cash crops for domestic and foreign markets, the need to feed expanding populations, and the depletion of forest resources for industrial and communications growth, which were initiated during colonialism and continued after independence, have steadly reduced women's access to basic resources. The withdrawal of male labour—for deployment in mining, roads and railway building, plantation of export crops and new industries—which was initiated by colonial regimes also increased women's burdens.

Despite international recognition of rural women's right to own land, attempts to incorporate this principle in land tenure and land development policies have been marginal. Forest policy, including policies for reforestation has yet to recognise the role of women in forest development, even though in some areas women have initiated major protest movement against deforestation, which have negatively affected their ability to feed their families and livestock. Case studies from Asia and Africa indicate that rural women are very dynamic and innovative in these fields when they are give the opportunity to participate collectively in such developmental activities. They also indicate a process of increasing self- confidence among women and an enhancement of their status within their families and the community. However, extension of such experiments to other areas will require uncorporation of women as a target group in policies and structures for agarian reform, and development of forests, agriculture, animal husbandry, silk production, fish culture, land development (including waste lands) etc.

Unless the structural constraints and the existing 'invisibility' of women in rural development policies and agrarian reform are removed, it is difficult to envisages an equitable growth and expansion of agriculture, food and forest production. It is important to take specific short-run measures to make them sensitive to women's potentials and the promotion of research and communication programmes for rural women in these areas. However, the solution to the problem lies in the establishment of long-term strategies and measures to implement them as a matter of national priority in the context of solutions to, for example chromic food problems deforestation and ecological imbalances, unemployment and poverty, and to enhance the process of corrective and individual self-reliance.

New initiatives are needed to reorient agricultural policies at the national level, which would give priority to a balanced approach to agricultural communities and food production. Within this policy restructuring process, a number of specific issues arise. A food strategy might be designed to support rural development and agrarian reforms and other relevant measures for strengthening and food sector recommended. Since food strategies are relatively new initiatives, whose policy guidelines are still being drawn up, they could provide an important policy intervention to strengthen women's role in food production.

In view of the role of women in farming and the inadequacy of access to services for expanding production the following measures could be fruitful:

— savings and investment programmes should aim at providing credit, finance and subsidies for women through various channels:

(*a*) regular agricultural financing institutions and credit programmes could include the elaboration of specific mechanisms for assisting farm women; and (*b*) revolving funds and credit subsidies extended to women through their associations net-works, and local level groups, as well as government offices at the local level, in conjunction with information campaigns to encourage women to use these services.

— new organisational schemes, especially those at the community level should be extended through women's groups and associations;

— current farmer training programmes, including the Technical Cooperation among Developing Countries (TCDC) programmes, could be reviewed and modified to cater for women farmers. An important elements of adjustment here would be to provide agricultural training programmes which would increase women's technical knowledge and allow them to combine mothering and training opportunities;

— increasing women's competence to participate in rural institutions, decision making and designs for agricultural and food programmes.

The persistence of the subordinate position of women in society, as illustrated by the experience in the agriculture and food sector, is a negation of the goals of development, which affects ill members of society equally, regardless of sex or creed.

Development Through Technology

In view of the importance of industrialisation, the pattern of industrial is at ion adopted in developing countries is most relevant. Differences in the socio-economic environment of individual developing countries resulted in various industrialisation strategies. However, regardless of the different industrialisation policies and practices of the individual developing countries, they have a common desire to generate national product, promote employment and secure the most dynamic possible modernisation, so as to secure a greater degree of technological and financial independence from the developed countries. The level and the features of the industrialisation of developing countries are usually determined by the individual country's resources, both material and human, and by its past experience of development.

The great dependence of the industrialisation processes in developing countries or developed countries, on technology transfer, capital investment, export. markets, etc., has resulted in a high degree of exploitation and in unbalanced industrial structures which are highly sensitive to international economic fluctuations. Thus, the introduction of new industries and changes. In the industrial structure of a developing country may profoundly and rapidly influence the overall economic structure. Such influences may bring about unexpected or unplanned changes and social life. Developing countries often find it difficult to fully control the structural changes in their industries and thus avoid industrial instability and exploitation of the workforce. This may to some extent be possible for those countries, which have large internal markets, strong public sectors, or were able to control investments in industrial development through generation of sufficient internal funds.

The share of women in industrial employment in developing countries rose from 21 percent to 26.5 percent in 1980. About two thirds of the net increase in the female industrial workforce (the number of women employed in industry in the world increased by 104 percent in the last two decades) took place in developing countries mainly in Asia. In contrast to Africa and Latin America, Asia has a higher share of the female than of the male world industrial labour force.

Women are usually engaged in labour-intensive industries with low productivity (*e.g.* processing industries—textile, food, leather, etc.). Their wages are influenced by their poor bargining position, and they have no influence at all on working conditions. Thus, for instance, although the working hours in manufacturing have generally tended to decline, in some developing countries working hours have tended to rise. The treatment of the female labour force is to a large extent a reflection of women's low status on the labour market, lack of proper education and training low or non-existent organisation, the lack of or non-implementation of protective legislation (particularly in export-oriented industries) and their generally unfavourable social position. The recent upward trend in women's employment in developing countries is not very significant in relation to the absolute size of the female population or workforce in these countries. Moreover, although this increase is in some of the most modern industries in the world, it does not appear to have made a substantial difference to women status, since it has done little to break the isolation and discrimination of women in the industrial workforce. The extension of the practice of subcontracting of home workers for certain stages of industrial production processes may have considerable counter-productive consequences,. for women's formal employment. Such organisational changes may sometimes lead to a circumvention of legal protective measures for labour, a deterioration of working conditions, lower wages within and outside industry, greater exploitation of women's and children's labour, diminishing union activity and, in the long run, also to increased formal unemployment of both men and women. While the short-term positive effects of income generation cannot be discounted, the negative effects of channelling or restricting women's employment to the informal sector make it considerably more difficult and could lead to a higher degree of isolation, exploitation and inequality of women, by excluding them from the mainstream of socio-economic activity.

It is unlikely that the position of women in the industries of developing countries can be changed without changes in the models of industrial development and organisation of industrial production. Therefore, formulation and implementation of national industrialisation policies based on the needs and interests of all strata of the population, as well as on an evaluation of domestic potentials continue to be priority tasks confronting developing countries. The existing potentials of developing countries are certainly conducive to positive changes. Balanced development planning and policies which aim at maximum utilisation of national resources and at an expansion of domestic demand are also the proper framework for the advancement of the role of women in this sector of the economic and for promotion within overall development.

To improve women's position in industry, a number of measures would have to be incorporated in the industrial policies of developing countries:

— changes in education, which would enable women to improve their position in industrial employment, and to acquire transferable skills through various forms of vocational and informal training;

— legal arrangements covering all aspects of industrialisation, from investment codes to regulations, which would provide for better general treatment of labour in industry. In this connection, there should be regulatory measures in free exporting zones to ensure that social costs are also covered. However, it must be recognised that collective action by the developing countries is needed for the successful legislation and implementation of such measures;

— adoption of technologies which ensure stability of employment and professional progress to women workers;

— extention of employment opportunities in accordance with human resources development policies;

— establishment of overall social control and of schemes for genuine workers' participation in management and decision making;

— selection, development and transfer of technology and know-how as well as training of personnel;

— elaboration of criteria for determining the size of enterprises in various industrial branches and the ways of organising them; promotion of small and medium-size enterprises in developing countries; establishment of industrial cooperatives;

— strengthening of self-reliance in industrial policy through industrial cooperation among developing countries, exchange of information and experience through ECDC/TCDC programmes and projects.

This would improve the bargaining position of developing countries *vis-a-vis* developed ones, particularly in case of transfer of technology or foreign investment, in enforcement of national legal mechanisms for the protection of the industrial labour force, including women workers. All this calls for urgent action among developing countries in the field of industrialisation.

Technological Development

The main issue connected with the utilisation of science and technology as a pool to speed up the development of the developing countries is, therefore, the transfer of technology and, in this respect, the choice of technology. Technology being a system consisting of hardware and software the transfer of technology must be viewed as a complex process, involving a range of economic, financial, legal and sociological factors.

In this connection, local inputs-primarily knowledge and information on technologies, trained cadres, legal and other regulations, etc.—are needed. The process of selection of technologies calls for an analysis and assessment not only of the economic impact, but also of the social impact. While must be kept in mind is that while technology itself is natural, the application of technology can have considerable social effects, since, through technology, a system of domination and exploitation, as well as a set of social norms and ethics may be transferred. A social impact analysis should be a constituent part of any transfer of technology arrangement.

Women are involved in science and technology through the structural transformations that occur with the transfer of technology and scientific and technological development, and as participants in research and technological activities; and experiencing the impact of the technologies on their everyday lives. In all cases, their involvement should be much stronger than it is at present. It is also very important that women understand scientific and technological innovations, because this enables them to influence the general social attitudes towards technological change through the existing non-formal education. The radical changes in the organisational pattern and activities of the society, associated with rapid scientific and technological change in the overall organisation, which are presently being experienced in the developed countries, may also dramatically affect all developing countries, and lead to either a more dynamic and humane development or to an ever higher degree of dependency and exploitation. The problem of the marginal position of some members of society, and of women specifically, cannot be solved unless the elements of these new technologies can be built into development strategies in accordance with the concept of integral development. Furthermore, the latest so-called frontier and trans-disciplinary technologies can be used in different ways and at different levels. Their use can serve to accontuate the productive role of women, because such technologies are applicable to a number of areas which are of relevance to the betters quality of life and to the integration of women in development, *i.e.* food production, clean water supply, improved housing conditions, use of alternative energy sources, in the services education etc.

It should be kept in mind that it is economic and political considerations, rather than social and cultural ones, which determine the availability and terms and conditions for the access of developing countries to new technologies and which are important for national development. Women's access to technological development thus also depends on the global relations between the technology owners and users and those who try to secure access to new technology and to processes of industrialisation.

Women have traditionally gained knowledge and experience (*e.g.*, in agricultural production, energy utilisation, running the household, manufacturing objects for everyday use, home medicine etc.,), which have not been, exploited from the developmental point of view. The application of new scientific and technological devices and knowledge may lighten household drudgery in urban and rural areas, providing better water, energy and other community facilities. This would release energies which women might be encouraged to direct forwards active and useful participation in other economic and social areas, and in the overall technological transformation of the society.

A greater involvement of women in scientific and technological development would therefore require:

— popularisation of scientific and technological knowledge and skills in order to enable their further development, by mass media, through changes in school programmes, and through all participatory and community development activities (especially in agriculture but also in other areas, *e.g.*, household activities, health, education, housing, etc.).

— changes in the traditional attitudes towards women by enabling them to fully participate in scientific and technological development by stimulating their involvement in various forms of education and training.

— an increase of the level of scientific and technological self reliance by developing national scientific and technological potentials, maximisation of the possibilities for technical proporation among developing countries and the introduction of selective transfer of technology systems.

— establishment of linkages between the existing traditional technologies and know-how and the new technologies. The involvement of women in the strengthening of these links could provide a firm basis for self-reliance and ensure a certain continuity in the development of authentic and original approaches, thus avoiding imitative modernisation, and developing participatory research as well as relating scientific and technological development to the specific needs of the country.

— establishment and strengthening of cooperation among developing countries in the areas of information on scientific and technological knowledge and devices transfer of technology and exchange of experience on application of science and technology in development, joint research, etc.

Skills and Services

The term services or tertiary sector encompasses a wide range of activities. Therefore, the analysis of the role of women in the services sector covers the generally complex problem of services classification and data, the identification of the manpower problem in general, and women's hidden economic role in particular, and the relationship between the services sector and the overall economy of the country.

Over the last decades this sector's contribution to GDP increased substantially, not only in developed market economies but also in developing countries, where this upward trend was evident even in the least developed countries. The services sector accounted for the largest share of GDP in both developed market economies (56.9 percent) as well as in developing countries (44.3 percent). In developing countries the services sector expanded at a past faster rate than the GDP in the period 1973-80, implying that the general slowdown of their economies during these periods affected the services sector less severely than other major economic sectors.

However, the expansion of the services sector in developing countries, particularly in least developed countries, is probably due to quite different economic causes and could the attributed to the marginalisation of the labour force in agriculture and industry. The development of services is partly due to major changes in agriculture and industry, and partly to their heterogenous production and consumption characteristics.

The role of women in the tertiary sector is very difficult to determine. However, the distribution of the female labour force may serve as an indicator. The total female labour force in developing countries was employed in agriculture, in industry and in services. This is very different from the situation in developed countries, where the shares are for agriculture, for industry and for services. In developing countries the share of females in the total labour force, by economic sectors, was highest in agriculture and much lower in the services sector.

There are considerable disparities between developing countries in the different regions-disparities between Latin America on the one hand and Asia and Africa on the other. In Asia the main feature is the relatively high share of women in the total labour force in industry (28.8 percent) and the lower share in services (23.2 percent). In Latin America the low share of women in the total agricultural labour force (9.3 percent) is in sharp contrast to the situation in the other two regions. In this region female employment in the services sector is as high as 38.3 percent. In Africa women account for 31.6 percent of labour in services, while their share in industry is only 19.7 percent. (UNIDO, 1984).

Many of the service activities in which women are employed do not require formal technical qualifications. Other activities such as health (especially nursing) and education (especially teaching) do require professional qualifications, but these are in many cases considered an extension of the essentially female role which has its origin in the household-the mother care offered to the family. Thus women's contribution in this sector has not really been adequately recognised.

Much of the productive activity of women in the services sector remains invisible because of its mainly traditional and informal nature in developing countries. Some thought should be devoted to the services, which this sector could provide to meet the needs of households in this countries, that is, what the services sector should produce for the household and its members.

In view of the importance of the role of women in this sector and of the significance of the services sector for the improvement of the status of women in developing countries, it is suggested that:

- — attention be paid to the analysis of the functioning, growth and development of the services sector (both public and private) in all developing countries, especially as regards the inter-linkages among this and all other sectors;
- — the position of women in this sector should be viewed as developmental and integrative of other activities, which means that the new developmental trends observed in this sector must be closely linked to overall development and the advancement of women;
- — services classification and data collection should be made more transparent and accessible;
- — cooperation among developing countries in this sector, which is scattered over different areas and usually invisible being traditional and informal;
- — women's hidden economic role in the services should be further studied and analysed;
- — could be pursued with a view to the development of self-reliant schemes. Cooperation among developing countries in this sector could contribute to exchange of experiences, to development of self-reliant schemes and linkages between micro and macro levels of implementation. This may be an avenue for the promotion of new approaches to the development of the services sector.

Education and Training

Education is a double-edged instrument: it can contribute to and be an ally of structural changes in society by training people in required skills-old, newly emerging and anticipated. It is also a value-generating process influencing the behaviour, norms and cultural attitudes of people, particularly younger ones. From the beginning of the movement for the equality of women in recent history, great emphasis was placed on education as the major instrument for the elimination of gender inequality. Developing countries have viewed education as an instrument to stimulate development in all fields, and to reduce their dependence on external advisers. The basic problems were to promote a rapid expansion of development and cultural structures to meet the manpower requirements of development and cultural progress in general. Scarcity of resources and the shifting priorities of development have constrained the balanced pursuit of these aims.

Illiteracy still remains a major problem in most developing countries and women constitute a large proportion of the illiterates. About 60 percent of the approximately 800 million adult illiterates in developing countries are women. Although the proportion of illiterates in the total adult population has decreased, the results are still unsatisfactory. The absolute number of illiterates in these countries is still increasing. Gender differences persist among illiterates, especially because the lower enrolment ratios for girls at the elementary level increase the number of illiterate women. The gender gap among illiterates is increasing in developing countries.

Trends in the process of equalising the access of men and women to different levels of the educational system, as measured through enrolment ratios, show some interesting results. Over two decades the gender gap in enrolment ratios for the age groups 6-11 and 12-17 has remained virtually constant in developing countries, although there is overall improvement in entrolment for both sexes. At the higher level of education, the gap is much narrower, in contract to developed countries, where the gender gap exists mainly at the higher level. At this level the gender gap has shrunk in the developed countries during the last decade, and it has slightly widened in the group of developing countries.

The persistence of these gaps prevents the equalisation of educational opportunities with consequent effects on employment, skill acquisition and participatory opportunities in all fields. The widening of the gap in higher education is a matter of serious concern, because this sector is the training ground for entry into many areas important development, *e.g.*, science and technology, communication industries utilising high level technology, professions such as law, medicine, etc. It is also the training ground for most managerial and decision-making occupations.

The participation of women in decision-making positions, which is already limited, could shrink still further if this gap were to expand. In addition to resource constraints, educational progress in developing countries has been impeded by many other problems. Lack of harmony with productive and other developmental activities, which is often a consequence of borrowed models of educational systems, imposed the need to reform and adapt educational systems and institutions, to turn increasingly to the informal aspects of education (vocational training, on the job-training, etc.), and to introduce mass media and other modern devices as useful means of spreading equcational programmes and contents in an effort to reach as many social groups as possible.

Developing countries have been experiencing great problems in education, reflected in poor material basis and functional difficulties, in sometimes alarming dropout levels (especially in Sub-Saharan Africa and South Asia), in the fact that a substantial proportion of children are unable to read and write even after going to primary school for four or five years, etc. Women are still mostly employed in traditional and informal sectors where there has been a lower level of technological and information support. This further compounds their educational handicaps. However, women with education have entered many new areas of occupation where their participation was virtually non-existent before.

The enable women to participate actively in all spheres of economic and social life, vocational and professional training must be further developed. In this respect, the training of trainers is of primary importance, as is the introduction of management training for women. Apart from the conventional types of training (seminars, workshops, export group meetings training through doing, etc.), the non-conventional types are often also suitable. Of special relevance are also the new participatory types of training, which include learner-centered methods developed in the framework of non-formal education in which trainers are facilitators, to elicit productive response and interaction-and local social and cultural forms that can be built upon for effective training. These include decision making patterns, social groupings and communications networks.

Culture

The major lacunae in educational development are in the areas of cultural change and promotion of social values, which support and reflect the goals of development. Cultural transformations are taking place in developing countries, but in many cases through processes over which the people and even the governments have little control. New values and aspirations are often promoted, directly or indirectly, for profit maximisation—by forces inside or outside the country Changes in consumption patterns and role models are stimulated by mass media, commercial interests and a process of borrowing or emulation of life styles from developed countries. In many countries such changes have contributed to a widening of the gap between the elites and the masses of the people between the rural and urban populations, between the rich and the poor. This presents a challenge to the educational system, which must correct the trend if it is to promote the goals of participatory development, and collective self-reliance, eliminate the dependency on external support and contribute to comprehensive integrated development.

While there is evidence that the process of unplanned cultural change helps to promote illusory images, which are far removed from the social realities of developing countries, cultural reaction, which tries to counter these influences by looking only to the past, may also have a negative impact on development. In their efforts to preserve their cultural identities developing countries have sought to reaffirm their attachment to their cultural heritage. While pride in this heritage can contribute to the spirit and the value of self-reliance, this process may also lead to distortions—to a withdrawal from present-day problems and realities to a glamorisation of the past, to the imposition of the culture of dominant groups on other culturally diverse groups and to a strengthening of some of the forces and institutions that oppose the goals of comprehensive, participatory development of all peoples, classes and groups.

In view of the crucial importance of culture values in the dynamics of development, it will be essential to enhance the role of the women and to promote new cultural values that take into account existing social realities and support the efforts to build a different future. Integral development, which subsumes equal participation in development *i.e.*, in production and decision making will enhance the role of culture in the development context. Women will no longer be viewed as marginal producers (or providers of an auxiliary workforce), but rather as equal partners in the promotion of development.

Educational institutions will have to play an active role in the promotion of the development of such new cultural values. Hitherto, their contribution has been inadequate. Structurally pedagogically and philosophically, educational institutions will have to play a far more active role in the development of a new cultural context that can contribute to the realisation of the goals of comprehensive development—human and material. This also requires that they internalise the concern for the equality of women and the enhancement of their role—in their curricula, pedagogic methods, organisation and research agendas.

A strategic interrelationship between education and cultural and socio-economic development which integrates concern for the emancipation of women would have to be characterised by respect for the specific cultural features of a particular environment and clearly define the cultural and developmental function of education in social transformation and support the process of educational reform.

In this connection, the promotion of new knowledge about women and new perceptions of the role of women in development could be viewed as an instrument for educational and cultural development with a view to:

- strengthening and extension of training activities so as to embrace all relevant problems, such as: improvement of professional skills, education for family life and responsibilities, training for community organisation and management, decision waking etc.;
- promotion of integral and interdisciplinary links among developing countries in the field of cultural transformation and education and especially in professional and vocational training as well as in all forms of non-conventional training, to ensure availability of cadres capable of handling the new technology.
- equal participation of the local population, and particularly of women, in devising, deciding upon

and implementing development programmes; this can be achieved by clearly defining the developmental interests of all groups of the population;

— enhancement of the collective self-reliance of nonaligned and other developing countries in culture and education by intensifying their communication in these fields, especially as regards the methodologies for educational reform which incorporates the advancement of women as one of its concerns.

Mass Media

This section focuses on the possibilities which the media offer provided they are used judiciously to reflect the contribution which women are making to the nation's development efforts. Communication media have been a powerful social influence, both as instruments of change and for maintaining *status quo*. In the last decade, an impressive amount of literature on the portrayal of women in the media has been produced. These studies have expressed concern about the stereotyped and negative images of women, which are being projected through the media without any cognizance of the new and expanded roles of women in society. Communication media are a powerful tool for the creation of an alternative and positive image of women and could promote new attitudes and strategies for action directed towards the achievement of the goal of equality for women. It is imperative to democratises the control over the communication media and to make them an instrument for the creation of an awareness of women's needs and problems.

Mass media, especially the audiovisual media, play an important role by influencing the consumption patterns and life-styles, and usually promote commercial interests (often of external producers), thus creating pressures to distort trade and industrial policies. They also contribute to the distortion of cultural development, promoting imported values, which militate against comprehensive integrated development and the principle of collective self-reliance. There has been a recent trend among media professionals in developing countries towards greater realism in their portrayal of social problems. Realism, however, must be used to inspire people to struggle for change. A search for new options in human relationships, the reshaping of social institutions, political and economic structures and cultural values, would go a long way towards integrating women into the world of the media, and enable the media to play a more positive role in integrated development.

In the past, there has been a one-way flow of information from the developed to the developing countries, and from government to the people. The goals of self-reliance and participatory development, which are being actively pursued by the non-aligned countries, involve a shift from excessive reliance of the developing countries on foreign resources towards a mobilisation of their indigenous resources, which would make these countries less vulnerable to external pressures and develop their own potential for growth. The new information and communication technology, the microchip revolution, has considerably magnified the power of the media. Satellite communication has exposed millions of people to new information.

Women are today an important factor in the strategy of self-reliance and the media could do much to create public awareness of the role of women and their potentials. There are a number of steps, which the media could take at various levels to strengthen the role of women as equal partners in development:

— a democratisation of the structures and control of the communication media could contribute to the representation and participation of women in the media at the decision-making levels;

- more women should be involved in media training programmes; communication and advertising policies involving participation by women could be developed;
- listeners and viewers from consumer groups or NGO action groups, etc., could be effectively utilised to create an awareness of women's issues and to evolve common strategies for the promotion of more positive approaches to women's issues;
- media content could be improved through coordinated efforts for increased interaction between nongovernmental organisations in formulating guidelines for monitoring programmes;
- various international seminars, conferences and expert group meetings, which have already covered a wide range of issues connected with women and the communication media indicate the need for further in depth studies, research training for women in communication technology, the organisational framework, including the development of a code of ethics with regard to the presentation of women in media and using traditional folk media to encourage participation of women.
- horizontal communication and cooperation among developing countries in this field could be strengthened in order to create an awareness of issues of common concern, identifying solutions to common problems and areas of cooperation.

Development Issues

The still largely unresolved problems of the inter-connections between economic and social development and the increasing concern for the distributional and human dimensions of development indicate the need to pay more attention to all aspects of social development. The issues of health, social security, population trends and family planning, housing urbanisation and the environment, are linked with the general problem of the level of socio-economic development of a country its resource base and social policies.

Health Delivery Systems

Millions of people in developing countries are trapped in poverty, malnutrition, hunger and disease, although there are regional variations in living conditions. It is estimated that acute forms of potential energy malnutrition affect 35 percent school children in Africa, 16 percent in Asia and 4 percent in of Latin America. Similarly, it is estimated that two-thirds pregnant women in the developing world suffer from nutritional anaemia. High maternal and infant mortality rates are closely linked with inadequate maternal and child health care services, lack of proper sanitation and a safe drinking water supply. By the end of the last decade, only 42 percent of households in developing countries had access to a potable water supply and over three quarters of the population lacked access to sanitary facilities.

A disaggregation of social indicators by regions reveals that not only is there a very great gap between the developed and developing countries but also that their is great diversity among the developing regions. The average life expectancy in Sub-Saharan Africa is 47.4 years while it is 63.9 years in some Asian countries. Similarly, infant mortality is highest in Sub-Saharan Africa, while it is more in South East Asia. In the South Asian region the mortality differentials by sex indicate higher infant mortality among females and empirical data also show sex-based health and nutrition related behaviour. In the health care subsystems, there are interesting variations: Latin America—with the highest per capita GDP— has 7.5 physicians and 11. 7 nurses per 10,000 population, followed by some countries in South East Asia, where despite low GDP per capita the averages are 5.4 physicians and 5.2 nurses per 10,000 population.

Most developing countries are faced with the problem of a decline or slowing down of the growth rate of production, rising unemployment, growing deficits in balance of payments and inflation. All these adversely affect the availability of resources for social services, *i.e.*, health, education and social security.

Despite the methodological weaknesses of the existing social indicators and an absence of data on access to and distributional characteristics of the social development infrastructure, the trends indicate that results differ sharply also within regions and that social improvements definitely do not come automatically as a by product of economic growth. In many cases health resources are disproportionately concentrated in big cities, at the expense of primary health care for the masses in rural areas Problems requiring careful study include disparities in increase and living standards, and the care available to different social groups, inadequate planning and management of health development, problems of inter and intra-sectoral coordination, administrative decentralisation and involvement of the people in the planning, programming and implementation of health care programmes.

Very few developing countries have systems of social security. Even where such systems exist, a large part of the population in the informal sector—a substantial proportion of which are women-is not covered by the existing systems of mater benefits, health insurance, old age benefits, etc. In some countries voluntary and philanthropic organisations supplement state action. However, their work is often uncoordinated and not adequate to deal with the increasing, demands of urbanisation and poverty. The development of social protection is linked to changes in the development strategies and orientation directed towards the satisfaction of basic minimum needs the reduction and elimination of poverty, promotion of employment opportunities and improvement other working conditions of labour.

The global strategy of Health adopted by the Thirty Fourth World Health Assembly in 1981, which emphasises basic health protection, the primary health care approach and organisation of an effective health care and health information system, identified priorities for health cooperation and drew up an Action Programme, stressing the need for a review of a number of policy orientations in the areas of primary health care, health information and monitoring system, community involvement in health programmes, prevention of infectious diseases, development of national services of health care and health education, production, distribution and consumption of drugs and protection of the human environment.

On the basis of the Medium-Term Programme for Technical Cooperation among Developing Countries for Health for All and in view of the calls for an acceleration of the development of national health care capabilities and the establishment of local points for TCDC in the area of health some priority activities may be identified:

— introduction of effective health surveillance systems at the national level, of health indicators for target setting and formulation of national priorities and plans of action, and of appropriate Systems for assessing strengths and weaknesses of national health programmes;

— linking of health policies and programmes with economic development and those facilities which can directly reduce women's drudgery and work burden and directly improve their health situation, *i.e.*, provision of adequate housing, water supply, sanitation, health regulations at the work-place, and health protection of women, particularly those working in the informal sector of the economy who are not covered by social protection policies;

- integration of maternal and child health care with family planning services and accelerated development of national capacities through development of health institutions and infrastructures and increase of the number of health experts and particularly health workers;
- promotion of health education and indigenous system of health care;
- involvement of women's organisations in primary health care activities and their representation on national and local health councils;
- promotion of health education and indigenous systems of health care;
- involvement of woman's organisations in primary health care activities and their representation on national and local health councils;
- introduction of TCDC programmes for the promotion of industries which are important for the development of health care systems. The developing countries could evolve suitable mechanisms for cooperation in training and development of human resources, collaborative research, joint programming, exchange of information and references, and exploring the application of low-cost technologies for water supply and waste disposal.

Demographic Factors

It is becoming increasingly obvious that population policies should be Implemented parallel with better health care and general socio-economic development as population Issues touch on very fundamental human values.

As the Mexico Conference on Population in 1984 stressed population strategies cannot be limited to the analysis of population trends, since there is a dynamic interrelationship between these and socio-economic transformations. Hence what is required is a set of coordinated strategies and activities for the promotion of economic development of the quality of life, human rights and in particular the fundamental right to individual choice.

The status of women and the advancement of their role in development remains a critical element in the achievement of these objectives. The persisting inequalities between men and women—which are evident in the higher incidence of poverty, unemployment and illiteracy among women—the limited range of employment categories offered to women, and the uneven sharing of borne and family responsibilities make it difficult for women to participate actively in the socio-economic development of the country.

There is sufficient evidence to show that it is lower income groups with a low level of literacy, low and insecure income and low health and nutritional levels which have larger families. This is points to a need for planning policies, which have a more integrated approach. Rapid population growth will affect the efforts of countries to achieve food security and to reduce pressure on the natural resources; also, its effects on urbanisation and on land and capital will exacerbate inequalities.

Many governments have launched subsidised family planning programmes. However, incentives are offered to encourage people to reduce family size. Experience has shown that a clinical approach, which threatens social values, beliefs and customs does not succeed and is actually a disincentive. To breakthrough the vicious circle of poverty, high fertility and mortality calls for a more careful and humane public policy with a judicious balance between individual choice and dignity and promotion of a sense of responsibility among parents to ensure a better future for all children. This could be further stimulated and promoted through various forms of technical assistance at various levels as well as enriched through mutual exchange of information and experience among developing countries.

Coping with Over Population: Women in the Cities

The rapid growth of cities in developing countries has created serious problems, since a large proportion of urban migrant workers are living in temporary hutments and settlements without adequate basic amenities. The growth of cities and the steep rise in rural-urban migration is a manifestation of imbalances in the location and expansion of productive activity. Women are particularly affected, as many of their activities are connected with their homes and bad housing and hygiene conditions are detrimental to both their own and their families health. The growth of cities has also created ecological problems. The growing demands of expanding cities have put undue pressure on natural resources, destroying the harmony between human beings and nature, and has led to a degradation of productive resources like water, land and forests.

The expansion of agriculture by clearing large tracts of forest has caused desertification due to severe soil erosion, a problem, which is extremely serious in Sub-Saharan Africa (Sahel), north-western Asia and the Middle East. Forests are crucial to the ecological life of many developing countries and deforestation has created serious problems, as the consumption of forest resources has exceeded replacement possibilities through natural growth. This has affected millions of rural households and the role of women in these households, as well as the nutritional level of the families. The human costs of malnutrition, famine and disruption in the lives of people seeking employment are a matter of serious concern.

Environmental issues conceiving the environment in its broadest social context are most relevant for women. The increasing marginalisation of certain sections of the population, growing poverty and deprivation of the masses, decreasing food production, the energy crisis and human environmental degradation in many developing countries are all symptoms of a pattern of growth and resource utilisation which is geared to existing power structures and prevents a large section of the population from satisfying its basic needs. The multidimensional problems facing developing countries are interconnected, but often these connection are not understood by those who formulate sectoral policies. In the long run, social development policies will have to be closely integrated with economic development policies and a strong commitment to the improvement of the quality of life. The methods and instruments of analysis and planning of socio-economic development should therefore take adequate account of environmental constraint.

INSTITUTIONAL ISSUES

Both the conceptual and sectoral parts of this study have indicated the basic features and tendencies of the changing role and status of women in developing countries. This was primarily the result of an analysis of the overall impact of development on the position of women in the societies of the developing countries and of the role of women in the developmental process. The effects of socio-economic development in individual sectors of the economy and public life have been identified and analysed. The endeavours at operationalisation of national development policies, including the integration of women in development raised the issue of instruments and institutions to implement these policies.

Issues addressed in this sections are: the role of government of public and private enterprises and of political participation and the role of women in decision-making processes as factors of development.

Government and Institution Effort

In principle, most governments have accepted the improvement of the social, political, economic and legal status of women, and the integration of women into development as desirable goals and planning objectives. The response of government, parliament and other political institutions at various levels to the need for the integration of women's issues into development plans is important for the effective implementation of appropriate strategies.

Country experiences indicate that during the UN Decade for Women many countries established governmental machinery, either as part of the existing administrative structures, as independent agencies (commissions, bureau, ministries) for women's affairs, or in the form of National Councils, which were extra-governmental organisations. Most of these mechanisms were created with the objectives of establishing responsibility and accountability within the government for planning, programming and implementing programmes for women and to act as a catalyst; providing the necessary infrastructure and resource support and training personnel: and reviewing, monitoring and evaluating policies and programmes and their impact on women.

The Mid-Decade review of the efficacy of these administrative and institutional mechanisms indicated that the constraints to action have ranged from conceptual of resource and organisational fractional factors. They do not have strong executive and resource support and have a limited mandate. The tendency has been to locate such units mainly within departments of social welfare and culture, which are considered non-productive and are usually not in the mainstream of the development effort and also suffer most from budgetary constraints during economic recession. The experience of some developing countries also indicates that the existence of governmental or state mechanism of this kind tends to reduce the concern of other administrative organs and of society as a whole for the advancement of women and leads to a diminution of activity in this direction.

As already indicated, the problems with regard to the role of women are closely linked with the problems of overall development. However, most of the governments have perceived the role of women as a specific interest issue without making any, attempt to integrate the problems involved into the mainstream of development planning. In many developing countries women-specific projects were designed to provide income-generating activities and basic needs to poor rural and urban women. These efforts basically addressed the immediate needs for survival faced by women in the poorer sections, without addressing the multidimensional and multisectoral processes and structures that marginalise these women. The governmental bodies deliberating on the crucial strategies of food production, industrialisation rural development, science and technology, and monetary reforms still face the problems connected with the integration of the role of women into their overall plans of action.

It is becoming increasingly evident that issues related to the position of women cannot meaningfully be dealt with only through specific projects, without effectively linking them to economic policies, plans and programmes, and making these projects an integral part of the long-term process of development. The typical women and development projects may, however, perpetuate the reformist stance by promoting marginal, often non-viable activities not linked to major sectors of development and sometimes lead to a considerable increase in women's burden without providing the necessary supportive institutions for their new role and expanded opportunities. They fail to deal with structural inequalities, which lead to changes in policies and programmes and affect the allocative, distributive and participatory processes.

The access of women to productive resources is a necessary precondition for their advancement. Recent discussions in both international and national flora have stressed issues such as title to land, access to credit and banking facilities, to employment on equal terms and under equal conditions, and to information and knowledge, education and training. Any policy aimed at improving the lot of poorer households should involve substantial changes in resource control, *e.g.*, land tenure, investment patterns, access to information regarding markets, technology, employment opportunities, availability of financial or other support, training etc., to increase women's control over their own labour and income.

During the UN Decade for Women, besides the integrative approach, arguments for specific transitional strategies and policies by the government to deal with the historically disadvantaged position of women were put forward. The approach was based on the assumption that the understanding of the role of women could be strengthened within the complex framework of government by setting time-specific and measurable goals within each important sector, thus operationalising the concern for the position and role of women and translating it into programmes of action. Further, recognising the close link between class and gender issues, it was expected that targetting for each group, in addition to the overall development target, would narrow the gender gaps in various sectors. To ensure a more meaningful intervention, a blending of the two approaches, *i.e.*, integral development with specific action, is suggested. Minor transitional activities should be in line with the long-term perspectives, if they are not to be counter-productive. A survey conducted by the ILO in mid-1984, on the integration of the question of women in national development plans, reveals that only 12 of 44 developing countries has incorporated employment of women by sectors in their national development plans, 28 countries had setup governmental bodies dealing with the question of female workers, and only 19 of 44 countries had undertaken sectoral surveys to investigate the problems and prospects of female workers. Much ground remains to be covered before the legal guarantees and administrative measures can be put into practice. Attempts at removing legal obstacles and improving access to education and other social services have not prevented growing poverty and malnutrition, rising unemployment and underemployment coupled with an increasing work burden, and persistent marginalisation of women in the economy and in decision making structures, although there have been varying results in the individual countries and regions.

However, governments have experienced considerable difficulties in their attempts to articulate these new approaches in policies and development action. These are due to a number of factors: the persistent invisibility of women as a critical and important factor within development structures; continued lack of awareness and understanding of the difficulties that women face even when they are participating on equal terms in development—both as beneficiaries and as agents; and delays in developing an adequate set of monitoring and evaluation measures and instruments to speed up effective implementation of adopted policies.

The most urgent task, which now faces governments is more innovative blending of the role of women into the design of action programmes, policy instruments and evaluation criteria or monitoring procedures in all sectors of development. The issue of women's role in development cannot be a concern of women only. The value-creating mechanisms, *i.e.*, the educational system, and the media, may be suitably modified to project values of sex equality. Governments could modify or eliminate legal provisions that still uphold the unequal status of women.

The strategies for action suggested in the sectoral chapters all call for operational instruments. Who is to initiate, implement and evaluate these measures at the national and at the regional and international levels? The emphasis should be on perceptional, organisational and infrastructural development. At the government level, executive and administrative measures need to be taken to ensure recognition of women's productive, reproductive and participatory roles and to provide supportive services such as child care and need social services, *i.e.*, health care, education, catering, housing and drinking water, etc., to reduce their work burden and enable them to assume wider responsibilities.

What kind of policy instruments have been effective in incorporating the role of women into sectoral structures? A concerted effort is needed to bridge the gap between the highest levels of government and the intermediate and lower levels where plans are operationalised. A comparicon of organisational and infra-structural models and approaches in different countries could provide an insight into the strengths and weaknesses of various arrangement.

The Mexico Conference had visualised the National Commission as watchdog bodies—to review and recommend measures necessary to enhance the equality and participation of women in development and decision making. Some countries have defined the functions of the national mechanisms in this manner and provided them with the requisite powers of resource support. At the same time the strength of the argument that women's affairs cannot be separated from the sectoral agencies responsible for planning and implementation of development in the fields of agriculture and rural development, industry, energy, science and technology, urban and rural development, education, health and other social services must be acknowledged. Since the objective is the integration of women in all these sectors of development, it could be useful to institutionalise this concern, or mandate—to continue the task of making the Sectoral agencies sensitive, concerned and accountable.

In view of the stagnation of overall development, the modest resource support has kept efforts to promote the role of women at a marginal level in most developing countries. Thus in some developing countries such efforts have been primarily dependent on international aid. Apart from the fact that this may have precluded the integration of these efforts into major development sectors, this dependence has in some cases also diverted attention from the goals of collective and national self-reliance, and sometimes also distorted national priorities.

Research on women in development, which has evolved during the Decade as an important instrument for the advancement of the role of women has been useful, since it has been instrumental in the collection of empirical information which has, to date, provided most of the data to assess the impact of various development policies on women; it has sensitised the people involved in development planning and administration by posing issue resulting from their empirical investigations and promoted an ideological climate and public concern thus raising the level of consciousness among women and others.

So far, such studies have primarily been confined to research and have made little impact on the training and value transformation of younger generations. The promotion of such studies as an instrument for enhancing the role of women in development, through educational and training institutions agencies responsible for research and information has emerged as a critical need. Such an approach would be most appropriate within the areas of cooperation among the non-aligned countries in order to eliminate the dependence on external aid-with the possible risk of distortions. In view of the fact that the role of women in development has been acknowledged as an important component of the research and information system that is being promoted within the movement of the non-aligned countries, it is suggested that this component could be included through a combination· of research, training and information dissemination.

The incorporation of the aspects of the role of women in development in existing teaching/training and research institutions may reduce investments in physical and administrative infrastructure—and improve the prospects for integrating/articulating women's problems, issues and concerns within all educational institution/disciplines, instead of allowing them to remain a separate, marginal activity, whose isolation makes it ineffective. National, regional and international networks of such institutions should be encouraged to share and expand share and expand their experiences, which would help to increase their competence, and strengthen the ties or intellectual and developmental co-operation among non-aligned nations. Such efforts would help to increase the extent and improve the quality of data needed by national governments. They would also make it possible to train an increasing number of cadres to take up the various functions identified as necessary for the advancement of women in development. Above all, the incorporation of studies of this kind within the educational systems and in training institutions would help promote the needed cultural transformation. Science and technology, which could be powerful instruments for the advancement of the role of women in development have so for usually by passed women because their educational and other handicaps. Science and technology have also often been misused to marginalise women and reduce their status. It is therefore important not merely to facilitate the access of women to science and technology, but also to ensure that practitioners will be aware of the problems involved in the employment of women in his areas. It would be useful to introduce these concerns as early as the training stage.

In particular, developments in the fields of communication technology and communication sciences pose a critical challenge to the decisions of the non-aligned Countries to enhance the role of women in development. If these new developments are not harnessed in accordance with the policies for the advancement of women, they will continue to be used by social forces, which oppose the equality of women and development, and help to strengthen and perpetuate values and behavioural norms that thrive on the subordination of women.

The improvement of the systems for data collection and development of quantitative and indicators for measuring women's development is another critical area. Despite repeated decisions at various international conferences many national data collection agencies still do not have adequate data on women, nor do they provide sex break-downs or gender differentiation in different fields. They continue to be pervaded with a biased understanding of what is important information regarding the status of women and its impact on the conditions and equality of life of families, communities and development in general. Similarly, there has been little follow-up action at the national levels to the very useful international efforts and decision to develop and compile comparable socioeconomic indicators to measure the role of women in development, as initiated recently by INSTRAW and the UN Statistical Office.

A system of reporting by sex disaggregated data would help the flow of information from the bottom up, monitoring the actual implementation of programmes and benefits accuring to women, and through women to the entire community, and increase the accountability of government agencies. Simultaneously, such a process would initiate improvement of data systems, concepts and methods of statistics and development of indicators.

●●

4

Entrepreneurship Approach

The word entrepreneur is derived from the French entrepreneure, meaning to undertake. The entrepreneur is one who undertakes to organize, manage and assume the risks of a business. In recent years entrepreneurs have been doing so many things that it is necessary to broaden this definition. Today, an entrepreneur is an innovator or developer who recognizes and seizes opportunities, converts those opportunities in to workable/marketable ideas, adds value through time, effort, money or skills, assumes the risks of the competitive marketplace to implement these ideas, and realizes the rewards from these efforts.

The entrepreneur is the aggressive catalyst for change in the world of business, and is the independent thinker who dares to be different in a background of common events. The literature of entrepreneurship research reveals some similarities, as well as a great many differences, in the characteristics of entrepreneurs. Chief among these characteristics are personal initiative, the ability to consolidate resources, autonomy, risk taking, competitiveness, goal-orientated behaviour, opportunistic behaviour, reality-based actions and the ability to learn from mistakes. It should be recognized that if some characteristics are taken to their extreme then entrepreneurs exhibit a 'dark side' which could result in destructive behaviours.

While no single definition or complete profile of an entrepreneur exists, research is providing an increasingly sharper focus on the subject. A brief review of the history of entrepreneurship illustrates this. In addition, entrepreneurship has now extended into major corporations where innovative activity is revitalizing organizations. Known as intrapreneurship, this entrepreneurial strategy inside established companies has become a major force for growth and development of organizations.

The entire world is currently in the midst of a new wave of business and economic development, and entrepreneurship is its catalyst. Yet the social and economic forces of entrepreneurial activity existed long before the 1990s. In fact, it has been the entrepreneurial spirit that has driven many of mankind's achievements.

The recognition of entrepreneurs dates back to the eighteenth century when the French economist Richard Cantillon associated the 'risk bearing' activity in the economy with the entrepreneur. In England during the same period the Industrial Revolution was evolving, with the entrepreneur playing a visible role in risk taking and the transformation of resources.

The association of entrepreneurship and economics has long been the accepted norm. In fact, until the 1950s the majority of definitions and references to entrepreneurship had come from economics. Cantillon mentioned above, the renowned French economist Jean Baptiste Say and twentieth-century economic genius Joseph Schumpeter all wrote about entrepreneurship and its impact on economic development. Thus entrepreneurship was introduced by the economists of the eighteenth century, and continued to attract the interest of economists in the nineteenth century. In present times the word has become synonymous, or at least closely linked, with free enterprise and capitalism. Also, it is generally recognized that entrepreneurs serve as agents of change, provide creative, innovative ideas for business enterprises and help businesses grow and become profitable.

Entrepreneurs today are considered the heroes of free enterprise. Many of them have used innovation and creativity to build multimillion dollar enterprises from fledgling businesses. These individuals have created new products and services and have assumed the risks associated with these ventures. Many people now regard entrepreneurship as a pioneership on the frontier of business. One definition, developed by Ronstadt (1984), summarizes some of the current thoughts concerning entrepreneurship:

Entrepreneurship is the dynamic process of creating incremental wealth. This wealth is created by individuals who assume the major risks in terms of equity, time, and/or career commitment of providing value for some product or service. The product or service itself mayor may not be new or unique but value must somehow be infused by the entrepreneur by securing and allocating the necessary skills and resources.

The Myths of Entrepreneurship

Throughout the years many myths have arisen about entrepreneurship. These myths are the result of a lack of research in entrepreneurship. As many researchers in the field have noted, the study of entrepreneurship is still in its infancy, and thus 'folklore' will tend to prevail until it is dispelled with contemporary research findings. Some of the major myths are discussed below.

'Entrepreneurs are Born, not Made'

This myth, which implies that the characteristics of entrepreneurs cannot be taught or learned, that they are innate traits with which one must be born, has long been prevalent. Today, however, the recognition of entrepreneurship as a discipline is helping to dispel this myth. Like all disciplines, entrepreneurship has models, processes and case studies that allow the topic to be studied and the traits acquired.

'Entrepreneurs are Academic and Social Misfits'

The belief that entrepreneurs are academically and socially ineffective is a result of some business owners having started successful enterprises after dropping out of school or quitting a job. In many cases such an event has been blown out of proportion in an attempt to profile the typical entrepreneur. Historically, in fact, educational and social organizations did not recognize the entrepreneur. They abandoned him or her as a misfit in a world of corporate giants. Business education, for example, was aimed primarily at the study of corporate activity. Today the entrepreneur is considered a hero socially, economically and academically. No longer a misfit, the entrepreneur is now viewed as a professional.

'Entrepreneurs Fit an Ideal Profile'

Many books and articles have presented checklists of characteristics of the successful entrepreneur. These lists were neither validated nor complete; they were based on case studies and on research findings among achievement-orientated people. Today we realize that a standard entrepreneurial profile is hard to compile. The environment, the venture itself, and the entrepreneur have interactive effects, which result in many different types of profiles. Contemporary studies being conducted at universities across the world will, in the future, provide more accurate insights into the various profiles of successful entrepreneurs.

'All you Need is Money to be an Entrepreneur'

It is true that a venture needs capital to survive; it is also true that a large number of business failures occur because of lack of adequate financing. Yet having money is not the only bulwark against failure. Failure due to a lack of proper financing is often an indicator of other problems: managerial incompetence, lack of financial understanding, poor investments, poor planning, etc.

'All you Need is Luck to be an Entrepreneur'

Being in 'the right place at the right time' is always an advantage, but 'luck happens when preparation meets opportunity' is an equally appropriate adage. Prepared entrepreneurs who seize the opportunity when it arises often appear to be 'lucky'. They are, in fact, simply better prepared to deal with situations and turn them into successes. What appears to be luck really is preparation, determination, desire, knowledge and innovativeness.

Approaches to Entrepreneurship

In the study of contemporary entrepreneurship, there is one recurring concept: entrepreneurship is an interdisciplinary concept. As such it contains various approaches that can be used to increase one's understanding of the field. Thus there is a need to recognize the diversity of theories as an emergence of entrepreneurial understanding. One way to examine these theories is with a 'schools of thought' approach that divides entrepreneurship into specific activities. Another way is through a process approach that blends the elements into multi-faceted models.

In this section we shall highlight the ideas emanating from the macro and micro views of entrepreneurial thought, and we shall further break down these two major views into six distinct schools of thought, three within each entrepreneurial view. While this presentation does not purport to be all inclusive, neither does it claim to limit the schools to these six, for a movement may develop for unification or expansion.

The Macro View

The macro view of entrepreneurship presents a broad array of factors that relate to success or failure in contemporary entrepreneurial ventures. These include external processes that are sometimes beyond the control of the individual entrepreneur, for they exhibit a strong external locus of control point of view.

Three schools of entrepreneurial thought represent a breakdown of the macro view: *(1)* the environmental school of thought; *(2)* the financial/capital school of thought; and *(3)* the displacement school of thought. The first of these is the broadest and most pervasive school.

The environmental school of thought deals with the external factors that affect a potential entrepreneur's lifestyle. These can be either a positive or a negative force in the moulding of entrepreneurial desires. The focus is on institutions, values and mores that, grouped together, form a socio-political environmental framework that strongly influences the development of entrepreneurs. For example, if a middle manager experiences the freedom and support to develop ideas, initiate contacts or create and institute new methods, the environment will serve to promote that person's desire to pursue an entrepreneurial career. Another environmental factor is the social group environment that often affects the potential development of entrepreneurs. The atmosphere of friends and relatives can influence the desire to become an entrepreneur.

The financial/capital school of thought is based on the capital seeking process. The search for seed capital and growth capital is the entire focus of this entrepreneurial emphasis. Certain literature is devoted .specifically to this process, whereas other sources tend to treat it as but one segment of the entrepreneurial process. In any case, the venture capital process is vital to the development of an entrepreneur. Business planning guides for entrepreneurs emphasize this phase, and there are development seminars focusing on the funds application process. This school of thought views the entire entrepreneurial venture from a financial standpoint.

The displacement school of thought focuses on group phenomena. It holds that the group affects or eliminates certain factors that project the individual into an entrepreneurial venture. Individuals will not pursue a venture unless they are prevented or displaced from doing other things. Three major types of displacement illustrate this school of thought.

1. Political Displacement. This type of displacement is caused by factors ranging from an entire political regime that rejects free enterprise (international environment), to government regulations and policies that limit or redirect certain industries.

2. Cultural Displacement. This type of displacement deals with social groups precluded from professional fields. Ethnic background, religion, race and gender are all examples of factors that figure in the minority experience. Increasingly, this experience will turn various individuals from standard business professions towards entrepreneurial ventures.

3. Economic Displacement. This type of displacement is concerned with the economic variations of recession and depression. Job loss, capital shrinkage, or simply bad times can create the foundation for entrepreneurial pursuits, just as it can affect venture development and reduction.

The Micro View

The micro view of entrepreneurship examines the factors that are specific to entrepreneurship and are part of the internal locus of control. The potential entrepreneur has the ability to direct or adjust the outcome of each major influence. In this view are presented the entrepreneurial trait theory, the venture opportunity theory, and the strategic planning theory. Unlike the macro approach, which focuses on events from the outside looking in, the micro approach concentrates on specifics from the inside looking out. The first of these schools of thought is the most widely recognized.

Since many researchers and writers have been interested in identifying those traits that are common to successful entrepreneurs, the entrepreneurial trait school of thought is grounded in the study of successful people who tend to exhibit similar characteristics that, if copied, would increase success opportunities for the emulators. For example, achievement, creativity, determination and technical knowledge are four factors that are usually exhibited by successful entrepreneurs. Family development and educational incubation are also examined. Researchers Contend that new programmes and new educational developments are on the increase because they have been found to aid in entrepreneurial development. The family development idea focuses on the nurturing and support that exist within the home atmosphere of an entrepreneurial family. This reasoning promotes the belief that certain traits, that are established and supported early in life, eventually lead to entrepreneurial success.

The venture opportunity school of thought focuses on the opportunity aspect of venture development. The search for sources of ideas, the development of concepts, and the implementation of venture opportunities are the important areas of interest for this school. Creativity and market awareness are viewed as essential. Additionally, according to this school of thought, developing the right idea at the right time for the right market niche is the key to entrepreneurial success.

Another development from this school of thought is the corridor principle. New pathways or opportunities will arise that lead entrepreneurs in different directions. The ability to recognize these opportunities when they arise, and to implement the necessary steps for action, are key factors. Proponents of this school of thought believe that proper preparation in the interdisciplinary segments of business will enhance the ability to recognize venture opportunities.

The strategic formulation school of thought emphasizes the planning process in successful venture development. Strategic formulation can be viewed as a leveraging of unique elements. Unique markets, unique people, unique products or unique resources are identified, used or constructed into effective venture formulations. The interdisciplinary aspects of strategic adaptation become apparent in the characteristic elements listed below.

1. **Unique Markets.** Mountain versus mountain-gap strategies, which refers to identifying major market segments as well as interstice (in between) markets that arise from larger markets.

2. **Unique People.** Great chef strategies, which refers to the skills or special talents of one or more individuals around whom the venture is built.

3. **Unique Products.** Better widget strategies, which refers to innovations that encompass new or existing markets.

4. **Unique Resources.** Water-well strategies, which refers to the ability to gather or harness special resources (land, labour, capital, raw materials) over the long term.

Without question, the strategic formulation school encompasses a breadth of managerial capability that requires an interdisciplinary approach.

While the knowledge and research available in entrepreneurship is in an embryonic stage, it is still possible to piece together and describe current schools of thought in the field. From this point we can begin to develop an appreciation for the schools and view them as a foundation for entrepreneurial theory.

Process Approaches

Another way to examine entrepreneurial activities is with a process approach. Unique to the process approach is its major focus on the start-up of a venture. Process approach models developed by various researchers are inter-disciplinary because entrepreneurship includes factors from numerous disciplines. These process approaches attempt to be integrative, while focusing on individual elements that harmoniously fit together. There are many methods and models that try to structure the entrepreneurial process and its various factors. For example, the assessment approach, developed by Ronstadt (1984), stresses assessments that must be made qualitatively, quantitatively, strategically and ethically with regard to the entrepreneur, the venture and the environment. The results of these assessments must be compared with stages of the entrepreneurial career early, mid-career or late. This process is called the entrepreneurial perspective.

A more detailed process approach to entrepreneurship is the multidimensional approach. From this viewpoint, entrepreneurship is a complex, multidimensional framework that emphasizes the individual, the environment, the organization and the venture process.

The process approaches to studying entrepreneurship Illustrate that three distinct variables are critical to any analysis: the individual, the venture and the environment. However, the stages of any venture (idea, preventure. start-up, early growth, harvest) are also critical to new venture analysis. In addition, a career perspective should be considered, which means that the entrepreneur's career stage (early, middle or late) can be a decisive factor in differentiating the variable with the venture development stages. Thus it may be necessary to visualize entrepreneurial strategies as contingencies. In other words all of the evolving and emerging conditions involved with any entrepreneurial pursuit cause a constant dynamism. If newly emerging entrepreneurial issues such as global expansion, the growth in numbers of women entrepreneurs and corporate entrepreneurship are also introduced, then a model of entrepreneurial strategy would be multidimensional, multi-staged, and contingency based.

The Dark Side of Entrepreneurship

There is a great deal of literature devoted to extolling the rewards, successes, and achievements of entrepreneurs. However, there also is a 'dark' side of entrepreneurship. This aspect of the entrepreneurial profile has a destructive source that exists within the energetic drive of successful entrepreneurs. In examining this dual-edged approach to the entrepreneurial personality there are a number of major traits that characterize this dark side.

The Need for Control

Entrepreneurs are driven by a strong desire to control both their venture and their destiny. This internal locus of control spills over into a preoccupation with controlling everything. An obsession for autonomy and control may cause entrepreneurs to work in structured situations only when they have created the structure on their terms.

Sense of Distrust

Entrepreneurs try to anticipate and act on developments that others will recognize too late. This distrustful state can result in their focusing on trivial things, causing them to lose sight of reality, distort reasoning and logic and take destructive actions.

Desire for Success

The entrepreneur's ego is involved in the desire for success. Thus, the entrepreneur rises up as a defiant person who creatively acts to succeed and takes pride in demonstrating that success. There in lie the seeds of possible destructiveness: the danger that the individual will become more important than the venture itself.

External Optimism

Entrepreneurs maintain a high level of enthusiasm that gives off an external optimism that allows others to believe in them during rough periods. However, when taken to its extreme, this optimistic attitude can lead to a fantasy approach to the business. A self-deceptive state may arise in which the entrepreneur ignores trends, facts and reports and deludes them-self into thinking everything will turn out fine.

Stress

In order to achieve their goals, however, entrepreneurs are willing to tolerate stress. It is important to recognize four causes of entrepreneurial stress: *(1)* loneliness; *(2)* immersion in business; *(3)* people problems; and *(4)* the need to achieve.

The Concept of Risk

Starting or buying a new business involves risk, and the higher the rewards, the greater the risk entrepreneurs usually face. This is why entrepreneurs need to evaluate risk very carefully. There are a number of different types of risk faced by entrepreneurs. These can be grouped into four basic areas: *(1)* financial risk; *(2)* career risk; *(3)* family and social risk; and (4) psychic risk.

Intrapreneurship—the Process of Corporate Entrepreneurship

The contemporary thrust in entrepreneurship as the major force in worldwide business has led to a desire for this type of activity inside enterprises. While some researchers have concluded that entrepreneurship and bureaucracies are mutually exclusive and cannot coexist, others have described entrepreneurial ventures within the enterprise framework. Successful corporate ventures have been used in many different companies, including 3M, IBM, Hewlett Packard, AT&T, General Electric and Polaroid. Today there is a wealth of popular business literature describing a new corporate revolution taking place, thanks to the infusion of entrepreneurial thinking into larger bureaucratic structures. This infusion is referred to as corporate entrepreneurship or intrapreneurship.

Pinchott (1985) coined the term intrapreneur as entrepreneurial activity inside the corporation where individuals (intrapreneurs) will champion new ideas from development to complete profitable reality. Other authors have expanded this definition to include sanctions and resource commitments for the purpose of innovative results.

Over the last few years there has been a growing interest in using intrapreneurship (corporate intrapreneurship) as a way for corporations to enhance employees' innovative abilities and, at the same time, increase corporate success through the potential creation of new corporate ventures. However, the creation of corporate entrepreneurial activity can be difficult because it involves radically changing traditional forms of internal organizational behaviour and structure.

The desire to pursue corporate entrepreneurship has arisen from a variety of pressing problems including: *(1)* required changes, innovations and improvements in the market-place to avoid stagnation and decline; *(2)* perceived weaknesses in the traditional methods of corporate management; and *(3)* the turnover of innovative-minded employees who are disenchanted with bureaucratic organizations. This loss of talented employees is intensified by entrepreneurship's new appeal as a legitimate career and the increased ability of the venture capital industry (as well as informal capitalists) to finance more new ventures.

The first step in planning an intrapreneurship strategy for the enterprise is sharing the vision of innovation that the corporate leaders wish to achieve. Since it is suggested that corporate entrepreneuring results from the creative talents of people within the organization, employees need to know about and understand this vision. The importance of shared vision is a critical element for a strategy that seeks high achievement. This shared vision requires identification of specific objectives for corporate entrepreneuring strategies, and the programmes needed to achieve those objectives.

The next step for a corporation seeking to establish an intrapreneurial strategy is to encourage innovation among employees as the key element in their strategy. The importance of developing innovation within the corporate environment is a critical component of contemporary competitive strategies. Innovation has been described as chaotic and unplanned by some authors, while other researchers insist that it is a systematic discipline. Both positions can be true depending on the nature of the innovation.

A third step in developing an intrapreneurial strategy is to focus on venture teams. Venture teams and the potential they hold for producing innovative results are being recognized increasingly as the productivity breakthrough of the 1990s. There is certainly little doubt that their popularity is on the rise. Companies that have committed to a venture team approach often label the change a 'transformation' or 'revolution'. This breed of work team is a new direction for many firms. The teams are often referred to as self-directed, self-managing or high performance, but usually a venture team includes all of these descriptions. By examining many of the successful entrepreneurial developments within established corporations, it can be shown that entrepreneurship is not the sole province of the company's founder or its top managers. Rather, it is diffused throughout the company where experimentation and development go on all the time.

In re-establishing the drive to innovate in today's corporations, the final, and possibly most critical, step is to invest heavily in an entrepreneurial structure that allows new ideas to flourish in an innovative environment. This concept, when coupled with the other elements of a strategy for innovation, can enhance the potential for employees to become venture developers. In fact, in developing employees as a source of innovations for corporations, it has been found that companies need to provide more nurturing and information sharing activities. In addition to establishing entrepreneurial ways and nurturing intrapreneurs, there is a need to develop a climate that will help innovative-minded people reach their full potential. The perception of an innovative climate is critical for stressing the importance of management's commitment not only to the organization's people but also to the innovative projects.

●●

5

Theory of Women Development

For women to become a vital force in their societies, change will have to be based on a new theory of development which embraces feminism. Feminism poses some challenges to development theory and praxis that must be addressed if any effective and inclusive work on bringing about a new order is to be done. It questions the artificial barriers between the political, social and economic aspects of society, and how individuals relate to these orders. Feminism asserts that the personal is political and personal change is a prerequisite to social change... the internalisation and subjectification of being a change agent. It insists that the experience of women be recognised and validated in all work related to change. Examples of how this theory can be developed already exist, in progressive women's movements all over the world that are challenging the power of patriarchy. Women are organising, speaking out against injustice in the home, workplace and society. These struggles are not restricted to upper and middle class women (as we are often told), but evident in working class and peasant women's groups, who have a long history of struggle against oppression.

At the same time, the struggle against patriarchy and economic oppression cannot be separated from the struggle of those who are poor and powerless. Progressive women's movements can be separate, and part of all those who work to bring about a just, participatory and sustainable society.

Income Generation

For mainstream development models, development has meant the "integration" of developing countries into the international market system, whereby the notion of "growth" was to be manifested in increased economic production. Towards this end, education and employment were considered a means for income generation. Therefore, it should come as no surprise that common indicators used to determine women's involvement in development have been employment and education. When most women live in rural areas and in a non-market economy (70 to 80 per cent are involved in subsistence work), these indicators have little validity. As women make up 60 to 90 per cent of the agricultural labour force and produce 44 per cent of all food, why is it crucial to talk of income generating projects? Rather, would it not be better to recognise women's current productivity? Most developing economies have moved or are moving from agrarian-based to industrial-based economies, in spite of what their governments may claim. During this process, the structure of agriculture has suffered. With growing emphasis on cash cropping and non-food crops, subsistence farming has suffered a major setback.

This has had serious repercussions on women and the rural communities. Through subsistence farming, most of a rural family's and community's needs were met. Excess edibles were sold or bartered in local markets for commodities such as soap and clothes. With increasing numbers 01 women having to shift to cash cropping, and with meager economic returns; the family's needs are not being met. Nutritionally this has taken a heavy toll on the health and well-being or rural communities. Former food-producing communities are not growing cash crops or non-food crop's for export to urban, national and international markets. Whereas once they were somewhat self-sufficient, they now mostly rely on government handouts or foreign aid. Income generating projects may be a godsend to women, with few opportunities for subsistence farming and few or no skills for alternative work in a limited job market, who have been forced into non-farm work. However, it further exacerbates the problem of vanishing subsistence farming and food dependence on foreign markets.

Enlisting women in new jobs, largely for manufacturing export items, often requires their migration to urban areas. Skills that women are taught are "female-prone" - a term used to describe skills which women are supposedly best at, such as sewing, knitting, embroidery, and which are low-skilled, low-paid and easily replaceable. Local and multinational industries such as textiles, electronics and agribusiness have capitalized on this shift and preferentially hire women. Paying low wages for long hours in unhealthy and hazardous working conditions, these industries claim they are liberating women. Multinationals have been keen advocates of this transfer of women's work from self-sufficient to market-oriented types. The industries well realise the gold mine they have struck with women who are usually the most willing to work, the easiest to fire and the least likely to unionize. Income generation advocates little realised the complexity of issues when they suggested this. With little or no protection for wages, benefits and work, women are the most abused section of the formal labour force.

Education

Education, along with income generation capacity, has been perceived as the key to the golden door of success and equal participation of women in the development process. It is true that women need education to be able to participate in society, but the nature of this education has not been sufficiently questioned.

In industrialised societies or urban areas of developing countries, education can be a stepping stone to economic self-sufficiency. However, the educational systems in most developing countries are relics of their colonial past, and irrelevant to the needs of most people, especially women. The education is either highly specialised (in which case women have to compete in a narrow job market) or too general (in which case women have access only to the lowest paid jobs). Economically, even such education is beyond the means of most people. If a child has to be educated, preference is given to the male child, who is a better asset in terms of financial returns. For the affluent, educating woman is an exercise that will increase their price in the marriage market. If education is to have any value for women, it must be a means to raise their consciousness about the oppressive structures that keep them in positions of powerlessness. Most educational systems do not provide a climate for such thinking skills to develop. In developing societies, most educated women—the leaders, academicians, professionals in establishment organizations—perpetuate the status quo. The reasoning behind this is that if the patriarchal system has worked for them, it should work for all women. Demands for traditional education from third world women and others come from a lack of perspective of what this limited privilege can be used for.

When a woman is relatively powerless and has little control over what is happening in her environment, education for literacy is meaningless. What she craves is knowledge of why she must bear so many children, work endless hours without respite, be beaten and raped, have an alcoholic husband, and go hungry. Existing educational systems have not provided women with the tools to understand and analyse the true nature of social, political and economic systems that govern their lives and oppress them, and this is why they have failed. If women are to be change agents in their societies, the education offered them must be a tool for consciousness raising and action. This end result cannot be brought about by learning the three rupees or being drilled in nutrition and family planning.

Appropriate Technology

Transfer of technology has been a major ingredient of mainstream development work. This transfer has filed the coffers of many multinational corporations that manufacture and export heavy equipment, has supported highly specialised and largely intellectual research and development institutions, and has meant large investments for developing countries. It has proved an expensive and futile exercise and developing countries are now demanding technologies that meet the needs of their budgets and projects.

Taking off from the "small is beautiful" ideology, the concept of appropriate technology emerged. Developed countries rushed into developing ones with new designs and innovations that would revolutionize the developing world. Recognising that women do back-breaking work for long hours, the women in development community sought solutions once again in technology. Instead of examining why women, after hard work in the fields and markets, have to return home to cook, care for children, gather fuel and water and take care of animals, the development planners seized upon appropriate technology. Smokeless stoves, grinders, seed hullers, weeders, hoes and suchlike were invented and improved upon to cut the time spent in these tasks. The inherent sexism in permitting men to return from the fields, bathe, eat and go visiting with friends has never been questioned. Job sharing of "women's work" is unheard of.

Similar questions can be raised regarding technical innovations that have supposedly eased the burden of women's work in developed societies. Have the vacuum clearner, dish-washer, blender, ice maker enabled a women to have a more equal relationship with a man? Equality cannot be achieved as long as women are seen as marginal to the existence of men, society or development.

The new directions in technology suffer from the same malady as development. They are male-dominated, designed mostly in developed societies, and often involve resources alien to the local environment. Even when the appropriate technologies are locally developed, they are often done in research laboratories and academic institutions with little' input from the women and men in the field who will be utilizing the technologies.

Health

Most of the health care focus around women has been in family planning and nutrition. While it is important for women to have access to information and services to control their fertility, much of the help offered has been misguided and controlled mainly by population specialists and family planning agents, who are usually men. Reproduction information and services made available to women are largely male and establishment-controlled, and unsuited to the lifestyles and bodies of the women receiving them. Additionally, services such as regular checkups and pre-and post-natal care are rarely available. Efforts by the overzealous and insensitive population community (with help from the pharmaceutical industry and national governments which work hand in hand with these organisations) have been based on the premise that it is better to have reduced fertility at any cost than overpopulation. Who makes this decision is quite clear certainly not the women on the receiving end of these programmes. In spite of the known dangers of synthetic contraceptives, the women in development community has further pushed for these programmes.

A similar situation exists in the area of nutrition. The popular thinking is that most people in developing countries do not have sufficient know-how to balance their diets and need to be educated. However, it can be said that development has done more to undermine the possibility of achieving a balanced diet than to help it. Development strategies, supported by international food politics, have pushed for the boost in food production of items for export (to earn foreign exchange for sophisticated technology and research), as well as non-food items. Towards this end, land once producing food to meet the needs of the community is being used for cash-cropping and income generation.

To alleviate this problem, solutions are being proposed and implemented such as food substitutes (*e.g.* soymeal) which are alien to the diet of the local people, and, therefore, rejected. Questions relating to the overall structures of agriculture, of land ownership, crop priorities, etc., are hardly ever raised. If they are, it is in the light of reformist measures such as land reform or water reallocation.

If a society were committed to maintaining a fair standard of health for its people, it would devise and implement systems of agriculture and health care that would make the goal possible. As long as foreign exchange earnings and modernisation are higher priorities for most developing societies, basic health care will remain an illusion. Research and development emphases will be on diseases which affect mainly the elites (*e.g.* cardiovascular diseases), with little attention to the politics of malnutrition and reproduction. Development experts, unwilling to question the power and control of medicine and researchers will continue to ignore the role of women in the health and planning process, except as a means to serve the experts' ends.

Women in Development

Since its conception, much of the mainstream women in development work has been like a long distance affair. Largely defined by western women and their elitist counterparts in developing countries, it has fallen prey to the same assumptions that development work has; *i.e.*, development is an overseas problem. All societies are developing societies. While it is true that most people in less developed countries live more precariously than their western counterparts, it is also true that marginalised sections of developed societies have much in common with their counterparts in developing countries. This relationship, a critical one if development were viewed as a class issue has been ignored by the experts. It is easier to deal with something which is not too close to home and which is also more exotic.

At the same time, this long distance strategy excuses governments of developed countries from dealing with issues of deprivation at home. With increasing internationalisation of capital and human resources as well as raw materials over the last decade, it has become detrimental to development work not to establish this link. As a result, the strategies in the past, as well as the ones being proposed for the future, lack validity. Case in point: the marginalisation of women in developing societies (so well elucidated in the women in development literature) cannot be overcome without examining the roots of marginalisation, which is the patriarchal system, not only in the developing societies but in the developed ones as well.

That some percentage of women in developed societies enjoy a certain level of economic independence must not be equated with the achievement of equality in the power structures that control their societies. This is evident in examining the position of the majority of women in developed societies, who are the poorest, most oppressed, overworked and marginalised sections of their society.

Decisions made in any country regarding woman in the garment industry affect women in the USA, Mexico, Britain, Italy, India, Sri Lanka, Korea, Taiwan and many other countries. Flight of capital and the internationalisation of trade has brought these women together-either to lose or gain from such investments or to collectively organise against the single-purpose of the multinational corporations: maximisation of profit.

Women working in the mainstream development community have largely failed to address these issues-at home or overseas. It is easier to propagate reformist measures such as income generating projects, job skills, nutrition education, welfare and the like than to examine the root causes of overt sexism, agricultural displacement, and the marginalisation of women in any society. If ever the issues of power and powerlessness are brought up at a national international forum, it is only at the theoretical level with little pragmatic follow up.

Women in development can have real meaning when the vital links between the local and global situations are made. For example, women in the USA must look at the struggles of women in their rural communities, women in Appalachia, Native American women, farm-worker women, working class women. Many of the problems these women are facing are similar to those being faced by their sisters overseas. As most women in the USA fall into the marginalised categories, the women in development community in the USA has gravely shirked its responsibility in neglecting these issues and failing to relate them to the marginalisation of women overseas.

Strategies for Change

There is no one strategy that will ensure equitable development for all. However, there are several directions that such strategies can go which could enable equitable development. If change were to be categorised in two broad areas—reform and radical-each category would have certain strategies that would enable change to be brought about.

Reformist strategies are those which are devised to alleviate problems (*e.g.*, food stamps for the hungry, unemployment compensation for the unemployed) without much attention to the cause of the problems. Radical strategies are devised by examining the root of the problem, and proposing alternatives to presently existing structures that are responsible for creating the problems. Whether strategies are reformist or radical in nature, they can go hand in hand, especially in societies where a total transformation of the political, social and economic system is not in sight, but there must be understanding of the means and the end.

The US 1980 Democratic Political Convention illustrated the need for such awareness. Political reforms meant that for the first time, women were half of the delegates to the national convention. However, as a columnist Richard Reeves pointed out, "Women, even when they share floor space at a convention, may never truly share political power of change politics. The game has rules made by men and they have a life and momentum of their own." Such reforms are important, but should not alone be taken as necessarily representing a real shift toward equality in decision-making.

Both reformist and radical movements share a common goal for change. The underlying ideologies of the two are different, but reforms rightly integrated can become steps to more long-term change.

Helping Shape this Future

Individuals and institutions interested in building this new just order need first of all to do more intentional thinking about the kind of political, social and economic order that will meet the needs of the all people. Towards this end, development must mean the production, distribution and consumption of goods and services in the most equitable manner possible, with maximum participation of all people. For those in the developing and developed world it means study, consciousness raising, dialoguing and brainstorming about how people can gain control over their economies, no matter where they are. It means concentrating on the problems locally, state-wide, nationally and internationally.

A feminist approach to this future would require that this process happen before "development" is planned. It would also require the participation of women in every step of the way.

And finally, women—and men who are concerned about development—must learn to stand fast. Too long the theory has prevailed that when other more pressing issues of politics and peace are dealt with, then humankind will be able to turn to the needs of women. The challenging idea of our times is a determination to build a world less divided between rich and poor, the weak and the powerful. In moving to this goal, the old theory can no longer hold. True development, just development, cannot happen when the needs, talents, and potentialities of half of the world's population are seen as secondary and marginal. That is why feminism is not a frivolous concern. It deals with work, with struggle, and above all with the dream of a new day for all peoples.

Managing Development in Women's Interests

A political challenge, reducing poverty involves overcoming class-based interests in inequality, and it requires effective public institutions to deliver resources to and create opportunities for the poor, frequently in the face or local opposition. When poor women are the target of these kinds of interventions, resistance can be ever more intense than opposition to pro-poor measures. If one of the objectives of promoting social and economic improvements in women's lives is greater gender equality, such interventions challenge the social prerogatives of men, even poor men. Considerable institutional capacity to resist local patriarchal interests is required to persist with these measures. Institutional capacity to deliver development resources effectively, and institutional autonomy from vested interests have been perennial preoccupations of development planners the world over. But discussions of institutional capacity-building in development rarely consider what this would mean from the point of view of women, except, sometimes, to assume that whatever is good for the poor will automatically benefit poor women too. But gender-equity programmes can arouse gender-based resistance as well as class-based resistance, even within the institution promoting these measures. It is time to ask what kinds of changes are needed to enhance the capacity of development institutions to respond to women's needs, and to represent their interests in development planning.

We have tried here to explore the question of institutional change from the point of view of women involved in development delivery: women field workers in rural development programmes. The location of this investigations are two rural credit and development programmes in Bangladesh, one a state programme, the other run by a non-governmental-organisation (NGO). Both programmes have implemented institutional changes which are known to improve the access of poor people, especially women, to credit. These include bringing banking to the village and substituting social for physical collateral. Pioneered in Bangladesh, these innovations have inspired micro-finance programmes for the poor all over the world, and are rightly celebrated as development success stories. But having women as the focus of credit-delivery efforts does not mean that these programmes necessarily put women's needs and interests as women, as a group with specific gendered interests, before other concerns, such as poverty reduction. For women's needs to find a response other kinds of institutional changes may be necessary; changes which institutionalise a capacity to promote women's rights and opportunities. However, many organisations have taken on gender and development goals without assessing the implications for management practices both inside the organisation and in relation to the way development is practised in the field.

The initial intention was to compare typical approaches of NGOs with state-bureaucratic approaches to rural development and credit provision to investigate the causes of any differences in delivery capacity to women. From the 1980s, widespread disappointment with the development capacity of state institutions has led to policies which cut back on the role and reach of the state and privatised some development delivery functions to NGOs, which are assumed to have a greater capacity to serve the poor. Initially, we tried to establish whether this presumed advantage in reaching the poor extended to a comparative advantage in promoting women's interests in development. But in the course of the research for this work an unexpected finding shifted the focus of the study to the attitudes and work practices of field-level staff in both types of organisation, as opposed to the structural characteristics of these institutions and the organisation of their programmes. Although administrative and cultural differences typical of NGOs and public-sector organisations did indeed result in efficiency differences, they did not necessarily result in major differences in the local-level receptivity of staff to the problems, needs and concerns of women clients. Instead, cutting across both of the organisations studied were differences in the perspectives and behaviour of women and men field workers towards women programme clients, suggesting that gender was an important factor determining how staff respond to organisational incentives and use their discretion to enhance institutional capacity to respond to poor women.

At the heart of these differences was a more critical attitude amongst some women staff towards existing gender relations, and a willingness to engage with women clients on matters which overstepped the bounds of the credit programme: matters such as domestic violence, reproductive health, children's well-being, and property-ownership rights. These are all matters which affect, one way or another, women's capacities to profit economically and socially from their access to credit. This study does not romanticise these attitudinal and behavioural differences. The class distance separating women staff from their clients allied them much more closely with their male colleagues than with their often impoverished women clients. The incipient alternative perspectives and practices of women field staff do, however, point to their potential to contribute leadership resources to gender-sensitive development practice. Their potential impact in this sense was hampered by gender biases in organisational cultures and structures which limit women's capacity to use their discretion in the field or to have an impact on decision-making within their organisations.

In the current context of liberalisation, it is almost an article of faith that constraints on the exercise of personal judgement and discretion of public workers are necessary usually, to limit opportunities for corruption, on the grounds that discretion is used by state agents to promote their own private interests at the expense of public welfare. In the context of rural credit programmes with a mass clientele, limits on the personal discretion of field workers are also considered necessary to ensure the delivery of a standardised package of services to clients. Yet these constraints go against the spirit of rural development service, where there is a huge variety in local conditions, requiring flexibility of response, and where field workers are in the best possible position to interpret changes in their clients' needs and devise appropriate responses to them.

Recent literature on institutional capacity-building in development is witnessing a revival of interest in the conditions for creating a commitment to public service, the creation of management, and clients, and the creative use consequently of local-level discretion (Grindle and Hilderbrand 1995; Jain 1996; Tendler 1998; Tendler and Freedheim 1994). There is another, less prescriptive and more critical tradition of analysing the interactions between service bureaucracies and their clients which investigates how these interactions—mainly struggles over authority and resources—create meanings or challenge or reproduce dominant social relationships (Arce and Long 1987; Long 1992; Long and van del' Ploeg 1989; Schaffer 1984; Wood 1988). This approach seeks to expand the space for constructive uses of field-worker discretion, by encouraging more participation by programme clients in establishing authoritative interpretations of their needs.

This work adds a gender dimension both to this interest in field-worker discretion as an element of responsive and effective development institutions, and to the interest in understanding how development bureaucrats contribute to official, authoritative interpretations of what people need. The evidence presented in the following chapters suggests that when the majority of an organisation's clientele is female, and when many staff are women too, the capacity issues which the organisation faces are not just about efficient service delivery, but also about promoting what can be a counter-cultural goal against social resistance. As other feminists analysing development institutions have pointed out, taking on gender and development goals can also mean an internal structural and cultural challenge for development organisations (Kardam 1991, Razavi alld Miller 1995; Staudt 1985), within development organisations, the goal of women's empowerment is experienced at a number of levels. It is not only a matter of working to empower women beneficiaries who are 'out there', beyond the organisation's boundaries. It can be about changes in the personal lives and beliefs of individual staff members, and changes in their work practices. At an organisational level, it is about changes in the structure and culture of the organisation, changes which will allow women staff to participate and flourish in the organisation, changes which will reward good performance on gender-equity work, changes which will accommodate the new values and perspectives which working in women's interests may bring to the organisation. Field workers playa critical role in communicating these changes—institutional and ideological—to their clients, and their own perspectives on the legitimacy of these changes will influence the way clients experience and benefit from participation.

This work is based on research conducted by the author and Rina Sen Gupta, a Bangladesh-based women's rights activist and development professional in 1993. The research focused on gender in credit programmes because these programmes provide rural women members with access to non-traditional resources and opportunities in development, and therefore can contribute to gender and development (GAD) goals by promoting transformation in gender relations. It focused on two well-known rural development and credit programmes, the Rural Development Programme of the Bangladesh Rural Advancement Committee (BRAC), an NGO, and the Rural Poor Programme of the government's Bangladesh Rural Development Programme. Both programmes were selected for study because they have characteristics which are generally representative of NGO and government approaches to rural poverty alleviation in Bangladesh, and both organisations made concerted efforts in the 1990s to integrate greater numbers of women staff to their field-level operations. These organisations were also selected because of an interest in investigating how gender issues and women staff are being 'mainstreamed' in important development institutions. We can expect to find women leaders, women staff, and a commitment to gender equity in many women's development organisations, but until recently, these were rare m mixed and more mainstream institutions.

Whether women development agents are able to manage development in women's interests? It considers problems of resistance to gender equity from colleagues within development organizations, and from interests within the rural environment in which they work. The focus is less on individual and visible women leaders than on the pursuit of women's interests at the local level, as experienced by women development agents. The work examines the nature of their interactions with their female clientele, the degree to which they develop perspectives on women's interests which differ from the views of their male colleagues, and the conditions in which they actually act upon these perspectives. The work also investigates the ways in which different organisational structures, practices, and cultures affect the capacities of women staff to act upon their interpretations of women's needs and interests at the field level and to channel their views to the management level.

●●

6

Social Causation of Love

It is now generally accepted that courtly poetry did not describe contemporary ways of courting and love making. Its non-realistic nature, however, does not indicate that it was intrinsically meaningless, as some modern authors have concluded. Even though the poems, as a rule, did not realistically portray any personal love experiences of the troubadours, and even though these lyrics were highly patterned according to literary conventions, some, and especially the greater, poets showed an unmistakable and deep emotional involvement and furthermore a strong sense of moral and cultural responsibility which is evidenced, for instance, by the earnest disagreements between Walther von der Vogelweide and Wolfram von Eschenbach regarding the concepts of courtly love and chivalry. Courtly lyrics clearly provided more than mere entertainment, since they did not offer simple fantasies of erotic wish-fulfillment, as did the contemporary pastourelle which described the easy success of a knight with a shepherdess. The fantasy content of the courtly love complex was not altogether pleasurable: To crave against hope the possession of an inaccessible woman, who usually was understood to be already married, to suffer agonising fears of rejection, and to gain the coveted approval of a protecting figure only at the cost of self-denial and frustration.

Any discussion of the social causation of the courtly love complex has to take into account the abiding interest of the public in this poetry. It was not read in privacy but presented at social gatherings. The majority of the troubadours and minnesingers and all of the performing *jongleurs* were poor and had to cater to the tastes of their audiences; even great noblemen, however, composed love songs in order to win the applause of noble society. Courtly poetry, in connection with courtly behavior and attitudes, became an intrinsic part of the value system of the new noble *genre de vie* in the "second feudal age". The courtly love complex no doubt has to be investigated in a socio-cultural context rather than by analysing individual poets, and the problem arises: Why did this configuration of specific anxieties and wishful fantasies appeal to a socially significant number of men of the secular upper classes? And what is the solution to the much debated question of the social background of troubadour poetry and *Minnesang?*

The major reason why the psychological meaning and the social basis of courtly love and *courtoisie* have never been satisfactorily explained lies in the dominance of the "philology of influences", which narrowed down the field of investigated reality to intercultural comparisons of ideas and poetical forms. This line of research with its quest for thematic similarities and chronological priorities is theoretically related to the sterile associationist psychology of the later 19th century and, while it gives the illusion of being free from any psychological and sociological presuppositions, it actually is built upon the assumption that imitation is the sole motive force in human history, interrupted only in rare moments by the appearance of unaccountable innovation. This type of comparative history, instead of aiming at discovering causations or dynamic interrelations, limits itself to the observation of surface similarities. The diffusion of culture traits, however, is never automatic but selective. Numerous—virtually innumerable—features are at any time available to be borrowed, but only a very few are chosen and assimilated;

and for any adoption as for any rejection there must be accountable reality factors.

The search for literary sources and possible borrowings and for avenues of transmission has certainly not proved that the troubadours and minnesingers were merely imitative craftsmen, but it has indeed shown that courtly poetry was not created without any poetical and intellectual traditions. The Platonic philosophy of love, Ovidian material, Neoplatonic thought, various Near Eastern ideas, early medieval Latin court poetry, Christian liturgy and drama, as well as autochthonous popular traditions have possibly contributed some thing to courtly literature. The most important single source of influences however, was the poetry' of Muslim Spain which experienced its greatest flowering in the 11th century, roughly one hundred years before courtly poetry developed in southern France. Hispano-Arabic poetry shows striking similarities in poetic forms and literary cliches; and many authors now accept as a fact that the troubadours were indebted to Muslim Spanish poetry to a similar extent as the German minnesingers, in turn, were influenced by the Provencals.

Hispano-Arabic poetry used the theme of "spiritualised" love *(hubb almuruwa)* which emphasised the avoidance of gross satisfaction, restraint, and tenderness in a "union of souls"; it also knew the desire for the approval of the beloved and the ennobling power of this tantalising love. It differed, however, from its Provencal and German counterparts, qualitatively, in that it lacked the idea that precisely an entirely unrequited love had an intrinsic educational value. Ibn Hazm states explicitly that love may change a lover morally for the worse as well as for the better. In Muslim Spain, the poet's love choice also was not limited to married ladies of the nobility; in fact, even slave girls qualified as objects of spiritualised love, while adulterous relationships were abhorred. Most important, the Muslim code of refined behavior did not have the social exclusiveness of Christian *courtoisie* which originally was a prerogative and a distinguishing characteristic of the knightly class over against *vilains.* Furthermore, there was a quantitative difference: In Andalusian poetry the essential features of spiritualised love occurred only sporadically and left room for a great variety of other amatory themes. If allowance is made for these dissimilarities, the occurrence of a strong and sometimes morbid interest in matters of sexual frustration and fantasied compensations is to be acknowledged for all three culture areas, Hispano-Arabic, Old Provencal, and Middle High German. The closeness of these culture areas in time and space, the limited dimensions of their disparities, and the existence of other culture areas which are not too dissimilar and can serve as controls, offer a good chance for a comparative set-up.

In the search for a specific social causation, the first step is the formation of a hypothesis which advances one factor or a combination of factors as the causative agent. In the social sciences, it is usually plausibility or empathetic insight into the situation which accounts for the formation of a hypothesis. The validation of the hypothesis, which in the natural sciences is obtained by experimentation with isolated factors, must be made in historical research by a comparison of cultural complexes. In either case certain correlations are being tested. The infinite variety of historical situations, far from making objective history-writing impossible, as the relativistic school has concluded, actually can have the same use for the historian as a vast laboratory has for those scientists who can isolate factors at will. As courtly poetry originated and flourished only during a certain period, in certain geographic areas, and in certain social strata, it will have to be shown that the hypothetic cause or combination of causational factors also was limited to the same time, areas, and social classes. A more or less perfect fit will spell the difference between verification or falsification of an otherwise merely plausible hypothesis. The most important precondition for a testable line of argumentation in historical research is the existence of quantitative factors. These may be discern able only in rough approximations indicating differential densities or frequencies, increases and decreases, spatial movements, and so on; but as long as any quantitative relationships are established, history has a scientific structure, *i.e.*, the relationships can be tested by anyone who wants to take the trouble to do so.

In order to detect the specific condition out of which the composition of love lyrics and the public interest in them developed, we have to look for factors which reached their greatest force in Muslim Spain in the 11th century, in southwestern France in the 12th century, and in southern Germany in the later 12th and early 13th centuries. In each of these three areas we may expect, and to a certain extent can prove, the existence of an earlier period during which the social emotional conditions were present, but during which the preoccupation with love lyrics had not yet crystallised into written literary production or rather had not yet received the social recognition which was the prerequisite for being committed to writing.

Hispano-Arabic love poetry with features foreshadowing the later troubadour lyrics is known to have been produced since about A.D. 820. The poetic forms known as *muwassaha* and *zajal* reportedly were invented in Spain at the end of the 9th century. Andalusian love poetry reached its greatest height in the 11th century. In or about 1022, Ibn Hazm wrote *The Dove's Neck-Ring* which in scope, realism, and beauty is vastly superior to *The Art of Courtly Love, a* stilted command performance, composed more than a century and a half later by Andreas, a chaplain at the court of Marie of Champagne. In Muslim Spain, love poetry was still popular after the coming of the Almoravides in 1086, but slowly waned in the 12th and 13th centuries.

As to the factor of causation, it appears that in Muslim Spain the inordinate preoccupation with uncontrollable eroticism, of which Ibn Hazm and other contemporary authors give many indications, conditioned by a chronic shortage of women. Among the Arabs of the Near East there was an older poetical tradition of frustrated and excessively sentimental love which appears to have been connected with the deprivations resulting from female infanticide and the increasing monopolisation of women by the wealthy and the powerful in a polygynous society. For Muslim Spain, there is ample proof that a high sex ratio, that is, a surplus of men over women, was created in the maniageable adult population by almost continuous migration into the peninsula. The invasion of Spain in 711-712 brought approximately 30,000 soldiers, both Arabs and Berbers. Thereafter Arabs came only as individual immigrants, but Berbers continued to arrive in large numbers; the great majority of them, as in most migrations of this type, were young males. The hoarding of women in harems increased the imbalance of the sexes in the unattached population. Both Arabs and Berbers married native Spanish women, as there was no prejudice against racial and religious intermarriage. During the 9th and early 10th centuries, immigration from Berber Africa seems to have somewhat diminished. Thereafter Muslim Spain became economically prosperous and attracted immigrants from the Near East and mercenary soldiers from Christian countries; most important among these were the *Sakaliba,* originally captives of war and imported slaves, among whom were Catalans, Basques, Frenchmen, Germans, Lombards, and particularly Slavs, who came to occupy a position similar to that of' the Janissaries. Furthermore African Negro slaves were imported from as far away as the Sudan and Guinea to be employed in agriculture, as house servants, and also as soldiers; there were mulattoes in 11th-century Spainy Since most slaves were captives of war, it can be assumed that their ratio was high. Muslim pirates were feared along the coastlines of Europe for their abductions of prisoners, and especially of girls. Ibn Hazm's *Dove's Neck-Ring* abounds with reports of men infatuated with slave women; these could be legally married if they were enfranchised.

Of greater importance than any of the aforementioned immigrants were the Berbers who in Spain were looked upon as unassimilable barbarians, though apparently one wave of them after another was in fact assimilated. They were brought into the country especially as mercenaries. Al-Mansur drew the Maghrib, even including Ifrikya, *i.e.*, modern Tunis, as an inexhaustible reverse of military manpower. After Al-Mansur's death in 1002, the mass influx of Berbers continued and led to an internal struggle and finally to the decomposition of the khalifate of Cordova in 1031 and the weakening of the Hispano Arab elements over against the Berbers. Muslim Spain then fell apart politically into some twenty petty kingdoms, some of whom were under Berber rulers 11th-century Spain exerted a strong pull on the surrounding populations as it was a wealthy country and offered many openings for soldiers, intellectuals, and others at the courts of the petty kings. Northwestern Africa, however was an overpopulated area with more or less continuous migrations northward. This northward push took on catastrophic proportions, when the nomadic Sanhaja tribes of the Sahara desert built an empire, were reinforced by Berbers from the Maghrib, and conquered the Spanish peninsula (1086-1106) Significantly, Ali, the son and successor of the great conqueror Yusuf Ibn Tashfin, had a Spanish Christian mother. The last warlike migration to cross the straits of Gibraltar was carried out, in 1147, by the Almohades who represented a nationalist movement of the sedentary Berbers; this new influx may have been counterbalanced by the mass flight of Almoravides and Mozarabs from the peninsula. For Muslim Spain there is thus a clear-cut parallelism between the incidence of amorous poetry and a high sex ratio owing to the masculinisation of the population through sex-selective immigration.

The lyrics of the troubadours and minnesingers, it will be remembered, have aptly been called "courtly", because they were definitely class poetry. Although in later centuries *courtois* behavior patterns and attitudes of "romantic" love were adopted by one social class after another, they were originally restricted to the nobility and knighthood; in fact, they served these people to define themselves as socially superior. In connection with this social limitation of courtly poetry, the emphasis on educational and moral uplift was incomparably stronger in the courtly culture area than in Muslim Spain, and tied up with it was the behavioral ideal of *courtoisie (cortezia; hofischeit).* Whatever were the specific causative agents that were operative in the formation of the courtly love complex, they must have been conterminous with the social confines of the secular upper classes and also, of course, with the chronological and geographical limits of courtly love attitudes.

Chronologically, troubadour poetry was restricted to the 12th and early 13th century, probably with some preliterary beginnings in the 11th century, at least in southwestern France. Duke William IX of Aquitaine was the first whose poems were transmitted to posterity; but the fact that of his eleven poems only four are of the tender genre and that he obviously did not write these poems out of inner necessity, and furthermore the fact that he wrote them in the dialect of the Limousin instead of that of his native Poitou make it likely that he used the pattern of a poetry which was already well developed at his time. Thus it may have begun at some time in the 11th century; it reached its apogee between 1150 and 1210, and rapidly lost its vitality thereafter Geographically, troubadour love poetry originated and experienced its vital flowering in Aquitaine, more exactly from the southern part of the Limousin and Perigord southward to Gascony, and in the county of Toulouse, From this nuclear area it radiated with diminished strength northward to Poitou, southwestward to Aragon, and eastward to Auvergne, Languedoc, and western Provence. In the, Rhone valley it found reception only in the last third of the 12th century. The Riviera and all of eastern Provence and Burgundy had no troubadours, so that the area of Provencal courtly poetry was not contiguous to that of German *Minnesang*.

The only other area where courtly poetry was cultivated with such force and originality as to indicate emotional involvement was southern Germany. According to Heinrich von Melk, the praise of women was already a typical trait of German knighthood in his day, about 1160. The first courtly poems which, in the 1180's, were committed to writing and considered worthy of preservation were the work not of professional entertainers or of the numerous knights, but of several noblemen of high lineage. Among those who wrote love poems around 1180 was Henry VI of Hohenstaufen. As in southwestern France, a personage of a great ruling house was among the first whose poems were preserved, but his models are unknown, though there was apparently an earlier tradition. In Swabia, *Minnesang* was produced to the middle of the 13th century. In Bavaria and Austria, it came to an end about twenty years earlier, when the moods of hopeless passion and plaintive yearning were no longer appreciated. About 1250, Tannhauser was a representative of the new attitudes of the south German nobility: *courtoisie* and knightly ideals were still valued highly as distinguishing marks of upper-class behavior, but love service in adoration of an unapproachable and demanding lady was rejected as whimsical. Poems were still written in the traditional manner, but they were artifacts devoid of emotional content.

The regional limits of German *Minnesang* are most important from the comparative point of view. Only the southern half of Germany produced courtly lyrics: the southwest corner of the Empire, Alsace and eastern Switzerland, the Rhine down to Worms, Rhenish Franconia and Swabia; farther east, Bavaria, Austria, Tirol, Styria, and Carinthia. Northern Germany, on the other hand, had no courtly poetry. The only Dutch poet who wrote courtly love poems in his native Low Franconian dialect was Heinrich von Veldeke. He introduced *Minnesang* concepts to his compatriots, but without any noticeable success; he did not find followers in his homeland Central Germany was intermediate between cultural extremes. There, lyrical love poetry was dependent on the courts of landgrave Hermann of Thuringia and his father-in-law, margrave Dietrich of Meissen, who attracted several outstanding poets to this region. But the mental climate differed greatly from that in the south. When Walther von der Vogelweide came to the Wartburg, he became keenly aware of the gap separating the literature which was appreciated in Thuringia from the expectations of his south German "courtly" public. He later ironically called the Thuringian knights "proud heroes" *(stolze helde)* which implied that their style of life was that of old-fashioned warriors and not sufficiently tempered by the influence of courtly love and courtliness. In this dissonant meeting of two subcultures, Wolfram von Eschenbach, a Bavarian, who had made his permanent home in Thuringia, defended the attitudes and tastes of the central German nobility and rejected the ladies' service of the minnesingers. Central Germany was, in fact, not as archaic as Walther intimated. In the life as well as in the literature of this area a complete blending was achieved between the old heroic and the modern courtly attitudes. In the new chivalrous epics, women were erotically on a par with men, neither negligible nor only demanding figures on a pedestal. Wolfram, the greatest of the central German poets, was the first to let courtly and marital affections merge.

Central German conditions resembled those of northeastern France where troubadours were attracted by Eleanor of Aquitaine and her daughters and where courtly poetry was cultivated by some of the so-called *trouveres* from about 1170. Chretien de Troyes, the most outstanding poet of this area, played a role similar to that of Wolfram in Germany, in that in his works the heroic and the tender aspects began to blend. For generations thereafter courtly poetry was produced in the north but, except in a very few individual cases, it remained uninspired and insincere. It owed its beginnings to the predilections of southern princesses, especially Marie of Champagne, and only to a minor extent can it be assumed that the stress on tenderness in amatory literature jibed with a real change in attitudes and coincided with a greater need for restraint in the later feudal period. The stronger motivation for the borrowing of southern material was its high prestige value among the nobility who appreciated cultural refinement as an expression of social exclusiveness. In northern France, more than anywhere else in Europe, the clergy as well as the bourgeoisie of the 12th and 13th centuries indulged in a rough and unbridled antifeminism, and even among the minor country nobles the doctrines of chivalry and the corresponding poetry had scarcely any success. By contrast, the greater nobles, ambitious knights, and self-conscious courtiers were intent on distinguishing themselves from the fast of the population and adopted from the south the new style of personality cultivation. Finally, from the middle of the 13th century, noble dilettantes all over Western Civilisation—from Silesia to Sicily, and from Spain to Cypress and Constantinople—wrote stilted courtly poetry, and the nobility everywhere adopted the corresponding behavior pattern. Thus it came to pass, through the overwhelming formative power of northern French culture, that a ritualised public adoration of ladies in combination with servant—like actions toward them—such as granting ladies precedence, picking up their things, performing all kinds of small personal services, etc. became a badge of social superiority men. The problem of this essay, however, is not the later functioning of *courtoisie* as a stereotyped pattern of upper-class behavior, but rather the origin of the courtly love complex in that period and in those regions where it had intrinsic strength as a live emotional reaction to the given situation, that is, in southwestern France and southern Germany.

What were the conditions that set off the southwest of France from the north and last, and southern from northern Germany? What specific regional factors were operative in producing the mental climate for the courtly love complex? It is the contention of this essay that the numerical increase of the nobility and knighthood provided the background for the courtly mentality, through a web of causation which will now have to be clarified.

It is well known that between the 11th and the 13th centuries a minor nobility was formed in most areas of Western Civilisation which finally merged with the high nobility and to a considerable extent even replaced it. For about 200 years, while Western society went through fundamental structural changes, there arose a need for a larger secular upper class of heavily armed knights and lay administrative personnel; during this period the nobility was an open class, both legally and in reality. This development, however, was greatly modified by regional diversities. Where the political powers could cooperate with the burghers and draw on their accumulating wealth, or where cities became more or less independent administrative units, it became possible to build up centralised administrations with paid officials and paid soldiers. The highest political functions, as a rule, remained reserved to the nobility, and this nobility, especially the princes, became even more powerful than they had been before; but their numbers did not grow significantly, since they delegated intermediate power increasingly and preferably to non-nobles. These economically most advanced areas were, first, Italy, and secondly, the Low Countries including Flanders with a wide are of surrounding regions: Southeastern England, Normandy, the Ile-de-France, Champagne, Westfalia, and Saxony. In these areas the courtly love complex had no native strength and was accepted only in its later conventionalised forms.

The process of the restocking of the nobility is most clearly traceable in Germany, as German feudal law was extremely heedful" of class distinctions. For several generations it preserved the term *ministeriales* for persons of unfree origin who filled important positions and were entrusted with power over men, but who had not acquired noble status, even after they had become socially acceptable to the old nobility and sometimes superior to many a minor nobleman in wealth and power. Conrad II was the first German emperor to organise *servitores* of his royal domain into an executive staff of officials, to equip others as knights, and to legalise them as a juridical class. These relatively few *ministeriales* of the Empire *(Reichsministerialen)* soon entrenched themselves in power and founded influential families. In the 12th century, and particularly in the lattel half, the number of imperial *ministeriales* grew, but also bishops, abbots, dukes, counts, and lesser barons surrounded themselves with *ministeriales* of their own. Intricate differences of juridical conditions and social distinctions developed within this class. At the top were those families who had transmitted their fiefs through a succession of generations and who in some territories had shaken off their servile condition. Others were well established but remained under certain restrictions recalling their servile status. There was a large contingent who were not born into this class, but were personally appointed and given a field consisting of land or rent; they might serve the emperor, a great lord, or a minor baron, which again made a great difference in their status; there also were men who were not enfeoffed but rather were highly trained mercenaries on horseback, castle guards, or men seeking services in some other capacity as, for instance, a minnesinger such as Walther von der vogelweide. Below these, there were aspirants to knighthood, teenagers serving their way up, lightly armed soldiers on horseback, and plain hangers-on and entertainers. While the number of old baronial families was steadily dwindling in Germany, the class of the *ministeriales* increased so that in the 12th and 13th centuries they vastly outnumbered the old nobles. When thousands of men had become knights whose parents or grandparents had been serfs, the avenues of advance became clogged; and from the end of the 12th century the dynasts increasingly resisted further upward mobility.

The spectacular growth of the upper class proceeded with great regional differences which were due not so much to any special laws or the absence of laws, but to the existence of different social needs and opportunities. The rise into the knighthood, ministeriality, and nobility was strongest in the areas where *Minnesang* flourished, that is, first in the area organised' by the Hohenstaufen: Alsace, Swabia, parts of Bavaria and of east central Germany; and secondly, in Austria and the other southeast German border regions. The *ministeriales* were the basis of Hohenstaufen policy, including their Italian imperialism, while the Welf party in northern Germany relied on a few wealthy cities as the centers of their power. The decisive reason for this disparity of social structures and political organisations was economic. Northern

Germany, from the lower Rhine area through Westfalia and Saxony to Lubeck, was part of the newly emerging north European economic boom area and excelled in trade and in textile and mining industries. Southern Germany, however, remained comparatively backward during the 12th century; its towns were small; the great days of the Upper German cities, Augsburg, Nuremberg, and others, were not to come before the 15th century. The Hohenstaufen were aware of the potential role of the cities for the building of a modern state; indeed, they made use of; and fostered, the humble towns existing in their areas. Yet since they failed to control effectively the wealthy north Italian communes, which alone could have given them the wherewithal for setting up a centralised government feudal conditions were given a new lease on life. The Hohenstaufen and other dynasts in southern Germany had to use *feudalministeriales* for the organisation of government. During the great period of castle construction from the 11th to the 13th centuries, by far the largest number of castles were built, by secular and ecclesiastical lords, in southern and particularly in south-western Germany which in the 12th century formed the center of the Hohenstaufens' expansionist policy. The new contingents of knights, who were needed to man the castles and to secure the imperial communication system, and the administrative, *ministeriales* were often promoted from lower social ranks or were moved in, usually from more northern locations.

Very different conditions prevailed in northern Germany (the lower Rhine area, Westfalia, Saxony). Even though the *ministeriales* of this region remained juridically unfree, there was less social distance between them and the old nobles. Significantly, the *ministeriales* became themselves a closed class as early as the 11th century and formed a quasi-nobility. In the archbishopric of Cologne, for instance, now *ministeriales* were no longer created in the 12th century except for a limited number chosen exclusively from among the sons of *ministeriales;* farther south, the bishop of Worms could still, at the same time raise any number of his serfs to the status of *ministeriales;* and in Bavaria the class lines between peasantry and lower nobility remained fluid well into the 13th century, when it was still easy for a peasanes son of some means to rise into the military class and lead the life of a nobleman. In northern Germany with its rapidly advancing urban economy, its spectacular conquest of the eastern and northern European markets, and its eastern colonisation, the upper classes played a different role than did those of the economically backward and of necessity feudal south; and ultimately this contrast accounts for the differences in mental climate and literary tastes.

Corresponding socio-economic disparities existed in France. Northeastern France and Flanders were important parts of the new prosperous northern industrial and trading area. The entire region from Anjou to Flanders was brought under the effective rule of a few dynasts who reduced the role of the feudal nobility and increasingly relied on salaried administrators, hired knights, and mercenaries. The term *ministeriales* occurred in France, but only in its original meaning, denoting servile agents of feudal lords or court officers; these people never developed into a separate juridical class. There were, to be sure, opportunities to rise into the higher ranks of feudal society, particularly for serf-knights and unfree *sergents* who did military service on horseback; but most of these persons were absorbed into the nobility as early as the 11th century without leaving any traces of their earlier condition. The northern French nobility tended to become a closed class since the 11th century. The knighting of serfs was abhorred, even though in later centuries, in individual cases, sons of non-noble fathers gained access to the knighthood. In Flanders likewise, the serf-knights merged with the older nobility during the 11th century. When the existence of nobles with servile ancestry was once more unexpectedly brought up in

1127, it led to a revolt against Charles the Good and to his assassination. After 1127, every trace of ministeriality disappeared also in Flanders.

It has often been tacitly assumed that the given social and cultural areas of the European Middle Ages coincide with the political boundaries of the modern nation states. Regarding the secular upper classes and their social mobility in the 12th century, the natural units for comparison are not France and Germany, but northern France, the Low Countries, and northern Germany on the one hand and southern France and southern Germany on the other. In contrast to the north of France, the south was politically an area which had become decentralised in the course of the 11th century. Outside their hereditary patrimony in Poitou, the dukes of Aquitaine had barely a nominal suzerainty over the vast area extending from the Loire to the Pyrenees, and from the Cevennes to the Atlantic coast. Likewise the counts of Toulouse, who until 1167 also held Languedoc, were weak overlords over a chaotic congeries of lordships whose numerous barons were resisting any central control and were fighting each other in local wars. The unification of Aquitaine by the Angevin administration became effective only in the 13th century, and that of Toulouse only after the Albigensian wars had decimated the nobility and brought southward the nobles of the north including the Capetians themselves. In the southwest of France, numerous castles were built during the 11th and 12th centuries which were controlled not by a few dynasts but by a large number of self-styled "princes", counts, viscounts, barons, and seigneurs. At the same time the Templars and Hospitalers built fortified monasteries, the *commanderies*. In this area the density of castles was no doubt higher than in any other part of France; most of them were built in isolation from other settlements, and each castle required its contingent of knights. Both Bertran de Born and Giraut de Borneth complained about excessive castle building, as it reduced the funds the lords had available for the remuneration of knightly services. In southern France as in southern Germany, aspirations for upward social mobility were predominantly focused on noble or at least knightly status. Mercantile and urban expansion was rapid only in Provence and along the coast of Languedoc, that is in those eastern parts of southern France where troubadour poetry did not flourish. In the rest of southern France, there was only an incipient urban renewal even in such cities as Toulouse and Bordeaux. Particularly in the southwest, urbanisation in the form of the *bastides* came only in the 13th and 14th centuries. The *sauvetes* of the preceding two centuries were agricultural settlements founded through baronial initiative; and any *bastidae* mentioned prior to the 13th century were mere isolated defense works.

As a result of these conditions, the southern nobility was an open class well into the 13th century, when nobles and prelates were still knighting at will any person they wished. There also were numerous adventurers who threaded their way into the knightly class by serving as soldiers and who then pretended to be noble. In Aquitaine, the nobility employed large numbers of castle guards *(milites castri)*, both knights and auxiliary soldiers, and mercenary knights who received a fief *(milites casati)*. Their status apparently was similar to that of the German *ministeriales*, even though probably the majority of them were not of servile but of free origin. The recruitment of a large number of knights and the multiplication of fiefs *(casamenta)* created an anarchic type of feudalism, similar to that of Swabia before it was consolidated by the Hohenstaufen. While the *milites castri* usually belonged to well-established native families, the *casati* were soldiers of fortune, frequently the sons or grandsons of rustics or of obscure origin. There is documentary evidence for the servile extraction of some of them, but many, especially those who came from distant baronies, escaped all investigations and with good luck became the ancestors of noble families. In addition to the fully armed knights, many administrative agents such as the *prevots, viguiers, juges, bailes,* and *forestiers* aspired to noble status and in the course of several generations, in the 11th and 12th centuries, often achieved it.

The regional disparities in the condition of the secular upper classes are reflected in their contrasting attitudes toward emigration. The peaceful and warlike migrations of this period are familiar ground and a few words will suffice to recall the facts. What is significant in the context of this essay is the geographical coincidence and, most probably, the causal connection between the very sizeble out-migration of knights and the economic prosperity and political consolidation of northern area, and by contrast in the south a lack of interest in distant settlement. From the northern area came the Normans who went to southern Italy, Sicily, and the Byzantine Empire, the invaders of England in 1066, Over 60 per cent of the participants of the First Crusade, and major though less exactly known proportions of the later crusades. The army of the Fourth Crusade was almost exclusively composed of nobles from northern France who established themselves in Greece and Constantinople. Finally their crusading zeal found an outlet in the Albigensian Crusade. From Burgundy came both the "imperialism" of Cluny and a heavy noble exodus to Portugal and Castile. Many descendents of north German *ministeriales* joined the *Orang nach Osten* and settled in the vast area of German colonisation and beyond in the Baltic countries where they became the nobility.

Southern Germany did not offer any comparable chances for expansion, but knights were needed at home and for the imperial expeditions and temporary occupation forces in Italy. In southern France, the nobility responded only reluctantly and ineffectually to the crusading appeal. Even the one really noticeable contribution made by the south, the large army led by Raymond of Toulouse in the First Crusade, proved to be short-lived, because these southerners soon returned home without sending replacements, so that their state, Tripoli, had to be taken over by northern Frenchman and Italians. Still more striking, southern France also did not send large numbers of knights to participate in the Spanish *reconquista,* while the farther distant northern French and Burgundians made considerable efforts in that area. It appears that the north had a spectacular surplus of knights and nobles who sought chances for advancement abroad, whereas the southern regions offered opportunities close at hand.

In sum, while in southwestern France and in southern Germany there were rising opportunities for knights and *ministeriales* and a subsequent enlargement of the nobility, in northern France, Flanders, and northern Germany such opportunities existed for comparatively fewer persons in the 11th century and rapidly diminished thereafter.

So far only a geographical coincidence has been established between a certain social structure and the prevalence of the courtly love complex. The connection between the two becomes more plausible in the field of marital conditions, selective mating, and amorous adventures. The continual rise of men to the lower nobility, to the *ministeriales,* and to the knights, and the existence of numerous aspirants to knighthood involved an extremely high sex ratio in the secular upper classes. Every castle also had its "bachelor" knights, boys of fourteen to twenty-one years of age, beginning their training for knight's service, or sometimes older men belonging to the lowest rank of the knights. From the latter half of the 11th to the early 13th centuries these *baccalarii, simples chevaliers, Knappen, etc.* became extremely numerous. Migration of knights to southwestern France and southern Germany also increased the sex ratio of this class, since among those who moved into these regions there will have been many young unattached males.

This high sex ratio became magnified and socially important in connection with the consequences of marriage for status and property. Even if we make the unlikely assumption that not more noble women than men entered monastic institutions, the shortage of marriageable women which existed in the lower stratum of the upper class affected also the old nobility. It was imperative for a nobleman, or a knight, or even a young aspirant to the knighthood to avoid a misalliance, lest he jeopardise his status or his chances for promotion and the status and inheritance of his children. It is true that in the 12th century there were not yet any clearly defined laws on these matters, nor were there any generally recognised rules of the Continental nobility regarding the status of children from an uneven marriage. But in this fluid situation, when the nobility was not yet a closed class, public opinion and usage insisted that a marriage to a woman of lower social status necessarily depressed the status of the issue from this union.

●●

7

Women Welfare Policies

Demographic indicators. *viz.*, female, maternal and infant mortality rates, and indicators of access to medical care, both reveal an increase in the neglect of female lives as an expendable asset. This is the only reasonable explanation for the declining sex ratio observed to persist over several decades. In our opinion, the neglect of maternity and child health serves and general public health services through over-concentration on efforts for family planning have contributed to this trend as well as defeated the ultimate objective of the family planning programme. We are entirely in agreement with the draft Fifth Five-Year Plan that integration of family planning with more positive health services like maternal and child health, and nutrition and improvement in the life expectancy of children and mothers will provide a far greater incentive to the adoption of family planning measures than the hitherto adopted negative approach. While welcoming this proposed integration, we with to offer certain suggestions wish regard to its organisation at different levels so that the objective of integration is not defeated by organisational separatism.

We recommended that:

(a) The rank of the Chief Executive for the integrated maternity and child health services, including family planning, should be upgraded to at least Additional Commissioner, so that this service does not again become subordinate to family planning. This procedure should be adopted at all levels of the administration at the Centre and the States.

(b) A separate budget head for maternity and child health services should be created, drawing on the provision now made for family planning and the general health services. It is important to increase the provision for these services to avoid their being neglected as has been the trend so far. Since programmes for immunisation and nutrition of infants yield better results when they form a part of general maternity and child health services, we see no difficulty in increasing the allocation for these services.

(c) At the level of the primary health centres, the maternity and child health service should be separated for purposes of administrative provision, medical personnel and budget. While they may share the same buildings and equipment, a separation of the administrative structure required for maternity and child health services will ensure greater priority of treatment. Facilities in the way of maternity beds, equipment for immunisation of children and family planning for women could be allocated to the MCR Unit. The P.R.C. could be made responsible for sterilisation operations for men along with other general health services.

The MCR Unit could coordinate the nutrition and immunisation measures, which form a basis component of the integrated child development programme. It could also collect and maintain fertility and morbidity statistics for women and children for better research and evaluation in these fields.

We recommend that each M.C.R. centre should collect this data, which should be studied and evaluated at the district level by persons of required competence. This will call for a health statistics Section at the district level.

(d) We recommend the abolition of the present practice of providing financial incentives to promoters of family planning. Incentives to women who accept family planning should be in the shape of a token or certificate to ensure them greater priority in health care facilities for both the mothers and their children. Such a step will promote greater acceptance of family planning and correct social attitudes towards these practices. Compensation for loss of wages during sterilisation operations should however be paid to daily wage labourers. Others should be given paid leave for this purpose.

(e) The qualifications prescribed for recruitment of personnel for these services in rural areas need to be gradually raised. Unit women of requisite higher qualifications are available, the present requirements may continue, but they should be reviewed and progressively increased after every 3 years. Attempts should also be made to obtain the services of older and mature women for these services in the rural areas.

(f) We disapprove the denial of maternity benefits to women in Government service after three children as adopted by some State Government and recommend rescinding of such orders.

(g) We further recommend the promotion of research in the field of female disorders *e.g.* puerperal psychosis and effects of family planning methods.

(h) We also recommend that mass campaigns for family planning should also aim to correct prevailing social attitudes regarding fertility and metabolic hereditary disorders and the sex of the child for which the women is generally blamed. Correct information in these matters would go a long way to improve the status of women.

Changes Needed in the Medical Termination of Pregnancy Act

(a) According to Section 4 (a) of the Act, consent of a minor girl is not required for this operation while in other surgical operations of children above 12 such consent is necessary. In our view this distinction is uncalled for and may lead to guardians compelling young girls to undergo this operation even when they do not want it. The consent of the patient should be essential. In the case of a minor girl nearing majority, if the doctor and the patient are in agreement, the consent of the guardian may be dispensed with. In all such cases, greater discretion should be permitted to the doctor.

(b) Sections 8 of the Act provides an overriding precaution to the doctor for any damage caused by the operation. Since no such protection is given for other operations, this Beems an unnecessary clause and may lead to negligence. It may, therefore, be dropped.

(c) While we appreciate the ethical considerations, which make many doctors reluctant to perform this operation, we feel that it is a woman's right to have control over the size of her family. At the same time it is important that doctors should have the authority to discourage such operations when they pose definite risk to the health of a patient. The condition being imposed in many hospitals that abortion will only be performed if the patient agrees to sterilisation, should not be compulsive. It would be far better to adopt methods of persuasion through expert counselling.

(d) The procedure and paper work involved in these operations need to be simplified. It is also necessary to extend facilities for authorised termination of pregnancies, particularly in the rural areas.

(e) Many hospitals continue to insist on the husband's consent before performing these operations though this is not required by the law. A special effort needs to be made to convince the medical profession of the social value of this law from the point of view both individuals and society.

(f) Most doctors are reluctant to perform these operations in the case of unmarried girls. It is necessary to clarify the point that rape is not the only ground to justify termination in cases of unmarried girls, nor is there any legal obligation on the doctor to inform the Policy of an operation done in a rape case.

Welfare and Development

In order to prevent any ambiguity in the understanding of what constitutes women's welfare and to prevent the development of policies that sometimes go against the basic objectives, we recommend that the Government of India should evolve a national policy on women's development in the light of the constitutional directives and pledges made to the women of this country and to the international community from time to time.

In view of the need to maintain links between governmental, voluntary and community effort for promotion of women's welfare and to assist the process of Government planning with actual knowledge and experiences of the problems and needs of women at different levels.

We recommend:

(a) Reorganisation of the Central Social Welfare Board as a statutory and autonomous specialised agency for planning, coordination and management of welfare and development programmes for women and children.

(b) Reorganisation of the State Welfare Advisory Boards as statutory autonomous agencies at the State level with similar functions. In addition, the State Boards may also serve as links between the Central agency, the State Government and the local bodies.

Need for Agencies for Coordination, Communication and Implementation of Measures to Improve the Status of Women.

The U.N. Commission on the Status of Women in its 25th Report has recommended establishment of a National Commission or similar bodies "with a mandate to review, evaluate and recommend measures and priorities to ensure equality between men and women and the full integration of women in all sectors of national life". We accordingly recommend the constitutions of statutory autonomous Commissions at the Centre and the State with the following functions:

(a) Collection of information on different matters, *e.g.* education, employment, health, welfare, political participation, impact of social legislation, etc., with the right to call for information on different matters from the concerned agencies of the Government and to suggest improved methods for collection of data in different fields.

(b) Evaluation of existing policies, programmes and laws that have a bearing on status of women with the following powers:

(i) The Commission's criticisms and suggestion made after due consultation with relevant Ministries or Departments of Government should be placed before Parliament or the State Legislatures. They would be answered by the Government within a states period with explanation or assurances.

(ii) To ensure non-implementation of these measures; to point out lacunae or deficiencies in such measures and suggest amendments.

(c) Recommendations of new laws, policies or programmes aiming to implement the Directive Principles of State Policy and the objectives of the U.N. Resolutions and Conventions regarding the status of women. These should be made to Parliament or the state Legislatures and Government will be statutorily responsible to consider such recommen-dations for action or to explain why they cannot be accepted.

(d) Redressal of grievances in cases of actual violation of existing laws.

The Commission may be empowered to take effective steps to redress the grievances of affected parties.

Composition of the Commissions

The composition of these Commissions should be broad-based, one category being selected for their representative status from different bodies like leading women's organisations, trade unions, legislatures, employers, etc., and the other group consisting of experts from the field of law, health education, social research planning and administration. The Chairmen and the majority of the members of all the Commissions should be women. The Chairmen should be non-officials, but on a full time basis.

We further recommend the establishment of special Tribunals for all violations of human rights, discrimination against women, violation or evasion of existing laws and policies for the protection of women and their rights in society.

BLUE PRINT OF ACTIONS POINTS

1. Legislative Measures

The existing legislations should be reviewed so that equality and social justice can be ensured to women of all communities and creeds. Where this involves amendments to existing personal Laws of minority group, initial efforts should be concentrated on arousing a desire for change from among the members of such minority groups. A vigorous campaign should be made to educated women about their rights, and to generate among all communities, a desire for a common civil code, to be achieved by the end of the U.N. Decade for Women in 1985.

Legal aid should be organised for women in need with the active assistance of the Bar Councils.

The setting up of family courts should be considered for speedy and effective adjudication in all cases concerning the family. Women, particularly in rural areas, should be protected against harassment.

The practice of dowry should be eradicated. The legislation should be strictly enforced. This is a social evil, which requires sustained action not only on the part of Governmental agencies, but also on the part of voluntary organisations and public leaders.

The provision of the existing Child Marriage Restraint Act should be reviewed. Special attention should be given to streamlining the enforcement machinery and involving local authorities and voluntary organisations in the implementation of the Act. Active public support should be mobilised by

Governmental agencies, voluntary organisations and public leaders against child marriage, particularly in rural areas. Simultaneously, systematic programmes of education and training should be developed for girls till they marry.

2. Administrative Measures

Education

Education is the greatest known catalytic agent for social change. All out efforts should therefore be made to achieve the goal of universal primary education as early as possible. The ideas of equality between the sexes and participation by women in development should be woven into the fabric of the educational system.

The employment of women teachers should be actively promoted. The existing employment procedures, including those for part-time employment, should be reviewed and, where necessary, relaxations in age, etc., made so that more women teachers, can be employed, and husbands and wives are posted in the same schools or at the same station.

The content of education should be strengthened in terms of both life and work relevance. Attention should be given to vocationalisation and diversification of courses, which should not only be limited to traditional women's vocations but also give emphasis on the preparation of women for participation in modern sectors of industrial production. Polytechnics (including mini-polytechnics) should be started for girls in the smaller urban centres to provide training facilities in trades crafts, which will prompt self-employment.

At the stage of higher education special incentives like freeships, scholarships, hostel facilities, and book loans should be made available to girls from rural, backward and hilly areas, from backward classes and from poor families. A greater diversification in the courses offered should be made to enhance work opportunities in nontraditional vocations in modern sectors of industrial production.

Adoption of multiple entry in education, non-formal part-time education facilities condensed courses for education correspondence courses and courses for continuing education should be made available in a larger measure to women in semi-urban and rural areas, and to working women in urban and semi-urban areas. Adult education and functional literacy programmes should be vigorously pursued through both official and voluntary agencies.

3. Employment

Equal Remuneration Act, 1976, has been passed, providing for the payment of equal remuneration to men and women workers and the prevention of discrimination on grounds of sex. Special steps should therefore be taken to review recruitment, promotion another personnel practices in all public and private sector undertakings to ensure that there is no discrimination against women candidates. Women apprentices should be taken without discrimination in industries. Representatives of women's voluntary organisations should be associated in the machinery set up to ensure adequate participation of women in employment.

Village industries, which provide scope for the employment of women should be further promoted. Special training services should be organised and credit, marketing facilities, etc. extended, specially in regard to crafts which can have a ready export market, through modernisation of design, etc. Integrated pilot projects to cover training, production and marketing should be started.

The existing recruitment procedures and employment conditions should be reviewed to encourage the re-entry of women into the work force. For this purpose, the provisions relating to maximum age of entry into service should be reviewed. Part-time employment of women should be promoted wherever feasible. Refresher courses and training programmes should be organised for adult women to make them fit for re-employment.

Organisations entrusted by the Government with the task of promoting self-employment opportunities should develop special women's entrepreneurial training motivation programmes and provide special assistance to women entrepreneurs and to women's co-operative in terms of credit, licensing, etc.

The existing legislation in regard to maternity benefits should be reviewed. It should simultaneously be ensured that there is no consequent adverse effect on the employment of women.

4. Health Care, Nutrition and Family Planning

Maternal and child health care facilities should be expanded, particularly in semi-urban and rural areas, and coverage provided to high risk pregnant women. Antenatal and post-natal clinics should be started in every Primary Health Centre and district hospital.

Nutrition supplementation should be provided to high risk pregnant mothers. Simultaneously, nutrition and health education should be given to girls and to mothers through all available media and institutions (school, hospitals, PHCs, etc.)

Family welfare planning services should be expanded and measures intensified to educate and prepare couples to avail them, specifically in rural, backward and tribal areas. The facilities under the Medical Termination of Pregnancy Act, 1971 should be made available in semiurban and rural areas and information regarding the provisions disseminated among women, immunisation facilities should be gradually extended to all children.

Facilities of Working Women

The establishment of day-care centres, creches, and balwadis should be promoted on a large scale in rural, semi-urban and urban areas to help working mothers and active women social workers discharge their duties, and enable the older children to attend school.

Hostel facilities for working women of the lower income groups should be expanded.

Care for the Socially Disadvantaged

Women without any means of support, and the physically handicapped should be provided services for education, training and rehabilitation so that they can become selfreliant. Old age homes should be opened for the aged and the infirm. Special programmes should be developed for unmarried mothers and their children.

The provision of the Suppression of Immoral Traffic Act (1956) should be reviewed to facilitate their more efficient implementation. Comprehensive rehabilitation programmes for victims of immoral traffic and their children should de developed. Special steps should be taken to prevent vulnerable young girls and women from becoming victims of this social evil.

EDUCATION

1. Introduction

In realisation of the importance of education in general and the need for equality in opportunities for the intellectual development of men and women, successive Five Year Plans have consistently placed special emphasis on the acceleration of women's education. The emphasis with regard to women's education has along been to equip her for the multiple roles as citizens, house-wives, mothers, contributors to family income and builders of the new society. Efforts have been made during the past two decades of planned development to enrol more girls in school; to encourage girls to stay in schools; to continue their education as long as possible; and to provide non-formal education opportunities for women. The Draft Fifth Five-Year Plan has declared that, "the outlays for the education of girls will be stepped up.... " The fulfilment of the constitutional directive in respect of providing free and compulsory education upto the age of 14 years has been included as one of the components of the Minimum Needs Programme.

These efforts have had a significant impact on the progress of women's education in India. For example, there is a primary school within the easy walking distance from the home of almost all the children. This has resulted in an increase in the enrolment of girls in classes I-V as a percentage of total enrolment in these classes. In respect of classes I-VIII, IX, XII, XII and university education also there has been an appreciable increase in the percentage of girls' enrolment to total enrolment. In fact, girls' enrolment is observed to be growing at a faster rate then those of boys.

Despite these encouraging trends and marked progress made in respect of women's education, the education status of women is still far from satisfactory for the following reasons:

(a) Literacy among women is generally lower than that among men. According to the 1971 Census data, only 13.4 percent of women in this age-group of 25+ are literate. According to 2001 census 62.3 percent of women in the age group of 25 + are literate.

(b) Enrolment of girls in classes I to V is only 66.4 percent of girls in the corresponding age-group, i.e. 6 to 11 years; while in repect of boys the relevant percentage is 100.2.

(c) Drop-out rate is also very high in classes I to V. A recent study has shown that the drop-out rate especially accentuated in the case of girls from rural areas and from the less privileged sections of society, is as heavy as 42.85 percent between classes I and II.

(d) In classes VI to VIII, percentages of enrolment of girls and boys to the total girls and boys in the relevant age-group (*i.e.* 11 to 14 years) are 22.2 and 48.3, respectively.

(e) At the secondary stage, *i.e.* classes IX to XIIXII girls enrolled constitute only 12 percent of girls in the relevant age-group 14 to 17 years as against 31 percent in respect of the enrolment of boys in this age-group.

(f) Enrolment of girls in Post-Matric classes constitutes only 2.3 percent of girls in the concerned age-group 17 to 23 years, while the enrolment percentage of boys in this age-group is 7.5.

2. Factors Retarding the Progress of Women's Education

Girls and women in India have thus not been able to take full advantage of the available opportunities/facilities for intellectual development. This is mainly because of several social and cultural factors in addition to various other reasons. Action plans and strategies for women's education should, therefore, aim at neutralising the effects of the factors, which have retarded the progress of women's education in India. With a view to facilitating the formulation of such a plan of action, in what follows, some of the major reasons which have operated against girls/women in taking full advantage of educational opportunities/facilities are listed below:

(a) General indifference to education of girls.

(b) Social resistance arising out of fears and misconceptions that education might alienate girls from traditions and social values and lead to maladjustments, conflicts and non-conformism.

(c) Early marriage and social inhibitions against girls pursuing education after marriage.

(d) Prevalence of child labour among girls belonging to weaker sections and the hard domestic chores which some of the unmarried girls—even in the middle class families—are required to perform.

(e) Discrimination effected by employers against women labour in both organised and unorganised sectors in matters of recruitment, training and promotion.

(f) The prevailing notion that the sole occupation of women is to bear children, look after her husband and children, and thus be restricted to domestic work.

(g) Many girls and their parents find that the school curriculum do not conform adequately to their needs and interests.

(h) Unsuitable and inflexible school timings and inadequate facilities for girls in schools, particularly in the co-educational schools.

3. Major Objective of Women's Education

It should be recognised here that the general objective of any policy towards women's education cannot be different from those relating to men. However, in view of the social and cultural handicaps that have operated against women in general and in view of the multiple role that women are required to play, the need for a set of objectives specific to women's education is imperative. The following major objectives are, therefore, considered here:

(a) Prepare women to fully participate in socially productive work, fully aware of family planning needs with a view to achieving her full integration with the democratic and developmental efforts of the country.

(b) Help break down over covert biases against women.

(c) Make women aware of the various legal, social and economic rights, provisions and privileges available to them and the way they can take advantage of them, for their advancement.

(d) Import the idea of equality between the sexes and participation by women in development through the educational system.

(e) Enable women to be self-reliant to achieve economic independence.

(f) And above all, to find full expression for her talent, ability and personality and for this purpose, enable her to adopt a discriminating attitude so that she can escape the bonds of superstition and obscurantism.

4. Action Plans

Action plans here are evolved within the general framework of major objectives mentioned above. In addition, the action plans have taken into consideration other objectives, which are specific of educational categories like elementary education, middle stage education, secondary stage education, middle stage education and non-formal education. For the sake of convenience, in what follows, action plans specific of each age-groups of girls, are all mentioned separately.

A. Elementary Education for Girls in the Age-Group 6-11 Years

Girls in this age-group constitute the population of girls of primary school going age. Action plans for this age-group will need to be in two directions:

(a) To universalise primary education for girls, and

(b) To strive for the retention of girls already enrolled.

Towards this end, the following action plans are suggested:

Administrative and Structural Measures

(i) State Governments should take note of the habitations without primary schools as indicated by the Third Educational Survey and make arrangements for providing primary school within a distance of 1.5 kms. of all habitations within next five years.

(ii) Girls in this age are often required to look after younger children and attend minor household duties, particularly in the rural areas and among the weaker sections of the society. As this is one of the major reasons that holds such girls from attending school, special efforts should be made to enlarge the scope and coverage of pre-school education programmes like balwadis and anganwadis, where the older girls can be given practical work experience and child care.

(iii) Mobile schools should be provided for children of all nomadic tribes, migrant labour and construction workers.

(iv) These pre-school education programmes should wherever possible, be attached to primary schools or at least located in the vicinity of primary schools, as that would help in cultivating a school going habit right from the childhood.

(v) Supervision and inspection of primary schools should give particular attention to the problem of enrolment of girls, their retetion, involvement of the community, etc.

Promotional and Motivational Measures

(vi) Special and sustained persuasive and motivational campaign and organisational drives should be undertaken among regions/communities which have shown markedly a low achievement in girls enrolment. Voluntary organisations at local level like Mahila Mandals and local bodies should be fully involved in this programme.

(vii) Promotion and support to girls' education should also be tackled through a multi-pronged programme of incentives—both for bringing girls to schools and for retaining them in schools. The incentives can be in the form of mid-day meals, free supply of books and reading materials, scholarships awards, etc.

Pedagogical Measures

(viii) The primary teacher training course should undergo a major revision with a view to adequately preparing the teacher for the promotion of girls' education. Emphasis should be more on the use of such non-formal methods of imparting education that would interest and attract more and more girls to attend schools.

B. Education for Girls in the Age-Group 11-14 Years

Population of girls in this age-group constitutes girls of middle school-going age. This group can be divided into three sub-groups:

(a) Girls students attending middle schools;

(b) Girl drop-outs at various stages from Class I to V;

(c) Girls who have never attended schools.

The objectives of education and training are different for each of the sub-groups.

(a) Middle School-Girl Students

Action plans for education of girls in this age-group should be concerned about:

(i) encouraging further enrolment of girls at this stage,

(ii) retention of girls already is middle schools, and

(iii) rendering the curriculum more relevant.

The following action plans are suggested:

Pedagogical Measures

(i) The content should be more oriented to the needs of girls in the village communities so that both the parents and the girls see relevance of this education for their own lives. The curriculum of the middle school stage needs to be given a strong work experience orientation, introducing girls to crafts and skills which will be of direct use to them in the family, community and farm, and help them in rural employment and self-employment.

(ii) *Women Teachers:* It is important for the promotion of girls' education to employ women teachers in schools. In fact, the general view is that women are more suited to be teachers and larger number of teachers should be women. However, the problem may come up in different ways. More number of men may be qualified and trained women may be not be in a position to accept employment as full time teachers due to personal problems; women also have difficulties in working in rural areas. There has to be relaxation from age restrictions. The States may consider reserving a certain number of posts of teachers for women and where there are not adequate number of trained teachers, untrained persons may be recruited and deputed for training.

It may also be worth while in those areas which have schools without women teachers, to select educated women in that area and send them for training and appoint them in the schools in that area. Where educated women are not available for posting in a school, local women may be selected and posted as school matas (school mothers) to keep the girl students company and induce parents to send their girls and children to schools. The rules relating to age and qualification of recruitment and service may have to be relaxed in these cases and the deficiency made up through in-service training. The question of giving posting to husband and wife both of whom are teachers int he same place may be considered.

Women should not be discriminated against in matters of recruitment. Selection and recruitment should be made on merit. No qualified meritorious woman candidate should be' over looked. State Governments may contemplate providing for 50 percent of teachers in schools being women and to look into this aspect while sanctioning grants to institutions.

(iii) The primary teacher training course needs to undergo a major revision to adequately prepare the trainees for their special responsibility for the promotion of girls education in rural areas, especially in adapting the content to suit the needs and interests of girls, in adopting non-formal methodologies and in linking with community and developmental activities.

(iv) Supervision and inspection of schools should give particular attention to the problem of enrolment of girls, their retention, factors contributing to wastage and stagnation, relevation of curriculum, involvement of the community, working conditions of women teachers, etc.

Promotional and Motivational Measures

(v) School timings should be flexible, as many of the girls in this age-group are required to help their mothers in routine domestic chores.

(vi) Incentives like mid-day meals, scholarships, free school uniforms, free books and study materials, stipend, awards, etc., should be extended to all girls in the rural areas and slums in the urban areas.

(vii) Adoption of multiple entry and part-time course is recommended.

(b) Middle School-Girl Drop-outs

Alternative Measures

(viii) For School drop-outs of girls, pre-vocational training programmes should be organised on an extensive scale to cover all girls in the rural areas and in the slums of urban areas. The objectives of such training should be to render them self-sufficient in home management, and help them to achieve economic independence. With this in view, such training programmes should include courses in sewing, knitting, cooking, nutrition, minor repairs of the house, motherhood, child care, etc.

(c) Girls Who Never Attended Schools

(ix) For the non-student girls in this age-group, the objective should be to provide adequate preparation in life through a combined three-year course in general education and vocational training. Vocational training should be on the lines of pre-vocational training mentioned above.

(x) Such training programmes should be extended to all girls in the rural areas. In the urban areas, preference should be given to girls in slum areas and destitute girls.

C. Education for Girls in the Age-Group 14-17 Years

4.4 Girls in this age-group also can be classified into three groups:

(a) Girl students with motivation to attend secondary school;

(b) Non-student girls, i.e., students who never attended schools.

(c) Girl drop-outs from classes VI to VIII.

(a) Girl Students

The action plans under this category should emphasise more on:

(i) facilitating more girls to pursue education at the secondary stage, and

(ii) strengthening the content in terms of both life and work relevance.

The following action plans are suggested:

Administrative and Structural Measures

(i) Separate girls schools or separate sections should be started where the social/cultural environment demands them.

(ii) In co-education schools special attention should be given to the provision of adequate toilet, rest and recreation facilities, separately for girls.

(iii) State Governments, which have not yet made high school education free for girls should do so on a priority basis.

(iv) Multiple entry system and part-time education may be provided.

Promotional and Motivational Measures

(v) All courses of training in vocational and technical schools at the secondary stage should be open to both boys and girls. There should be no discrimination in this regard.

(vi) Liberal incentives in the form of book allowances, book-bank facilities, etc., should be extended to encourage more girls in rural areas and backward areas to pursue secondary education.

(vii) Separate hostel facilities should be provided particularly in rural areas and residential scholarships should be offered.

Pedagogical Measures

(viii) The curriculum should be more diversified taking into consideration the various occupational opportunities available, to women and the interests and aptitudes of girls.

(b) Girl Drop-outs

Alternative Measures

(ix) Condensed courses of education started in 1958 were found very useful. Under this scheme women in the age-group 13-30 years who have had some schooling are prepared for middle school, matriculation or equivalent examinations within a period of 2 years' duration. The minimum age limit here should be reduced to 15 years. This scheme should be extended to cover all rural areas and weaker sections of the urban community.

(x) The condensed course should be organised for smaller groups, say 5 to 7 persons, using the community resources like girls' high schools and girls' colleges.

(xi) Correspondence courses and self-study programmes may be introduced.

(xii) Apart from imparting general education, condensed course should also aim imparting job-oriented training with the active cooperation of existing vocational training institutions.

(xiii) Efforts should be made to cover at least about 215 lakhs of girls in the age-group 15-30 under the condensed courses programme during the Fifth Plan period.

(c) Non-student Girls

(xiv) Fourth Plan introduced a programme of functional literacy with the objective of imparting elementary general education and vocational training-related to the functions performed-to men and women in the rural areas who never attended schools. This programme should be expanded to cover all rural areas.

(xv) Apart from imparting general elementary education and knowledge about farming techniques, the curriculum for women should include courses of training in occupational skills like kitchen, gardening, food processing, poultry keeping, animal husbandry; household arts like cooking nutritional values of foods locally available, sewing, knitting etc., and motherhood, child care and family planning as also electronics and like fields.

(xvi) Similar programmes should also be designed for girls in this age-group and under this category belonging to urban areas.

D. Education for Girls in the Age-Group 17 Years and Above

4.5 Education for girls in this age group also can be divided into three groups, as in the case of other age-groups:

(a) Education of girls at the higher education stage.

(b) Education for non-student girls-girls who who never had any education.

(c) Education for girl drop-outs from the educational system beyond the secondary stage.

In respect of the last category here, the education for non-student girls, action plans are the same as those concerning non-student girls in the age-group 14-17 years. Hence, this category is not dealt with separately here.

(a) Education for Girls at the Higher Education Stage

Action plans in this area should aim at:

(a) Making the curriculum more relevant and responsive to the cultural and occupational needs of women.

(b) Making higher education available to the less privileged sections of the society, particularly girls from the rural areas.

The following action plans may be taken up for consideration:

Administrative and Structural Measures

(i) The general policy here should be to discourage separate institutions for women and to promote coeducational facilities. However, in areas where separate institutions are required to promote education of women, they may be permitted on the merits of such cases.

(ii) Vocational counselling and guidance services should be organised in a more meaningful way to help girls-in college and universities-opt for suitable courses relevant to their talent, interests and needs.

Promotional and Motivational Measures

(iii) Incentives like scholarships, freeships, etc., should be provided to enable girls from rural areas to pursue highl education.

(iv) Provision of self-cooking facilities in hostels for girls should also be considered.

(v) For girls belonging to weaker sections, in-addition to freeships and scholarships, bursaries should also be provided to meet their expenses on food and lodging.

(vi) Girls pursuing higher education should be provided easy access to text-books and other reference material through book-bank facilities.

(viii) Girls should be encouraged to enter professional courses. If necessary, reservation of seats for girls in professional courses may be considered.

Pedagogical Measures

(viii) Diversification of courses at the junior college level and undergraduate level should be undertaken on a priority basis with a view to preparing the girls for the various employment opportunities open to them.

(b) Education for Girl Drop-outs

Girls in this age-group drop-out of educational system for various reasons. Marriage is one of the reasons, which force girls in this age-group to discontinue further formal education. Economic hardship is another reason, which forces some girls to a drop-out and seek jobs, with a view to supporting their families. Social prejudices and cultural attitudes also force some of the girls to leave the formal educational system. For girls in this category, therefore, the policy should be to extend non-formal educational facilities on a large scale.

The following action plans are suggested:

(i) Facilities for part-time self-study and correspondence courses should be expanded on a large scale to enable working girls and non-working-married and unmarried girls to enhance their educational qualifications.

(ii) In addition to course leading to degree/diploma, short courses in specific subjects through summer schools/sessions, ad hoc programmes like seminars, laboratory work, workshop experience, etc., should be organised for working girls, with a view to upgrading their professional skills and qualifications. Facilities for further education not necessarily leading to a degree, but for upgradation of knowledge and skills could be provided.

(iii) While the initiative for organising such programmes should be taken by the Central and State Governments, the employees should also be increasingly involved.

(iv) Entrepreneurship development programmes should be organised separately for educated women in the age-group 18-30 years with an minimum of matriculation level of education.

(v) Pre-examination training facilities should be orgnaised on a large scale for educated women from the rural areas and those belonging to weaker sections with the objective of equipping them to successfully compete in examinations for public jobs.

The objective of such training programmes should be:

(a) Make them aware of the various opportunities for self-employment;

(b) Motivate them to take up self-employment;

(c) Impart needed skills/training; and

(d) Promote achievement motivation among them.

E. Administrative Measures

To make the various action plans successful and to achieve a real breakthrough in women's education, there is urgent need for a matching and effective administrative set up, both at the central and state levels. With this in view, the following suggestions are made:

(i) In the Union Ministry of Education and Social Welfare, a special unit/cell may be setup to be in charge of women's education to review and initiate follow-up action.

(ii) As the district is the operational unit for all educational programmes and as the needs of girls vary in extent and kind from area to area within a district, a separate cell for girls' education-formal and non-formal-may be created within the purview of the district educational officer at the district headquarters.

(iii) In each State education department, a senior officer should be placed in charge of girls' education in order that it may receive adequate emphasis, execution and co-ordination.

(iv) School supervisory system should be staffed with more women.

(v) A suitable machinery may be set up at the Centre and the States to help in the formulation of plans for women's education-formal and non-formal to monitory, co-ordinate and evaluate progress of women's education from time to time, to create public opinion in favour of women's education etc.

Report of Working Group on Employment of Women (set up by the Planning Commission), September 1978. Government of India, Department of India, Department of Social Welfare, Women's Welfare and Development Bureau, New Delhi

In the context of the preparation of the Sixth Five Year Plan, the Planning Commission set up a Working Group on Employment of women to examine ways and means of increasing the employment of women. The Group scrutinised statistics on women's existing programmes/schemes of the Government pertaining to women, development of self-employment and enterpreneurship among women, skill development, and development of Cadres for promoting employment of women.

Their findings indicated that the problems of women's employment were characterised by *(i)* The inability of women to reach for services and assistance programmes offered by government and semi-government institutions; *(ii)* A lack of awareness among institutions about the need to promote employment of women; *(iii)* The tendency of economically powerful organisations to obtain financial and other assistance in the name of women but diverting it to other areas of investment; and *(iv)* The failure of technological modernisation of several industries in expanding employment opportunities for women, widening of skill training opportunities, and upward mobility of women workers.

The Group recommended earmarking of funds in sectoral plans; increasing their participation in decision-making processes; and collecting of micro-level data on employment conditions, unemployment situation and skill profile of local women, amongst others.

Development of Village Level Organisations: Report of the Working Group on Development of Village Level Organisation of Rural Women, June 1987, Government of India, Ministry of Agriculture and Irrigation, Department of Rural Development, New Delhi

A Working Group was constituted by the Department of Rural Development with two-fold purposes. One of the purpose was to review the objectives and functioning of associate organisation. Mahila Mandals and Youth clubs as well as their links with other agencies. The second purpose was to make recommendations on the basis of the findings especially about programmes to be implemented through the organisation, coordination with the work of other agencies, association of weaker sections with the associate organisations, and strengthening the cadre of workers or extension agents.

For detailed deliberations three sub-groups were constituted. These included sub-groups on the needs of rural women, objectives of Mahila Mandals and their involvement in rural development; sub-group on rural youth, their promotion, strengthening and training for participation in rural development programmes; and subgroup on block, district and state level functionaries for women's programmes and their training.

The report was submitted in two parts. Part I dealt with village level organisations for rural women including indicators of neglect, assessment of existing programme, new programmes, implications, and so forth. Part II dealt with development of rural youth organisation particularly to promote and strengthen. Yuvak Mandals.

●●

8

Humanists and Traditinalists

Feminists have taken a range of positions on this dilemma. Here are two extremes, both prominent in the international debate. The values of women's equality and dignity, and of the basic human rights and capabilities more generally, so outweigh any religious claim that might conflict with them that the conflict should not be seen as a serious conflict, except in practical political terms. Indeed, the secular feminist tends to view religion itself as irredeemably patriarchal, and a powerful ally of women's oppression throughout the ages. She is not unhappy to muzzle it, and does not see it as doing a whole lot of good in anyone's life.

Many secular humanist feminists are Marxists; if they follow Marx on religion, they are bound to take a negative view of religion's social role, and are unlikely even to give the free exercise of religion a high degree of respect. But some liberal feminists also take a secular humanist line. These feminists—usually comprehensive rather than political liberals—will be committed to preserving the liberty of conscience, but only within limits firmly set by a secular moral understanding of basic human rights and capabilities: religion, as Kant would have it, "within the limits of reason alone." This was in effect the position of J. S. Mill in On Liberty, where he excoriates Calvinism as an "insidious... theory of life" that creates a "pinched and hidebound type of human character."

Mill holds that it is perfectly proper for public policy to be based on the view that by teaching obedience as a good, Calvinism undermines "the desirable-condition of human nature." He thus advocates liberalism as a comprehensive doctrine of life, rather than (in political-liberal fashion) as simply the basis for core political principles. Some secular humanists in this comprehensive liberal tradition have, like Marxists, a general hostility to religion; Bertrand Russell is just one obvious example of a widely held view among liberal intellectuals. Others are not hostile to religion as such, but simply insist that it fall into line with a rational secular understanding of value; Joseph Raz and Susan Okin would seem to be in this group.

The second approach, traditionalist feminism, also sees the dilemma as basically a non-dilemma. The understandings of each community, both religious and traditional, are our best, perhaps our only, guides in charting women's course for the future. All moral claims not rooted in a particular community's understanding of the good are suspect from the start; but those that challenge the roots of traditional religious practices are more than usually suspect, since they threaten sources of value that have over the ages been enormously important to women and men, forming the very core of their search for the meaning of existence.

Some traditionalist feminists are cultural relativists, who hold that as a matter of theory it is impossible to justify any cross-cultural moral norms. Some, on the other hand, are worried more about normative moral substance than about justification: they just think local sources of value are more likely to be good for people than are international human rights norms, more in tune with and beneficial to the real lives they lead. In Indian terms, traditionalist feminists typically make—common cause with other "nativist" defenders of tradition, opponents of secularisation and modernisation, who hold that the essence of Indian national identity resides in Hindu traditions, and that traditional female roles are lie at the core of a Hindu identity. Nativists often support their attack on human rights norms by holding that Indian values are radically different from Western values.

Secular humanism is deeply appealing for feminists, since there is no doubt that the world's major religions, in their real life historical form, have been unjust to women both theoretically and practically. In contemporary politics, religious groups have frequently had a pernicious influence on women's lives, as our three cases from India suggest. It is indeed very tempting to say, fine, let religion exist, but let it clean up its act like anything else, bringing its own norms and conduct into line with a basic set of international moral standards, without receiving any special protections from the state. When religion is clearly doing wrong, this position seems sensible. This was, it seems, the position of Chief Justice Chandrachud in the Shah Bano case, when he called for an end to state protection for religious courts.

There are deep pragmatic difficulties with secular humanism, the Shah Bano case show us. It is rash and usually counterproductive to approach religious people with a set of apparently external moral demands, telling them that you know that these norms are better than the norms of their religion. In the Indian situation it was bad enough when the demands were made by Hindus to Hindus; but when similar demands were made by Hindus to Muslims, they were read, to some extent correctly, as both insulting and threatening, showing a lack of respect for the autonomy of a minority cultural and religious tradition.

Today, such demands are all the more clearly threatening, since the call for reform of Muslim personal law has been taken up as a rallying cry of Hindu nationalist forces, eager to portray Hinduism as enlightened toward women, Islam as backward and oppressive. Although the goal of a uniform code continues to be backed by many feminist and otherwise progressive thinkers, in practice it is so prominent a part of the goals of Hindu fundamentalism that it is difficult to dissociate it from the idea of Hindu supremacy and a relegation of Muslim citizens to second-class status.

A related pragmatic error of the secular humanist is to fail to pursue alliances with feminist forces within each religious tradition. Religious traditions have indeed been powerful sources of oppression for women; but they have also been powerful sources of protection for human rights, of commitment to justice, and of energy for social change. For example, they have been primary sources of U. S. abolitionism and of the more recent civil rights movement, and they are primary sources of the Gandhian anti-colonialism and of the contemporary Gandhian SEWA movement.

Muslim feminists like Heera Nawaz find ideas of justice in their religion important sources of empowerment. By announcing that she wants nothing to do with religion, or even (in the milder cases) by announcing that religion will be respected only insofar as it lives up to a comprehensive (liberal view of life), the secular humanist dooms herself to a lonely and less than promising struggle, and insults many people who would otherwise be her allies. In the Indian context especially, secularist grass-roots politics has had a hard time capturing people's imaginations. By ceding religion's moral authority and all its energy of symbol and metaphor to the side of patriarchy, or even (in the milder cases) by insisting that religions be feminist or liberal in all respects, the secularist further compromises her own political goals. Finally, she abandons the terrain of argument on which she is strongest, namely sex equality, and wades into contentious metaphysical issues. Why do this, when she doesn't need to?

But the difficulties with secular humanism are not merely pragmatic and political. Three arguments cast doubt on it at a deeper level. First is an argument from the intrinsic value of religious capabilities. The liberty of religious belief, membership, and activity is among the central human capabilities. To be able to search for an understanding of the ultimate meaning of life in one's own way is among the most important aspects of a life that is truly human. One of the ways in which this has most frequently been done in human history is through religious belief and practice; to burden these practices is thus to inhibit many people's search for the ultimate good. Religion has also been intimately and fruitfully bound up with other human capabilities, such as the capabilities of artistic, ethical, and intellectual expression. It has been a central locus of the moral education of the young, both in the family and in the larger community. Finally, it has typically been a central vehicle of cultural continuity, hence an invaluable support for other forms of human affiliation and interaction. To strike at religion is thus to risk eviscerating people's moral, cultural, and artistic, as well as spiritual, lives. Even if substitute forms of expression and activity are available in and through the secular state, a state that deprives citizens of the option to pursue religion in these important areas has done them a grave wrong.

For political purposes, the capabilities approach aims at religious capability or opportunity, rather than religious functioning, in order to leave to citizens the choice whether to pursue the pertinent human functions at all, and whether to pursue them through religion or through secular activity. But the very defense of religious capability as central involves the recognition that religious functioning has in many cases had high intrinsic value: religious conceptions of value are among the reasonable ones that we want to make room for, as expressions of human powers.

Because religion is so important to people, such a major source of identity, there is also a strong argument from respect for persons that supplements these considerations of intrinsic value. When we tell people that they cannot define the ultimate meaning of life in their own way-even if we are sure we are right and that their way is not a very good way-we do not show full respect for them as persons. In that sense, the secular humanist view is at bottom quite illiberal. It is precisely this consideration that led me to prefer political liberalism to comprehensive liberalism in the first lecture; the secular humanist view is a form of comprehensive liberalism. Obviously no state can allow all citizens to search for the ultimate meaning of life in all ways, especially where these ways involve harm to others. But secular humanism frequently errs in the opposite direction, taking a dismissive and disrespectful stance to religion even when no question of harm has arisen. Even were such a position correct, even if a certain group of religious beliefs (or even all beliefs) were nothing more than retrograde superstition, we would not be respecting the autonomy of our fellow citizens if we did not allow them these avenues of inquiry and self-determination.

As Roman Catholic thinker Jacques Maritain expressed the point:

> There is real and genuine tolerance only when a man is firmly and absolutely convinced of a truth, or of what he holds to be a truth, and when he at the same time recognises the right of those who deny this truth to exist, and to contradict him, and to speak their own mind, not because they are free from truth but because they seek truth in their own way, and because he respects in them human nature and human dignity and those very resources and living springs of the intellect and of conscience which make them potentially capable of attaining the truth he loves, if someday they happen to see it.

Secular humanists who marginalise religion tend to treat religion as an enemy of women's progress. In so doing, they make a most unfortunate concession to their traditionalist opponents: they agree in defining religion as equivalent to certain reactionary, often highly patriarchal, voices.

No religious tradition consists simply of authority and sheep like subservience. All contain argument, diversity of belief and practice, and a plurality of voices-including the voices of women, which have not always been clearly heard. All, further, are dynamic: because they involve a committed search for ultimate meaning, they shift in at least some ways in response to participants' changing views of meaning; and because they are forms of communal organisation, they shift in response to their members' judgments about the sort of community in which they want to live. What counts as Jewish, or Muslim, or Christian is not in any simple way read off from the past: although traditions vary in the degree and nature of their dynamism, they are defined in at least some ways by where their members want to go.

Thus any account of Judaism that fails to include the fact that Reform and Reconstructionist congregations address God as "you" rather than "he," and acknowledge the (four) mothers alongside the (three) fathers, is a false account of what the Jewish tradition is. By this argument, secular-humanist feminists are giving a false account of Judaism when they call it inherently patriarchal; equally false is the account given by political forces in Israel that would refuse recognition to non-Orthodox branches of Judaism. Any account of the Roman Catholic tradition that treats it as in principle anti-Semitic neglects a recent evolution in doctrine prompted by statements and actions of the current Pope. Jews may have good historical reasons for doubting whether the leopard can change his spots, but they also should not be deaf to what is going on.

A similar evolution may eventually take place with regard to women's role in the priesthood; many Catholics support such a change. Such changes, of course, have already been made in most major Protestant denominations. Any account of the Hindu tradition that holds that Rama is the one central divinity, or that Hinduism is in principle inseparable from the tradition of misogyny exemplied in the Laws of Manu, is again a false account, one that neglects the tremendous regional, temporal, and ideological diversity that has always obtained within Hinduism: including the deep religious commitments of campaigners for sex equality such as Rammohun Roy in the eighteenth century, Rabindranath Tagore in the early twentieth, and Ela Bhatt in our generation, all of whom understand themselves to be representing an authentic Hinduism, freed from historical and cultural distortions. Any account of Islam that holds it to be essentially and irredeemably misogynistic once again confuses fundamentalist voices (which frequently purvey their own highly synthetic accounts of tradition) with the whole of a tradition, and displays considerable ignorance about the texts (for example, about the fact that equal inheritance for women was secured by a return to the Quran from less authoritative interpretations, and that both Quran and Hadith regard men and women as sharing a single essential nature). Such ignorance is offensive to fellow citizens, and is objectionable for that reason alone; but it is also simply bad to be wrong!

If secular humanism has these practical and theoretical problems, how does traditionalist feminism fare? Interestingly enough, it suffers from very similar problems. In practical terms, as we shall soon see in more detail, it is highly divisive to neglect critical and dissenting voices within a religious tradition, equating it with its most patriarchal elements, and failing to acknowledge each tradition's dynamic character. Such ways of thinking about both Islam and Hinduism are implicated in the current bad state of group relations in India; narrow and static representations of tradition by the members of the traditions themselves are at least as much to blame for this as are ignorant representations by outsiders. Similarly, traditionalists about women's role have also made the pragmatic political error of dividing where they could fruitfully pursue alliances, since feminists of all stripes share certain common goals in the areas of material wellbeing.

In the theoretical domain too, similar problems can be identified. The traditionalist feminist seems to slight the intrinsic value of women's religious capabilities just as much as does the secular humanist, if refuses to acknowledge the many ways people search for religious meanings outside the most patriarchal element of a tradition. The ultra orthodox in Israel slight the intrinsic value of religious capabilities when they deny Conservative and Reform Jews the free exercise of their religion in areas such as marriage, divorce, and conversion; in similar ways, traditionalist Hindu, Islamic, and Christian authorities slight the value of dissident types of functioning in their own traditions, defining their way as the only legitimate way. This error is not only an assault on intrinsic value, it is also very much an assault on one's fellow citizens, who ought to be respected when they search for the good in their own way, even if one should hold, as fundamentalists typically do, that critical ways are erroneous departures from the correct way. Finally, it is evident that these traditionalists are frequently engaged in massive simplifications and rewritings of their own traditions, which distort and deform tradition and history by denying both diversity and dynamism, just as surely as do secularist feminists' misreadings.

The traditionalist view has one further difficulty that does not appear to be present in the secular humanist view. Namely, at least in some of its political forms, it rides roughshod over other human capabilities, giving religion (tendentiously interpreted) broad latitude to determine a woman's quality of life, even when it threatens not only dignity and equality, but also health, the wherewithal to live, and bodily integrity. The secular humanist is at least motivated by an admirable goal: to guarantee to women the full range of rights and capabilities, including both those already on the agenda for men and those that involve women's freedom from gender-specific abuses. It is rare to find a serious argument to the effect that a certain type of harm or inequality toward women is required, as such, by the spiritual or moral values inherent in a religious tradition. It was not argued that unequal inheritance rights for Mary Roy were a noble goal, essential to Christian worship; that polygamy and child marriage were of the essence of Hindu spiritual values; or that the failure to pay a monthly maintenance to Shah Bano was a high moment in Islam. Usually, instead, even the overt arguments of traditionalists allude to the value of preserving the power of traditional religious courts of law and traditional religious authorities—a value far more dubious in moral terms than the value of the basic human capabilities! And frequently their arguments have the paradoxical result of allowing women to suffer discrimination in property rights, or maintenance, or whatever, just because they happen to be members of that particular religion—surely a dubious way of showing respect for the moral values inherent in that tradition. Insofar as there is a moral argument of substance, it is likely to be an indirect one, alleging that the power of traditional authorities or courts is necessary for the maintenance of other valuable aspects of tradition. But such claims are empirical, and should be tested.

ORIENTING PRINCIPLES

Like all the central capabilities, religious capabilities are capabilities of individual people, not, in the first instance, of groups. It is the person whose freedom of conscience and freedom of religious practice we should most fundamentally consider. Although religious functioning is usually relational and interactive (like political functioning and functioning in the family), and although it often involves shared goals and ends, the capabilities involved are important for each, and it is each person who should not be prevented from having access to these capabilities. As with politics and the family, so here: an organic good for the group as group is unacceptable if it does not do good for the members taken one by one. In liberal democracies we standardly hold that not just some but all citizens should enjoy the political rights and liberties.

The religious analogue is the idea that all (in the sense of each and everyone) should enjoy the liberty of conscience and religious exercise (and the other human capabilities). Thus, any solution that appears good for a religious group will have to be tested to see whether it does indeed promote religious capabilities (and other capabilities) in the group's members, taken one by one. To subordinate the capabilities of some to the organic purposes of the whole is to violate people with respect to a capability that may lie at the core of their lives.

All religious functioning, to be acceptable, must be individualistic, in the sense that the individual regards herself as an independent and self-willed member of the religious group. Such an account of religious functioning and capability would obviously leave out many of the ways in which people search for the good by subordinating themselves to authority or hierarchy, or by joining up with the purposes of a corporate body. Israel's failure to give legal recognition to Reform and Conservative Judaism, for example, violates this principle: for it says, for the sake of a strong Judaism let us forbid individual Jews to worship in their own way, where marriage, conversion, and divorce are concerned. Whether this is indeed conducive to a strong Judaism may be doubted; but it certainly falls afoul of my principle. So does the refusal of Muslims in India to permit individual Muslims to adopt children, a practice that is controversial within Islam and accepted in many Islamic nations. So does the failure of the Indian system generally to allow individuals free egress from one religious tradition into another, given the impossibility of extricating ancestral property from the system of personal law into which one is born.

The motivation behind the establishment clause is to prevent citizens from being violated in conscience and practice by the pressures of a dominant religious group with political and legal power behind it; the motivation behind the free exercise clause is to prevent belief and worship from being impeded or burdened by public action. The history of these clauses is notoriously difficult and tortuous. At times they have appeared to be on a collision course with one another; at other times it is difficult to separate the strands of argument that the two clauses suggest.

But in the most abstract terms we can say that together they aim at a regime in which each citizen's liberty of conscience is preserved inviolate, despite the pressures that corporate bodies of various types, whether religious or secular, may bring to bear. As we shall see, this tradition has been cognisant of the fact that one way of denying individuals the free exercise of their religion would be to destroy a group or tradition of which that person is a member; so group values do enter into the equation. But they are not considered to be ends in their own right, and certainly they are not permitted to trump the value of the individual person's conscience.

The second orienting principle is the principle of moral constraint. Religion is given a high degree of deference and protection in many constitutional conceptions, as it will be in mine. One reason for this deference is surely that religion is extremely important to religious people, as a way of searching for the ultimate good. But another important part of this deference surely involves the role religions play in transmitting and fostering moral views of the conduct of life. As Heera Nawaz says: the major religions are all, at their heart, concerned with the conduct of life, and all the major traditions can plausibly be seen as attempts to reform or improve the conduct of life. Furthermore, it would not be too bold to add that all the major religions embody an idea of compassion for human suffering, and an idea that it is wrong for innocent suffering to occur. All, finally, embody some kind of a notion of justice. This doesn't mean that religions do not concern many other things, such as faith and ritual practice and celebration and pleasure and contemplation; but at least a part of what they are is moral.

When we give deference to religion in politics, we do not do so simply because of the moral role of the religion; nor need the political liberal assert that this moral role is the central object of the state's interest. To say such things would involve an unacceptably paternalistic stance toward religious traditions and what is central in them. We may and do, however, judge that any cult or so-called religion that does not contain this conduct-improving element does not deserve the honorific name of religion. Thus U.S. law has persistently refused to give religion status to Satanist cults and other related groups. Controversies over scientology have a similar character: insofar as state judge that this is really a money-making scheme, they refuse to give it the honorific status of religion.

Comprehensive ethical or political views do not suffice for religion under U.S. law. But systematic views of the conduct of life that are non-traditional, and in the end rather hard to distinguish from comprehensive ethical views, have been termed religion in two draft-board cases. It has been explicitly stated that belief in a deity is not required: otherwise Buddhism and Taoism would not get protection, as they clearly do. A moral constraint is applied, then, to the definition of what counts as religion when we protect religion. And further-what interests me here-such a constraint is also applied to more fine-tuned distinctions involving state protection of religion. Even when a group clearly counts as religion, we may judge that it forfeits its claim to state deference when it goes outside of certain moral understandings, especially those that are protected in the core of the basic constitutional conception.

Thus U.S. constitutional law has consistently denied that expressions of racial segregation or hierarchy are legitimate prerogatives of religion as such, when the state gives religion special tax benefits. The Indian Constitution made a similar move when it offered religion protection similar to that given it under the U.S., and yet made untouchability illegal: Hinduism gets protection only within moral constraints supplied by the core constitutional understanding of the equal worth of citizens. Laws against sati express a similar idea. In keeping with the idea of political principles' developed in the first lecture, we understand the moral constraints in terms of the list of central capabilities, in the following way.

We should refuse to give deference to religion when its practices harm people in the areas covered by the major capabilities. Obviously problematic will be practices involving harm to non-members of the religion (*e.g.*, a refusal by Hindus of a certain caste allow any woman to go outside because their own caste norms forbid that); but practices involving harms to co-religionists will also be problematic, where they significantly infringe a central capability (particularly where there is reason to doubt the voluntariness of the practice), especially when it is not established that individual members have the opportunity of exiting from the religion should they disapprove of it. Thus refusals by Hindus to allow Hindu women to go outside to work will also get critical scrutiny, especially when we feel that women are under duress and threat in this matter, and also when we have doubts about their opportunity to define themselves as non-Hindu should they wish to.

Formally and in the core of the political conception, the principle of moral constraint says nothing about matters internal to the religion itself. Political liberalism prevents this: the public political conception should take no stand on disputed issues of the good outside the core of the constitutional principles. But the principle of moral constraint has an informal' social corollary, which members of the religion may use in discourse with one another, and which may also be used across religious lines in informal social deliberation. One of our greatest problems, in talking about the prerogatives of religious actors and groups, is to decide when there is a legitimate religious issue on the table, and when the issue is, instead, cultural or political.

Religions are intertwined in complex ways with politics and culture. Even when a religion is based on a set of authoritative texts, culture and politics enter into the interpretation of texts and the institutionalised form of traditional practice. Jews differ about where to draw the line between what is genuinely religious in the tradition and what is the work of specific contextual and historical shaping. Similar debates arise in Christianity and Islam. In all cases, many interpreters are inclined to regard at least a part of tradition or even text as a historical or cultural artifact, expressive of human ideas of the good at a particular time, but not binding without translation for our time. Where Hinduism is concerned, the absence of scriptural authority makes it all the more difficult, if not virtually impossible, to identify a necessary religious core distinct from layers of history and culture, all powerfully infused with imperfect people's desire for political power.

When we are thinking, then, of curtailing some activity highly desired by some religious actor or actors speaking in the name of religion, it is useful to determine whether they are really speaking religiously, accurately understanding the core of that religion, or just going all out for political power.

But it is not just difficult to discover this; sometimes there may be no determinate answer to be discovered. Judges are not well qualified to judge in such matters, and in general they are rightly deferential to the claims of religious actors about what a legitimate claim of free exercise in their religion is. They should stick to a strictly limited political use of the principle of moral constraint. But in more informal social discourse it is sometimes important to take a stand. Do the Christians have a case that Mary Roy's inheritance claim jeopardises Christian worship, or is this simply a ploy on the part of Church leaders to keep tax revenue? Do Nehru's and Ambedkar's opponents have superior insight into the essence of Hinduism, or are they just trying to shore up power for religious courts?

The social version of the principle allows us to go further in commenting on these questions. It suggests that when we assess such debates we should be skeptical of any element that seems prima facie cruel or unjust-again, especially in the areas of the central capabilities. But now, in addition to saying that we may not give such elements state deference, we press the question whether that is really a core element in the religion. You say that your religion is dedicated to the good, we argue. But this is so patently bad that it seems dubious that it can really be a part of the religion, as we understand its central purposes. This social principle would strike me as a valuable one even if major religions had not endorsed it. But it clearly has deep roots in Indian religious history, as well as in the West. When the emperor Ashoka (a convert to Buddhism, in the third century B.C.) saw acts of religious intolerance being carried out in the name of religion, he invoked the principle of the moral core in order to conclude that damage to other religions is simply not a way of expressing or exalting one's own:

> ... the sects of other people all deserve reverence for one reason or another. By thus acting, a man exalts his own

> sect, and at the same time does service to the sects of other people. By acting contrariwise, a man hurts his own sect, and does disservice to the sects of other people. For he who does reverence to his own sect while disparaging the sects of others wholly from attachment to his own, with intent to enhance the splendour of his own sect, in reality by such conduct inflicts the severest injury on his own sect.

In other words, no matter what religious actors say about their conduct, we may conclude that they are in error about what religion requires: acts of intolerant harm damage, and do not express or glorify, one's own religion, Hindu or Buddhist. Had he been a state actor in a political-liberal state, Ashoka would have been well advised to speak in a more restrained way, simply saying that when people behave this way they forfeit a claim to state protection. But his informal social use of the stronger social version of the principle is highly effective.

A similar appeal to the principle of moral constraint was made by U.S. President Abraham Lincoln, in his Second Inaugural Address, delivered at the end of the Civil War. Speaking of the fact that both (former) slaveholders and abolitionists think of themselves as Christian and their cause as a Christian cause, he commented:

> Both read the same Bible, and pray to the same God; and each invokes His aid against the other. It may seem strange that any men should dare to ask a just God's assistance in wringing their bread from the sweat of other men's faces; but let us judge not that we be not judged.

Lincoln, like Ashoka, says in effect: whatever they think about the religious character of their acts, if the acts are unjust we must be highly skeptical. The idea that God is just lies behind and constrains more specific ideas of what God does and does not endorse. That God is really a backer of slavery is simply implausible. Again, U.S. courts speak more agnostic ally, simply saying that segregationists lose a claim to state protection in tax matters; but Lincoln's use of the stronger form of the principle is valuable, when religion is being invoked to back evil. For a Christian leader to say that slavery is anti-Christian does not seem to exceed the boundaries of public reason.

Moral-constraint arguments naturally arise in the context of women's livelihood. A young wife in Bangladesh, told by local mullahs that religion forbade her to work in the fields alongside men, said that if Allah really was requiring them to stay hungry, then" Allah has sinned." She meant, of course, to express skepticism about the mullah's interpretation. Her view of her religion was that a just and good god would not permit women to starve simply on the ground that it seems to some men improper for a woman to go out of the house. A just god, presumably, would let her gain her livelihood and ask men to conduct themselves modestly toward her (as the Quran, in any case, explicitly requires). Since Allah, by definition, does not sin, then any statement that implies that he does sin must be false. In general, this is the style of argument feminists in all religions have typically used to bring about change: if we're agreed that God is just and good, and if we can show you that a certain form of conduct is egregiously bad, then it follows that this conduct does not lie at the heart of religion, and must be a form of human error, which can be remedied while leaving religion itself intact. Again, it was a bad idea for the Chief Justice to say something like this; in his judicial role, especially as a Hindu, he should have confined himself to the more restricted political version of the principle. But these women, speaking socially and within their own religion, make a powerful use of its stronger social version.

Such arguments are common in both the Hindu and Muslim traditions in India, where women's issues are concerned. Nineteenth Bengali reformers Rammohun Roy and Iswarchandra Vidyasagar, campaigning against sati, child marriage, and polygamy, based their campaign on a recalling of Hindu tradition to its moral core. Similar moral arguments about Muslim conceptions of modesty are made by reformers, such as Rokeya Sakhawat Hossain, who challenged the seclusion of women from within religious orthodoxy, by pointing to its morally objectionable consequences, as well as its non-necessity for truly moral conduct. The Indian Constitution uses the more restricted political version of the principle, as seems appropriate for basic constitutional matters in a pluralistic democracy. It makes no pronouncements about what Hinduism is or is not, it simply makes untouchability illegal. But moral-constraint arguments do valuable work socially, in connection with such constitutional reforms.

To invoke the principle of moral constraint, we need not deny that a given form of immorality may at one time have been absolutely central to the beliefs and practices of the religion. It would be foolish, for example, to deny that the subordination of women was central in many religions' at many times, that the caste system was a core feature of Hinduism, that racial hierarchy was a prominent feature of the Church of Jesus Christ of Latter-day Saints, and so forth. What we are saying is that what makes religion worthy of a special place in human life (and of special political and legal treatment) is something having to do with ideals and aspirations, something that remains alive even when formerly core understandings shift in the light of moral debate, and indeed, something that guides that evolution.

Central Capabilities as Compelling State Interests

We have two constraints that limit interference with religion: respect for the intrinsic value of religious capabilities, and respect for religious people as citizens. Next, we have a constraint that pushes the other way, toward at least some scrutiny of religion and religious actors: respect for the other central human capabilities. Next, we have two orienting principles: the principle of each person's capability, and the principle of moral constraint, which we now interpret in terms of the central capabilities. And finally, we have a fact that both secular humanists and traditionalists generally neglect, the internal diversity and plurality of the religions themselves.

This proposal is conceived of as a good idea, not necessarily as the best reading of any particular constitutional tradition. It draws on ideas in U.S. Law, and it is very easy to adapt to the Indian constitutional tradition, which in most cases draws heavily on U.S. constitutional jurisprudence for precedents involving the interpretation of fundamental rights. But obviously interpreting a particular constitutional tradition involves asking questions other than whether something is a good idea, questions about precedent, text, history, and institutional competence.

The United States Religious Freedom Restoration Act of 1993 act prohibits any agency, department, or official of the United States, or any State, from "substantially burden[ing] a person's exercise of religion even if the burden results from a rule of general applicability," unless the government can demonstrate that this burden "*(1)* is in furtherance of a compelling government interest; and *(2)* is the least restrictive means of furthering that compelling governmental interest."

We now need some background on the origin and current fate of this law, in order to see how it grew out of a concern for the protection of minority religion, a central concern in my own argument. For some years there had been an issue, in First Amendment jurisprudence, about how far laws "of general applicability" might be upheld against a religious group or religious individuals, when those individuals claimed that the law imposes a "substantial burden" on their exercise of their religion. For quite a few years, the legal situation was, theoretically at least, more or less as RFRA later reestablished it: the Supreme Court consistently held that laws of general applicability might impose a substantial burden on an individual's free exercise of religion only if the law furthered a compelling state interest, and in the least burdensome manner possible.

The governing case was Sherbert v. Verner. A South Carolina woman refused to work on Saturday, because her Seventh-Day Adventist beliefs forbade it. Fired, she was also refused state unemployment benefits on the grounds that she had refused suitable employment. She claimed that the State had violated her religious free exercise; the U.S. Supreme Court agreed. The Court held that to attach to a benefit a condition that required violation of a religious duty did impose a substantial burden on her free exercise of her religion; the problem was compounded, the Court held, by the discriminatory impact of the benefits laws on workers who celebrate the Sabbath on Saturday.

In 1990, however, the Supreme Court changed course with its decision in Employment Division v. Smith. Significantly, this case involved an unpopular minority religion and the scary topic of legalised drug use. The case concerned native American tribes in the state of Oregon, who claimed that it was essential to their religion to use peyote in a particular ceremony, and thus claimed exemption (not generally, but in this one ceremonial instance) from the drug laws of the State of Oregon. The sincerity of their religious claim was not disputed, nor the centrality of the peyote ceremony to their religion. In a lengthy opinion by Justice Scalia, the Court held that the free exercise clause did not protect the plaintiffs, since "[w]e have never held that an individual's religious beliefs excuse him from compliance with an otherwise valid law prohibiting conduct that the State is free to regulate."

The Court explicitly rejected the" compelling government interest" requirement, as making the lawmaker's job far too difficult. The dissenters, however, emphasized the danger of disfavouring minority religions, and invoked the Founders' interest in securing "the widest possible toleration of conflicting views." Justice O'Connor, who joined this part of the dissenting opinion, concluded: "The compelling interest test reflects the First Amendment's mandate of preserving religious liberty to the fullest extent possible in a pluralistic society. For the Court to deem this command a 'luxury,' is to denigrate '[t]he very purpose of a Bill of Rights." This is an important moment for my approach, because the need to protect minority religion is my central motivation in favoring the ample protection of RFRA to the regime inaugurated by Smith. The decision generated public outrage.

RFRA was passed in 1993 by an overwhelming bipartisan majority in both houses, and signed into law by President Clinton. It was declared unconstitutional in June 1997, on grounds relating to the scope of Congress's powers under the Fourteenth Amendment. The principle involved in RFRA continues to enjoy strong support, including, it would appear, the support of a vast majority of the American people. The unresolved issue is how to translate this support into law, and, in particular, how to resolve the thorny issues of institutional competence raised by the clash between the legislative and the judicial branches.

No compelling government interest was established in the case as argued, nor would thinking about the central capabilities help us to make a stronger argument than was in fact made. One might point to the parallel Indian case of the legalisation of marijuana use during Holi, the Hindu spring festival: it seems just right to say that there is no compelling government interest in forbidding this festival use, and that forbidding it would impose a substantial burden on Hindu religion. (It's obvious, indeed, that Holi raises a far more serious issue of public order than the Native American ceremony, to put it mildly: for when a majority of the population is getting stoned, that can and does led to rioting and looting. Nonetheless, the Indian government is correct, in my view, to tolerate this exception and to focus on controlling disorder.) Other areas in which this principle would support an exemption would include the wearing of yarmulkes in the military, the wearing of religious jewelry in prisons, and reasonable accommodations to the religious dietary needs of prisoners.

On the other hand, a case like Bob Jones would come out as it did: the government's interest in eradicating humiliating and stigmatising racial discrimination would count as a compelling interest, in connection with the account of the central capabilities. We now face an important issue: does the approach require equality in basic capabilities, or only a basic minimum threshold? In other words, does sex discrimination with respect to the basic capabilities trigger a claim of compelling state interest; or only discrimination that pushes women into a situation of destitution or extreme capability failure? Let's try to get at this by looking at things in the other direction. Typicany, the state has been held to impose a substantial burden on religion when it treats members of one religious group unequally to others. The plaintiff in Sherbert v. Verner was losing a benefit that the state might not have offered at all; but the holding was that; so long as it does offer such benefits, to condition them on a practice that violates some people's religious freedom is to impose a substantial burden on the free exercise of religion. Forcing her to choose between the exercise of her religion and forfeiting benefits was said to be equivalent to fining someone for Saturday worship—a practice that we be unacceptable no matter how small the fine and no matter how great the individual's ability to pay. The inequality of treatment is itself a violation; to make X jump through hoops that Y is not forced to jump through on account of X's religion, *ipso facto* to burden the exercise of that religion. The very singling out of women for differential treatment in a central of human functioning is itself unacceptable, and gives rise compelling state interest in eradicating that discrimination, even if women are not by this means pushed into a basement level of functioning. Here we have the Indian constitution on our side, since, unlike the US constitution, it contains an explicit provision of non-discrimination on the basis of sex, listing this among the fundamental rights of citizens.

Finally, we face two very difficult questions. First, should religion be singled out for specially protective treatment, or should the same protections apply to all other expressive or ultimate-troth-pursuing activities? But there are other ways, some involving comprehensive ethical views, some involving less systematic forms of personal search, some involving poetry, music, and the other arts. It seems difficult to distinguish religious belief-systems from the non-religious beliefs and practices in any principled and systematic way. The features that make religion worthy of deference are frequently found in non-religious belief-systems or practices.

Moreover, even if one were to argue that religion is to be preferred not because of its role in people's search for meaning and community, but because it involves loyalty to a transcendent source of authority, this still would not yield a principled way of dividing what is conventionally called religion from what is conventionally called non-religion: not all religions are theistic, Buddhism and Taoism being only two examples. One attractive feature of the Smith decision, for some of its supporters, is its fairness to non-religious belief systems. To accommodate religion and to reject a similar accommodation for Thoreau's philosophy seems arbitrary and unfair.

U.S. constitutional law has handled this question in a very complex and sometimes quite murky manner, through the twin principles of non-establishment and free exercise. With respect to free exercise claims, religion is given special deference. But any privileging of religion over non-religion can potentially trigger an establishment clause issue, and with respect to establishment issues, religion is in some respects more curtailed' than non-religion. Thus a public display honoring Thoreau would present no problem; such a display honoring Moses, or Jesus, would potentially raise an establishment issue. Government endorsement of environmentalism is appropriate; government endorsement of Christianity is not. The two clauses to some extent balance one another; thus, it has recently been argued that any free exercise exemption to laws of general applicability "offends Establishment Clause principles" and "connotes sponsorship and endorsement." Sticking to the free exercise side of the issue, however, we may still feel uneasy when a religious capability is supported and another highly similar human capability is impeded.

We have two distinct issues, a theoretical/moral issue and a practical issue. On the side of theory, there seems little to be said in favor of privileging religion over non-religious beliefs and practices. A political liberal political conception based on an idea of human capability should not play favorites among the comprehensive conceptions of the good citizens may reasonably hold; my approach reflects this by making religion one of the permissible ways of pursuing a wide variety of human capabilities, rather than a separate capability all its own.

On the practical side, however, there are enormous difficulties involved in treating religious and nonreligious conceptions equally. Religion is usually organised and involves some publicly accepted body of doctrine and/or practice. It is not open to any and every believer to state ad hoc that a given law offends against his religion; however difficult such an inquiry may be, and however problematic an exercise of judicial faculties it may involve, such an inquiry must and frequently does take place. The Court in Yoder satisfied itself of the centrality of work in the Amish understanding of community; the Court in Smith granted the centrality of the peyote ceremony in Native American religious ceremonies.

With non-religion, such inquiries become absurdly taxing, and frequently they will yield no definite answer. If the belief system is comprehensive and textually based (as, for example, in the Thoreau case), things may not be too bad; but in many other perfectly legitimate cases the task of assessing the claim will be absurdly difficult, beyond the competence of any court or legislative body. If X says that his personal search for the meaning of life requires him to get stoned and listen to Mahler, he may be entirely sincere, and he may well have just as good a case morally as those who use drugs in a religious context; but ascertaining the centrality of this practice to his search for meaning will be virtually impossible, and granting exemptions in this way would quickly make a mockery of the drug laws, of mandatory military service, and many other laws of general applicability.

For some, these difficulties provide a strong reason to prefer Smith. First, we confine the explicit area of potential exemptions to religion; but we allow religion to have a somewhat broad definition, including non-theistic belief systems such as the one that won Seeger his draft exemption. It remains essential, however, to determine that the exercise of freedom of conscience is religion-like in having a systematic and non-arbitrary character; thus my Mahler fan, however sincere his practice, would still be excluded. The disadvantage that would thereby be incurred by the non-religious can to at least some extent be remedied by adopting strong protections for expressive speech and conduct. Thus, although the Mahler fan will not get an exemption from the drug laws, he can at least count on the protection of his right to listen to the music of his choice, to read the books of his choice, and so forth.

This approach suggests to me that it should be a contingent contextual question whether that protecting is best done through a regime of non-establishment or through a regime of limited establishment with sufficient safeguards for citizen equality and free exercise. Given our specific history of intolerance toward minority religion, it seems wise for the U.S. to support a strong form of non-establishment; only this regime, in the social context, guarantees the equal worth of religious liberty for all citizens.

In the Scandinavian states, however, it seems plausible that the established Lutheran Churches actually protect religious pluralism more effectively than would a purely secular regime: they have been staunch defenders of religious pluralism in education, for example, and of other measures favorable to minorities. This is absolutely crucial to the case of India, because the existing regime of secularism in India involves a type of limited plural establishment: certain religions are entitled to maintain their own systems of civil law, and others (those too small or new to have a codified system of personal law) use the secular system.

Children and Parents Approach

The Children and premts approach will protect the capabilities of adult women as fully equal citizens. But the upbringing of children is equally important and still more complex. In one way, the state has an especially strong interest in protecting the capabilities of children: for they are its future citizens; nor are they voluntary members of the family unit. But in another way, the state should acknowledge at least some limits to its power to intervene in children's lives, given its interest in the maintenance of the family. Parents have an extremely strong interest in bringing up children in their own religion and continuing traditions to which they are attached. The state should acknowledge this interest, and must treat children somewhat differently from adult women-both because their parents have at least some legitimate rights over them and because it is difficult to ascertain the child's own choice, given parental power and the child's economic dependency. Although the larger issue of children's capabilities deserves closer attention, we need to approach it now in the context of religious education.

Numerous conflicts have arisen between parents' religious education of their children and the state's interest in its future citizens. Many of the most interesting cases involve compulsory education and child labour. India has laws mandating compulsory education, usually up to age 14, but the nation is in no position to enforce either these laws or laws against child labour at this time; the constitutional tradition has therefore not yet articulated clear boundaries in this area.

In Pierce v. Society of Sisters the Court invalidated an Oregon law that required parents to send their children to the public school system, and forbade them to elect a religious school. The Court argues that parents have a fundamental liberty interest in directing the education of their children "by selecting reputable teachers and places." The law was held to be an unreasonable interference with that liberty interest: the state cannot "standardise its children by forcing them to accept instruction from public teachers only." The Court was careful to limit the latitude given to parents:

> No question is raised concerning the power of the State reasonably to regulate all schools, to inspect, supervise and examine them, their teachers and pupils; to require that all children of proper age attend some school, that

teachers shall be of good moral character and patriotic disposition, that certain studies plainly essential to good citizenship must be taught, and that nothing be taught which is manifestly inimical to the public welfare.

Nonetheless, the opinion is a fundamental affirmation of the right of parents to choose religious schooling for their children.

John Rawls's suggested requirement that all students be taught the rudiments of civic affairs and of the existing public constitutional order seems a bare minimum, and this teaching would include, in India' as in the U.S., the teaching that women, under the public constitutional order, are fully equal citizens with equal rights and responsibilities. This teaching about the public political conception is fully consistent with the religion's teaching, as well, its own comprehensive view. Given that the religion has agreed to sign on to a constitution of a certain type, it will figure out how to square this overlapping consensus of public political matters of basic justice with the rest of what It teaches. Within these constraints, religious schooling should be a protected option.

Sometimes compulsory education appears to interfere with religious requirements.

Capabilities and Loss

What is lost, if we follow my approach? Do these proposals involve a tragic aspect? The principle of the moral core informs us that nothing of value is lost when we tell people that they cannot lord it over other people in immoral and harmful ways. By using the central capabilities as our guide, we allow considerable latitude for the preservation of tradition in cases that do not involve grave harms to others. And yet one should nonetheless acknowledge that there are some valuable ways of life that will become difficult to sustain for oneself in a climate of choice.

Although an emphasis on the capabilities does not in :my way preclude the choice to live a traditional hierarchical life, and indeed is intended to protect that opportunity; although we carefully create spaces within which such forms of life may continue and be supported; and although we stress that religion has always been a diverse and changing set of practices, and therefore won't be killed off by being nudged in the direction of support for the capabilities-nonetheless, despite all this, we should acknowledge that at least some price will be paid for the sheer emphasis on choice and capability. There are some ways of life that people find deeply satisfying, and that probably do not involve unacceptable levels of indignity or capability inequality, which are likely to cease to exist in a regime of choice, simply through social pressure and the availability of alternative choices. Veiling is available in a regime that does not make veiling mandatory, and it seems quite wrong of a regime to impose veiling by force on women who do not choose it. And yet the motivation for this move can at least be comprehended, when we recognise that women who may wish to remain veiled have an extremely difficult time doing so in a fast-moving capitalist society in which their husband is likely to be working for a multi-national corporation many of whose members view veiling as primitive.

Brought up in an educated family in north India, Hamida Khala had a fine education under her father's supervision, and longed to wear the burqua as a sign of maturity. At the age of thirteen she was betrothed to a much older widower in the civil service, reputed to be of "modern" views. Hamida consented to the marriage on the condition that if he asked her to stop observing purdah she would return to her family. She began living with her husband at the age of fifteen, and he took her to Calcutta, far away from her family. As a civil servant, he worked with British, Hindu, and Muslim colleagues, and social life was organised around couples who typically attended dinners and tea parties together. Her husband began to resent her seclusion, which was cramping his own social life and his professional advancement. Although some colleagues arranged dinner parties at which women sat in a separate room, many refused to do so. And at last one host played a trick.

One night the women were seated at a table with empty seats at every other place. Suddenly a group of men came in and sat in the vacant seats. Hamida recalls this event with tremendous pain:

> What I experienced, I just can't tell you. There was darkness all around me. I couldn't see anything. I had tears in my eyes... What I ate I don't remember... All my attempts, my endeavours to keep my purdah were over. I felt I was without faith, I had sinned. I had gone in front of so many men, all these friends of my husband. They've seen me. My purdah was broken, my purdah that was my faith.

Her husband insisted that he was not aware of the plan, and apologised profoundly to her. Nonetheless, she recognised that her life would have to change if she were to stay with him. She wrote to her father, asking his advice. He told her that if her marriage might be endangered, she would have to leave purdah, adding that her extreme type of purdah does not represent an ancient Islamic tradition; she could behave with reticence and modesty even after leaving it. After reading sacred texts on her own, she came to the conclusion that there was a way of living as a devout Muslim outside of strict purdah. She worked out her own rules of modest dress and demeanorlong-sleeved blouses, downcast eyes, no makeup or jewelry and followed them the rest of her life, while going outside and learning how to conduct daily business and social affairs. Her husband supported her and showed respect for her religion.

Hamida reports some good aspects of the change. She developed greater physical agility and strength by walking outside. She learned how to manage accounts, which came in handy when her husband died prematurely of a heart attack. Coming to the conclusion that" the real purdah is modesty", she refused to lend her support to a political campaign to bring back widespread purdah in Pakistan, when a conservative leader asked her for help. She feels that she has been able to define successfully a Muslim identity that included the central precepts of her religion—and yet, she acknowledges that there has been a real cost. "It was a big sacrifice for me to leave purdah." If that is so even in this very favorable case, where, because of Hamida's personal strength and her husband's respect, she was able to construct a viable religious alternative, we can easily imagine that other women might experience the sacrifice without discovering a viable alternative.

••

9

Technical Development Scenerio

The main issue connected with the utilisation of science and technology as a pool to speed up the development of the developing countries is, therefore, the transfer of technology and, in this respect, the choice of technology. Technology being a system consisting of hardware, software and orgware, the transfer of technology must be viewed as a complex process, involving a range of economic, financial, legal and sociological factors.

In this connection, local inputs—primarily knowledge and information on technologies, trained cadres, legal and other regulations, etc.—are needed. The process of selection of technologies calls for an analysis and assessment not only of the economic impact, but also of the social impact. While must be kept in mind is that while technology itself is natural, the application of technology can have considerable social effects, since, through technology, a system of domination and exploitation, as well as a set of social norms and ethics may be transferred. A social impact analysis should be a constituent part of any transfer of technology arrangement.

Women are involved in science and technology through the structural transformations that occur with the transfer of technology and scientific and technological development, and as participants in research and technological activities; and experiencing the impact of the technologies on their everyday lives. In all cases, their involvement should be much stronger than it is at present. It is also very important that women understand scientific and technological innovations, because this enables them to influence the general social attitudes towards technological change through the existing non-formal education. The radical changes in the organisational pattern and activities of the society, associated with rapid scientific and technological change in the overall organisation, which are presently being experienced in the developed countries, may also dramatically affect all developing countries, and lead to either a more dynamic and humane development or to an ever higher degree of dependency and exploitation. The problem of the marginal position of some members of society, and of women specifically, cannot be solved unless the elements of these new technologies can be built into development strategies in accordance with the concept of integral development. Furthermore, the latest so-called frontier and trans-disciplinary technologies can be used in different ways and at different levels. Their use can serve to accontuate the productive role of women, because such technologies are applicable to a number of areas which are of relevance to the betters quality of life and to the integration of women in development, *i.e.* food production, clean water supply, improved housing conditions, use of alternative energy sources, in the services education etc.

It should be kept in mind that it is economic and political considerations, rather than social and cultural ones which determine the availability and terms and conditions for the access of developing countries to new technologies and which are important for national development. Women's access to technological development thus also depends on the global relations between the technology owners and users and those who try to secure access to new technology and to processes of industrialisation. This implies that major efforts should be made to maximise the utilisation of the existing knowledge in developing countries and to lessen the technological dependence on developed countries.

Women have traditionally gained knowledge and experience (*e.g.*, in agricultural production, energy utilisation, running the household, manufacturing objects for everyday use, home medicine etc.,) which have not been, exploited from the developmental point of view. The application of new scientific and technological devices and knowledge may lighten household drudgery in urban and rural areas, providing better water, energy and other community facilities. This would release energies which women might be encouraged to direct forwards active and useful participation in other economic and social areas, and in the overall technological transformation of the society.

A greater involvement of women in scientific and technological development would therefore require:

- popularisation of scientific and technological knowledge and skills in order to enable their further development, by mass media, through changes in school programmes, and through all participatory and community develoPIll.ent activities (especially in agriculture but also in other areas, *e.g.*, household activities, health, education, housing, etc.).
- changes in the traditional attitudes towards women by enabling them to fully participate in scientific and technological development by stimulating their involvement in various forms of education and training.
- an increase of the level of scientific and technological self reliance by developing national scientific and technological potentials, maximisation of the possibilities for technical proporation among developing countries and the introduction of selective transfer of technology systems.

- establishment of linkages between the existing traditional technologies and know-how and the new technologies. The involvement of women in the strengthening of these links could provide a firm basis for self-reliance and ensure a certain continuity in the development of authentic and original approaches, thus avoiding imitative modernisation, and developing participatory research as well as relating scientific and technological development to the specific needs of the country.
- establishment and strengthening of cooperation among developing countries in the areas of information on scientific and technological knowledge and devices transfer of technology and exchange of experience on application of science and technology in development, joint research, etc.

Skills and Services

The term services or tertiary sector encompasses a wide range of activities. Therefore, the analysis of the role of women in the services sector covers the generally complex problem of services classification and data, the identification of the manpower problem in general, and women's hidden economic role in particular, and the relationship between the services sector and the overall economy of the country.

Over the last decades this sector's contribution to GDP increased substantially, not only in developed market economies but also in developing countries, where this upward trend was evident even in the least developed countries. By 1980, the services sector accounted for the largest share of GDP in both developed market economies (56.9 per cent) as well as in developing countries (44.3 per cent). In developing countries the services sector expanded at a past faster rate than the GDP in the period 1973-80, implying that the general slowdown of their economies during these periods affected the services sector less severely than other major economic sectors.

However, the expansion of the services sector in developing countries, particularly in least developed countries, is probably due to quite different economic causes and could the attributed to the marginalisation of the labour force in agriculture and industry. The development of services is partly due to major changes in agriculture and industry, and partly to their heterogenous production and consumption characteristics.

The role of women in the tertiary sector is very difficult to determine. However, the distribution of the female labour force may serve as an indicator. In 1980, 66.3 per cent of the total female labour force in developing countries was employed in agriculture, 16.3 per cent in industry and 17.4 per cent in services. This is very different from the situation in developed countries, where the shares are 13.7 per cent for agriculture, 29 0 per cent for industry and 57.3 per cent for services. In developing countries the share of females in the total labour force, by economic sectors was highest in agriculture (36.4 per cent, even with universed figures) and much lower in the services sector (26.9 per cent) and industry (26.5).

There are considerable disparities between developing countries in the different regions—disparities between Latin America on the one hand and Asia and Africa on the other. In Asia the main feature is the relatively high share of women in the total labour force in industry (28.8 per cent) and the lower share in services (23.2 per cent). In Latin America the low share of women in the total agricultural labour force (9.3 per cent) is in sharp contrast to the situation in the other two regions. In this region female employment in the services sector is as high as 38.3 per cent. In Africa women account for 31.6 per cent of labour in services, while their share in industry is only 19.7 per cent. (UNIDO, 1984).

In relation to the integration of women in development some partial issues arising in the service sector have been studied. These include trade (women being active internal trade, mostly in the petty trade of the informal sector); transport Oinks between rural and urban areas, developed and underdeveloped regions, formal and informal sectors); banking (mainly in connection with the problems of access to credit); tourism (increased opportunities for productive employment, provision of lodging, catering, etc., could discourage some negative forms of tourism).

Many of the service activities in which women are employed do not require formal technical qualifications. Other activities such as health (especially nursing) and education (especially teaching) do require professional qualifications, but these are in many cases considered an extension of the essentially female role which has its origin in the household—the mother care offered to the family. Thus women's contribution in this sector has not really been adequately recognised.

Much of the productive activity of women in the services sector remains invisible because of its mainly traditional and informal nature in developing countries. Some thought should be devoted to the services which this sector could provide to meet the needs of households in this countries, that is, what the services sector should produce for the household and its members. In view of the importance of the role of women in this sector and of the significance of the services sector for the improvement of the status of women in developing countries, it is suggested that:

- attention be paid to the analysis of the functioning, growth and development of the services sector (both public and private) in all developing countries, especially as regards the interlinkages among this and all other sectors;

- services classification and data collection should be made more transparent and accessible;
- the position of women in this sector should be viewed as developmental and integrative of other activities, which means that the new developmental trends observed in this sector must be closely linked to overall development and the advancement of women; women's hidden economic role in the services should be further studied and analysed;
- cooperation among qeveloping countries in this sector, which is scattered over different areas and usually invisible being traditional and informal;
- could be pursued with a view to the development of self-reliant schemes. Cooperation among developing countries in this sector could contribute to exchange of experiences, to development of self-reliant schemes and linkages between micro and macro levels of implementation. This may be an avenue for the promotion of new approaches to the development of the services sector.

Education and Training

Education is a double-edged instrument: it can contribute to and be an ally of structural changes in society by training people in required skills-old, newly emerging and anticipated. It is also a value-generating process influencing the behaviour, norms and cultural attitudes of people, particularly younger ones. From the beginning of the movement for the equality of women in recent history, great emphasis was placed on education as the major instrument for the elimination of gender inequality. Developing countries have viewed education as an instrument to stimulate development in all fields, and to reduce their dependence on external advisers. The basic problems were to promote a rapid expansion of development and cultural structures to meet the manpower requirements of development and cultural progress in general. Scarcity of resources and the shifting priorities of development have constrained the balanced pursuit of these aims. One of the objectives which had a low priority in the allocation of efforts and resources was the elimination of gender inequality.

Illiteracy still remains a major problem in most developing countries and women constitute a large proportion of the illiterates. About 60 per cent of the approximately 800 million adult illiterates in developing countries today are women. Although the proportion of illiterates in the total adult population has decreased, the results are still unsatisfactory. The absolute number of illiterates in these countries is still increasing. Gender differences persist among illiterates, especially because the lower enrolment ratios for girls at the elementary level increase the number of illiterate women.

The gender gap among illiterates is increasing in developing cauntries. In 1960 the share of women among illiterates was 57.9 per cent. This increased to 59.5 per cent in 1970. (UN, 1980, p. 81).

Trends in the process of equalising the access of men and women to different levels of the educational system, as measured through enrolment ratios, show some interesting results. Over two decades (1960-80) the gender gap in enrolment ratios for the age groups 6-11 and 12-17 has remained virtually constant in developing countries, although there is overall improvement in entrolment for both sexes. At the higher level of education, the gap is much narrower, in contrast to developed countries, where the gender gap exists mainly at the higher level. At this level the gender gap has shrunk in the developed countries during the last decade, and it has slightly widened in the group of developing countries.

The persistence of these gaps prevents the equalisation of educational opportunities with consequent effects on employment, skill acquisition and participatory opportunities in all fields. The widening of the gap in higher education is a matter of serious concern, because this sector is the training ground for entry into many areas important development, *e.g.*, science and technology, communication industries utilising high level technology, professions such as law, medicine, etc. It is also the training ground for most managerial and decision-making occupations.

The participation of women in decision-making positions, which is already limited, could shrink still further if this gap were to expand. In addition to resource constraints, educational progress in developing countries has been impeded by many other problems. Lack of harmony with productive and other developmental activities, which is often a consequence of borrowed models of educational systems, imposed the need to reform and adapt educational systems and institutions, to turn increasingly to the informal aspects of education (vocational training, on the job-training, etc.), and to introduce mass media and other modern devices as useful means of spreading educational programmes and contents in an effort to reach as many social groups as possible.

Developing countries have been experiencing great problems in education, reflected in poor material basis and functional difficulties, in sometimes alarming dropout levels (especially in Sub-Saharan Africa and South Asia), in the fact that a substantial proportion of children are unable to read and write even after going to primary school for four or five years, etc. Women are still mostly employed in traditional and informal sectors where there has been a lower level of technological and information support. This further compounds their educational handicaps. However, women with education have entered many new areas of occupation where their participation was virtually non-existent before.

The enable women to participate actively in all spheres of economic and social life, vocational and professional training must be further developed. In this respect, the training of trainers is of primary importance, as is the introduction of management training for women. Apart from the conventional types of training (seminars, workshops, export group meetings training through doing, etc.), the non-conventional types are often also suitable. Of special relevance are also the new participatory types of training, which include learner-centered methods developed in the framework of non-formal education in which trainers are facilitators, to elicit productive response and interaction-and local social and cultural forms that can be built upon for effective training. These include decision making patterns, social groupings and communications networks.

Culture

The major lacunae in educational development are in the areas of cultural change and promotion of social values which support and reflect the goals of development. Cultural transformations are taking place in developing countries, but in many cases through processes over which the people and even the governments have little control. New values and aspirations are often promoted, directly or indirectly, for profit maximisation-by forces inside or outside the country. Changes in consumption patterns and role models are stimulated by mass media, commercial interests and a process of borrowing or emulation of life styles from developed countries. In many countries such changes have contributed to a widening of the gap between the elites and the masses of the people between the rural and urban populations, between the rich and the poor. This presents a challenge to the educational system, which must correct the trend if it is to promote the goals of participatory development, and collective self-reliance, eliminate the dependency on external support and contribute to comprehensive integrated development.

While there is evidence that the process of unplanned cultural change helps to promote illusory images which are far removed from the social realities of developing countries, cultural reaction, which tries to counter these influences by looking only to the past, may also have a negative impact on development. In their efforts to preserve their cultural identities developing countries have sought to reaffirm their attachment to their cultural heritage. While pride in this heritage can contribute to the spirit and the value of self-reliance, this process may also lead to distortions-to a withdrawal from present-day problems and realities to a glamorization of the past, to the imposition of the culture of dominant groups on other culturally diverse groups and to a strengthening of some of the forces and institutions that oppose the goals of comprehensive, participatory development of all peoples, classes and groups.

In view of the crucial importance of culture values in the dynamics of development, it will be essential to enhance the role of the women and to promote new cultural values that take into account existing social realities and support the efforts to build a different future. Integral development, which subsumes equal participation in development *i.e.*, in production and decision making will enhance the role of culture in the development context. Women will no longer be viewed as marginal producers (or providers of an auxiliary workforce), but rather as equal partners in the promotion of development.

Educational institutions will have to play an active role in the promotion of the development of such new cultural values. Hitherto, their contribution has been inadequate. Structurally pedagogically and philosophically, educational institutions will have to playa far more active role in the development of a new cultural context that can contribute to the realisation of the goals of comprehensive development-human and material. This also requires that they internalise the concern for the equality of women and the enhancement of their role—in their curricula, pedagogic methods, organisation and research agendas.

A strategic interrelationship between education and cultural and socio-economic development which integrates concern for the emancipation of women would have to be characterised by respect for the specific cultural features of a particular environment and clearly define the cultural and developmental function of education in social transformation and support the process of educational reform.

In this connection, the promotion of new knowledge about women and new perceptions of the role of women in development could be viewed as an instrument for educational and cultural development with a view to:

- strengthening and extension of training activities
- so as to embrace all relevant problems, such as: improvement of professional skills, education for family life and responsibilities, training for community organisation and management, decision waking etc.;
- equal participation of the local population, and particularly of women, in devising, deciding upon and implementing development programmes; this can be achieved by clearly defining the developmental interests of all groups of the population; promotion of integral and interdisciplinary links among developing countries in the field of cultural transformation and education and specially in professional and Vocational training as well as in all forms of non-conventional training, to ensure availability of cadres capable of handling the new technology.

- enhancement of the collective self-reliance of nonaligned and other developing countries in culture and education by intensifying their communication in these fields, especially as regards the methodologies for educational reform which incorporates the advancement of women as one of its concerns.

Mass Media

This section focuses on the possibilities which the media offer provided they are used judiciously to reflect the contribution which women are making to the nation's development efforts. Communication media have been a powerful social influence, both as instruments of change and for maintaining status quo. In the last decade, an impressive amount of literature on the portrayal of women in the media has been produced. These studies have expressed concern about the stereotyped and negative images of women which are being projected through the media without any cognizance of the new and expanded roles of women in society. Communication media are a powerful tool for the creation of an alternative and positive image of women and could promote new attitudes and strategies for action directed towards the achievement of the goal of equality for women. It is imperative to democratises the control over the communication media and to make them an instrument for the creation of an awareness of women's needs and problems.

Mass media, especially the audiovisual media, play an important role by influencing the consumption patterns and life-styles, and usually promote commercial interests (often of external producers), thus creating pressures to distort trade and industrial policies. They also contribute to the distortion of cultural development, promoting imported values which militate against comprehensive integrated development and the principle of collective self-reliance. There has been a recent trend among media professionals in developing countries towards greater realism in their portrayal of social problems. Realism, however, must be used to inspire people to struggle for change. A search for new options in human relationships, the reshaping of social institutions, political and economic structures and cultural values, would go a long way towards integrating women into the world of the media, and enable the media to play a more positive role in integrated development.

In the past, there has been a one-way flow of information from the developed to the developing countries, and from government to the people. The goals of self-reliance and participatory development, which are being actively pursued by the non-aligned countries, involve a shift from excessive reliance of the developing countries on foreign resources towards a mobilisation of their indigenous resources, which would make these countries less vulnerable to external pressures and develop their own potential for growth. The new information and communication technology, the micro-chip revolution, has considerably magnified the power of the media. Satellite communication has exposed millions of people to new information. The strengthening of the autonomous capacities of the individual countries and improvement of the organisational framework and media content will depend on the socio-political context of each country.

Women are today an important factor in the strategy of self-reliance and the media could do much to create public awareness of the role of women and their potentials. There are a number of steps which the media could take at various levels to strengthen the role of women as equal partners in development:

- a democratisation of the structures and control of the communication media could contribute to the representation and participation of women in the media at the decision-making levels;

- more women should be involved in media training programmes; communication and advertising policies involving participation by women could be developed;
- media content could be improved through coordinated efforts for increased interaction between nongovernmental organisations in formulating guidelines for monitoring programmes;
- listeners and viewers from consumer groups or NGO action groups, etc., could be effectively utilised to create an awareness of women's issues and to evolve common strategies for the promotion of more positive approaches to women's issues;
- various international seminars, conferences and expert group meetings, which have already covered a wide range of issues connected with women and the communication media indicate the need for further in depth studies, research training for women in communication technology, the organisational framework, including the development of a code of ethics with regard to the presentation of women in media and using traditional folk media to encourage participation of women.
- horizontal communication and cooperation among developing countries in this field could be strengthened in order to create an awareness of issues of common concern, identifying solutions to common problems and areas of cooperation.

Crucial Development Issues

The still largely unresolved problems of the inter-connections between economic and social development and the increasing concern for the distributional and human dimensions of development indicate the need to pay more attention to all aspects of social development. The issues of health, social security, population trends and family planning, housing urbanisation and the environment, are linked with the general problem of the level of socioeconomic development of a country its resource base and social policies.

Health Delivery Systems

Millions of people in developing countries are trapped in poverty, malnutrition, hunger and disease, although there are regional variations in living conditions. It is estimated that acute forms of potential energy malnutrition affect 35 per cent school children in Africa, 16 per cent in Asia and 4 per cent in of Latin America. Similarly, it is estimated that two-thir.ds pregnant women in the developing world suffer from nutritional anaemia. High maternal and infant mortality rates are closely linked with inadequate maternal and child health care services, lack of proper sanitation and a safe drinking water supply. By the end of the last decade, only 42 per cent of households in developing countries had access to a potable water supply and over three quarters of the population lacked access to sanitary facilities.

A disaggregation of social indicators by regions reveals that not only is there a very great gap between the developed and developing countries but also that there is great diversity among the developing regions.

The average life expectancy in Sub-Saharan Africa is 47.4 years while it is 63.9 years in some Asian Countries Similarly, infant mortality is highest in Sub-Saharan Africa (127.1 per thousand live births), while it is 56.2 in South East Asia. In the South Asian region the mortality differentials by sex indicate higher infant mortality among females and empirical data also show sex-based health and nutrition related behaviour. In the health care subsystems, there are interesting variations: Latin America with the highest per capita GDP—has 7.5 physicians and 11.7 nurses per 10,000 population, followed by some countries in South East Asia, where despite low GDP per capita the averages are 5.4 physicians and 5.2 nurses per 10,000 population.

Most developing countries are faced with the problem of a decline or slowing down of the growth rate of production, rising unemployment, growing deficit in balance of payments and inflation. All these adversely affect the availability of resources for social services, *i.e.*, health, education and social security.

Despite the methodological weaknesses of the existing social indicators and an absence of data on access to and distributional characteristics of the social development infrastructure, the trends indicate that results differ sharply also within regions and that social improvements definitely dò not come automatically as a by-product of economic growth. In many cases health resources are disproportionately concentrated in big cities, at the expense of primary health care for the .masses in rural areas Problems requiring careful study include disparities in increase and living standards, and the care available to different social groups, inadequate planning and management of health development, problems of inter and intra-sectoral coordination, administrative decentralisation and involvement of the people in the planning, programming and implementation of health care programmes.

Very few developing countries have systems of social security. Even where such systems exist, a large part of the population in the informal sector-a substantial proportion of which are women-is not covered by the existing systems of mater benefits, health insurance, old age benefits, etc. In some countries voluntary and philanthropic organisations supplement state action However, their work is often uncoordinated and not adequate to deal with the increasing, demands of urbanisation and poverty. The development of social protection is linked to changes in the development strategies and orientation directed towards the satisfaction of basic minimum needs the reduction and elimination of poverty, promotion of employment opportunities and improvement of the working conditions of labour.

The global strategy of Health for All by 200'0 adopted by the Thirty Fourth World Health Assembly in 1981, which emphasises basic health protection, the primary health care approach and organisation of an effective health care and health information system, identified priorities for health cooperation and drew up an Action Programme, stressing the need for a review of a number of policy orientations in the areas of primary health care, health information and monitoring system. community involvement in health programmes, prevention of infectious diseases, development of national services of health care and health education, production, distribution and consumption of drugs and protection of the human environment.

On the basis of the Medium-Term Programme for Technical Cooperation among Developing Countries for Health for All (1984-89) and in view of the calls for an acceleration of the development of national health care capabilities and the establishment of local points for TCDC in the area of health some priority activities may be identified:

- introduction of effective health surveillance systems at the national level, of health indicators for target setting and formulation of national priorities and plans of action, and of appropriate Systems for assessing strengths and weaknesses of national health programmes;
- integration of maternal and child health care with family planning services and accelerated development of national capacities through development of health institutions and infrastructures and increase of the number of health experts and particularly health workers;

- linking of health policies and 'programmes with economic development and those facilities which can directly reduce women's drudgery and work burden and directly improve their health situation, *i.e.*, provision of adequate housing, water supply, sanitation, health regulations at the work-place, and health protection of women, particularly those working in the informal sector of the economy who are not covered by social protection policies;
- promotion of health education and indigenous system of health care;
- involvement of women's organisations in primary health care activities and their representation on national and local health councils;
- involvement of woman's organisations in primary health care activities and their representation on national and local health councils;
- promotion of health education and indigenous systems of health care;
- introduction of ECDC/TCTC programmes for the promotion of industries which are important for the development of health care systems. The developing countries could evolve suitable mechanisms for cooperation in training and development of human resources, collaborative research, joint programming, exchange of information and references, and exploring the application of low-cost technologies for water supply and waste disposal.

Demographic Factors

It is becoming increasingly obvious that population policies should be implemented parallel with better health care and general socio-economic development as population issues touch on very fundamental human values.

As the Mexico Conference on Population in 1984 stressed, population strategies cannot be limited to the analysis of population trends, since there is a dynamic interrelationship between these and socio-economic transformations. Hence, what is required is a set of coordinated strategies and activities for the promotion of economic development of the quality of life, human rights and in particular the fundamental right to individual choice.

The status of women and the advancement of their role in development remains a critical element in the achievement of these objectives. The persisting inequalities between men and women-which are evident in the higher incidence of poverty, unemployment and illiteracy among women-the limited range of employment categories offered to women, and the uneven sharing of borne and family responsibilities make it difficult for women to participate actively in the socio-economic development of the country. Population policies should be viewed as an integral part of overall socio-economic development.

There is sufficient evidence to show that it is lower income groups with a low level of literacy, low and insecure income and low health and nutritional levels which have larger families. This is points to a need for planning policies which have a more integrated approach. Rapid population growth will affect the efforts of countries to achieve food security and to reduce pressure on the natural resources; also, its effects on urbanisation and on land and capital will exacerbate inequalities.

Many governments have launched subsidised family planning programmes. However, incentives are offered to encourage people to reduce family size. Experience has shown that a clinical approach which threatens social values, beliefs and customs does not succeed and is actually a disincentive. To breakthrough the vicious circle of poverty, high fertility and mortality calls for a more careful and humane public policy with a judicious balance between individual choice and dignity and promotion of a sense of responsibility among parents to ensure a better future for all children. This could be further stimulated and promoted through various forms of technical assistance at various levels as well as enriched through mutual exchange of information and experience among developing countries.

Coping with Over Population: Women in the Cities

The rapid growth of cities in developing countries has created serious problems, since a large proportion of urban migrant workers are living in temporary hutments and settlements without adequate basic amenities. The growth of cities and the steep rise in rural-urban migration is a manifestation of imbalances in the location and expansion of productive activity. Women are particularly affected, as many of their activities are connected with their homes and bad housing and hygiene conditions are detrimental to both their own and their families health. The growth of cities has also created ecological problems. The growing demands of expanding cities have put undue pressure on natural resources, destroying the harmony between human beings and nature, and has led to a degradation of productive resources like water, land and forests. With increasing pressure on the land, overgrasing and deforestation, severe environmental damage has followed.

The expansion of agriculture by clearing large tracts of forest has caused desertification due to severe soil erosion, a problem which is extremely serious in Sub-Saharan Africa (Sahel), north-western Asia and the Middle East. Forests are crucial to the ecological life of many developing countries and deforestation has created serious problems, as the consumption of forest resources has exceeded replacement possibilities through natural growth. This has affected millions of rural households and the role of women in these households, as well as the nutritional level of the families. The human costs of malnutrition, famine and disruption in the lives of people seeking employment are a matter of serious concern.

Environmental issues conceiving the environment in its broadest social context are most relevant for women. The increasing marginalisation of certain sections of the population, growing poverty and deprivation of the masses, decreasing food production, the energy crisis and human environmental degradation in many developing countries are all symptoms of a pattern of growth and resource utilisation which is geared to existing power structures and prevents a large section of the population from satisfying its basic needs. The multidimensional problems facing developing countries are interconnected, but often these connection are not understood by those who formulate sectoral policies. In the long run, social development policies will have to be closely integrated with economic development policies and a strong commitment to the improvement of the quality of life. The methods and instruments of analysis and planning of socio-economic development should therefore take adequate account of environmental constraint.

●●

10

Psychological Gender Differences

The existence of a gender difference does not necessarily identify whether the trait is due to nature or environment. Some traits are obviously innate (for example, reproductive organs), others obviously environmental (for example, given names), while for others the relationship is either multi-cause or unknown.

From the viewpoint of evolutionary psychology (championed by David Buss, Steven Pinker, Desmond Morris, Daniel Dennett, and others) modern humans have inherited natural traits that were adaptive in a prehistoric environment, including traits that had different advantages for males versus females (see Sexual selection). Evolutionary theory of sex considers gender differences as a result of distinct specialization of the sexes, performing relationship with preceding generations (inheritance) and with the environment (variability). Theory explains ethological and psychological sexual dimorphism, more efficient "education" or "training" of females during the course of ontogenetic adaptation as well as greater conformism of females well known to psychologists. Gender role theory and Alice Eagly claims that boys and girls learn the appropriate behavior and attitudes from the family and overall culture they grow up with, and so non-physical gender differences are a product of socialization.

Some feminists see gender differences as caused by patriarchy or discrimination, although difference feminism argues for an acceptance of gender differences. Conservative masculists tend to see gender differences as inherent in human nature, while liberal masculists see gender differences as caused by matriarchy or discrimination.

Traditional Abrahamic religions see gender differences as created by God: "He made them in his image: man and woman He made them" (Genesis 1:27) or, among egalitarian Christians, as being a result of humankind's fall from grace (interpreted from Genesis 3:15-17, Galatians 3:27-28) (see Role of women in Judaism, Christian views of women, Gender roles in Islam).

Physical Health

From conception to death, but particularly before adulthood, females are less vulnerable than males to developmental difficulties and chronic illnesses. This could be due to females having two x chromosomes instead of just one, or in the reduced exposure to testosterone.

Neurology

Female brains are more compact than male brains in that, though smaller, they are more densely packed with neurons, particularly in the region responsible for language. Also, females have language functions evenly distributed in both cerebral hemispheres, while in males they are more concentrated in the left hemisphere. This puts males more at risk for language disorders like dyslexia.

Psychology

In one large scale study, most cognitive abilities and psychological traits showed little or no average difference between the sexes . Where sex differences exist, there is often considerable overlap between the sexes; in addition, it is unclear how many of these differences hold true across different cultures. Nevertheless, certain trends tend to be found.

Personality Tests

- In the big five personality traits, women score higher in Agreeableness (tendency to be compassionate and cooperative) and Neuroticism (tendency to feel anxiety, anger, and depression).
- Demographics of MBTI surveys indicate that 60-75% of women prefer feeling and 55-80% of men prefer thinking.

Aggression

Males are generally more aggressive than females (Coi & Dodge 1997, Maccoby & Jacklin 1974, Buss 2005). There is evidence that males are quicker to aggression (Frey et al. 2003) and more likely than females to express their aggression physically (Bjorkqvist et al. 1994). However, some researchers (such as Rachel Simmons) have suggested that females are not necessarily less aggressive, but that they tend to show their aggression in less overt, less physical ways (Bjorkqvist et al. 1994, Hines and Saudino 2003). For example, females may display more verbal and relational aggression, such as social rejection. High agression has been correlated with high testosterone levels. This would expain men generally having higher levels of agression in adolescence and manhood than in boyhood than females.

Systematizing and Empathizing

Females score higher on self-report scales of empathy, on samples ranging from school-age children to adults. Empathy scales include measures of perspective taking, orientation towards another person, empathic concern, and personal distress. However, such measures are subjective and empathy may be more related to gender role rather than sex.

Simon Baron-Cohen's EQ SQ Theory claims that, in general, men are better at systematizing (the desire to analyze and explore systems and rules) and that women are better at empathizing (the ability to identify with other people's feelings).

More males than females are diagnosed with autism and Asperger syndrome. According to Cohen, autistic and Asperger individuals are examples of an "extreme male brain." Autistic and Asperger individuals are very high in systematizing, albeit often in a manner which is hyperfocused, and may even oversimplify more complex systems due to missing certain details. Autistic and Asperger individuals are also very low in empathizing.

Intelligence

Many recent studies have concluded that IQ performances of men and women vary little. Other studies show a greater variance in the IQ performance of men compared to that of women, *i.e.* men are more represented at the extremes of performance, and less represented at the median.

Communication

Deborah Tannen's studies found these gender differences in communication styles:

- Men tend to talk more than women in public situations, but women tend to talk more than men at home.
- Females are more inclined to face each other and make eye contact when talking, while males are more likely to look away from each other.

- When listening, women make more noises such as "mm-hmm" and "uh-huh", while men are more likely to listen silently.
- Boys tend to jump from topic to topic, but girls tend to talk at length about one topic.
- Women are inclined to express agreement and support, while men are more inclined to debate.

The studies also reported that in general both sexes communicated in similar ways. Critics, including Suzette Haden Elgin, have suggested that Tannen's findings may apply more to women of certain specific cultural and economic groups than to women in general. Although it is widely believed that women speak far more words than men, this is actually not the case.

Stereotypes

Stereotypes create expectations regarding emotional expression and emotional reaction. Many studies find that emotional stereotypes and the display of emotions "correspond to actual gender differences in experiencing emotion and expression."

Stereotypes generally dictate how and by whom and when it is socially acceptable to display an emotion. Reacting in a stereotype-consistent manner may result in social approval while reacting in a stereotype-inconsistent manner could result in disapproval. It should be noted that what is socially acceptable varies substantially over time and between local cultures and subcultures.

According to Niedenthal *et al.*:

- Women are more emotionally expressive.
- Women are more emotionally responsive.
- Women are more empathetic.

- Women are more sensitive to others' feelings.
- Women pay more attention to body language.
- Women judge emotions from nonverbal communication better than men do.
- Women are more obsessed with having children.
- Women express their feelings without constraint, except for the emotion of anger.
- Women anticipate negative consequences for expressing anger and aggression.
- Men are overwhelmed by women's expressions of emotion.
- Women express more love, fear, and sadness.
- Women laugh, gaze, and smile more.
- Men restrain from expressing their feelings.
- Men are stoic.
- Men express more anger.
- Men control their feelings.
- Men show emotion to communicate dominance.

Experience and Expression

When measured with an affect intensity measure, women reported greater intensity of both positive and negative affect than men. Women also reported a more intense and more frequent experience of affect, joy, and love. Women also reported a more intense and more frequent experience of embarrassment, guilt, shame, sadness, anger, fear, and distress. Experiencing pride was more frequent and intense for men than for women.

Men and women use different cognitive strategies when coping with emotional situations. Women are more prone to depression because of their tendency to dwell on the causes of negative emotions while men distract themselves from dwelling on these emotions.

Women have a greater affect intensity, which makes them more prone to "self-referring, overgeneralizing, and selective attention to emotional information, which may lead to more intense emotional reactions." (282) Women also have a tendency to catch others' emotions, known as emotional contagion.

Heuristic Devices

When lacking substantial emotion information they can base judgments on, people tend to rely more on gender stereotypes. Results from a study conducted by Robinson and colleagues showed that participants relied more on stereotypes when imagining the average man or woman's emotional reaction than when imagining their own emotional reaction. The study also showed that when placed in the same situation men and women experience parallel emotions.

Some observers were placed in a hypothetical situation. These observers believed that male players would display more masculine emotions while female players expressed feminine emotions. The observers that watched an actual game failed to evaluate the female and male players' emotions differently.

The findings of this study imply gender stereotypes as more influential when judging others' emotions in a hypothetical situation. Also, with minimal or no available relevant emotional information, men and women depend on gender stereotypes to fill in lacking information.

Context also determines a man or woman's emotional behavior. Context-based emotion norms, such as feeling rules or display rules, "prescribe emotional experience and expressions in specific situations like a wedding or a funeral," (290) independent of the person's gender. In situations like a wedding or a funeral, the activated emotion norms apply to and constrain every person in the situation. Gender differences are more pronounced when situational demands are very small or non-existent as well as ambiguous situations. During these situations, gender norms "are the default option that prescribes emotional behavior." (291)

Decoding Emotion

Decoding can be defined as a "capacity to judge, to interpret and to identify others' emotions from nonverbal cues." (295) Typically, women are more accurate in decoding nonverbal cues' emotional meaning than men. Developmental research suggests that a woman's ability to identify another's emotion is not innate but instead caused by the socialization process.

Studies

- In 1980, 3- to 5-year-old children and adults identified the sex of "gender-neutral puppy dogs depicting happy, angry, fearful, and sad emotions" for Birnbaum and colleagues. This experiment measured the children's and adult's stereotypes concerning sex differences in emotional expression. Both children and adults attributed the happy-, sad- and fearful-looking puppies with the female sex and the angry-looking puppies with the male sex.

- A Cambridge University lab showed that at birth girls gaze longer at a face, whereas suspended mechanical mobiles, rather than a face, keep boys' attention for longer. The Cambridge team also found that the amount of eye contact children make is partially determined by prenatal testosterone, a biological factor.

- According to a study done by Hall and Matsumoto, "women are more accurate than men in judging emotional meaning from nonverbal cues even under situations of minimal stimulus information."
- Studies that measure facial expression by the use of electromyography recordings show that women are more adequately able to manipulate their facial expressions than men. Men, however can inhibit their expressions better than females when cued to do so. In the observer ratings women's facial expressions are easier to read as opposed to men's except for the expression of anger..
- In a study where researchers wanted to concentrate on nonverbal expressions by just looking at the eyebrows, lips, and the eyes, participants read certain cue cards that were either negative or positive and recorded the responses. In the results of this experiment it is shown that feminine emotions happen more frequently and have a higher intensity in women than men. In relation to the masculine emotions, such as anger, the results are flipped and the women's frequency and intensity is lower than the men's.
- In imagined frightening situations, such as being home alone and witnessing a stranger walking towards your house, women reported greater fear. Women also reported more fear in situations that involved "a male's hostile and aggressive behavior" (281) In anger-eliciting situations, women communicated more intense feelings of anger than men. Women also reported more intense feelings of anger in relation to terrifying situations, especially situations involving a male protagonist.

Emotion, Gender, and Culture

A number of studies have been conducted in western cultures for the most part, specifically North America and Western Europe. Most of the research has indicated that sex differences in expressing emotion tend to be greater in North America than in other cultures, particularly Asian culture.

Culture impacts gender differences in the expression of emotions. This may be partly explained by the different social roles men and women have in different cultures, and by the status and power men and women hold in different societies, as well as the different cultural values various societies hold.

Happiness

A commentary released by Pew Research Center addressed some questions about the way men and women view their lives:

- Overall, women claim to be far happier than men with their lives, and reported more often that they had made personal progress in the last five years.
- Women show greater concern about family and home life issues, while men express more concern about political issues. Men are happier with their family life and more optimistic about their personal future and that of their children.

Problems with Research

Studies of psychological gender differences are controversial and subject to error. Many small-scale studies report differences that are not repeated in larger studies. Self-report questionnaires are subject to bias, particularly if the subjects are told that the questionnaire is testing for gender roles. It is also possible that commentators may exaggerate or downplay differences for ideological reasons.

Income

In many countries, there is a gender income gap which favors males in the labour market. For example, the median full-time salary for U.S. women is 77% of that of U.S. men. Several factors other than discrimination may contribute to this gap. On average, women are more likely than men to consider factors other than pay when looking for work, and may be less willing to travel or relocate. Thomas Sowell, in his book Knowledge and Decisions, claims that this difference is due to women not taking jobs due to marriage or pregnancy, but income studies show that does not explain the entire difference. The U.S. Census's report on the wage gap reported "When we account for difference between male and female work patterns as well as other key factors, women earned, on average, 80 percent of what men earned in 2000...Even after accounting for key factors that affect earnings, our model could not explain all of the differences in earnings between men and women." The income gap in other countries ranges from 53% in Botswana to -40% in Bahrain.

In the United States, among women and men who never marry or have children, women make more than men. Additionally, women who work part-time make more on average than men who work part-time.

Employment

According to a 2004 report by the US department of labour :

- 52.9% of American women are in the labour force versus 73.3% of men.
- 70.7% of women with children under 18 are in the workforce (up from 47% in 1975), compared with 94% of men with children under 18.
- 5.6% of employed women and 8% of men are self-employed.

- Approximately 26 percent of employed women usually work part time, compared with about 11 percent of employed men.
- Women account for more than half of all workers in the following industries: financial activities, education services, healthcare, leisure and hospitality, and office and administrative support. Women are far more likely than men to be social workers, paralegals and legal assistants, teachers, nurses, speech pathologists, dental hygienists, maids and housekeeping cleaners, and childcare workers.
- Women in nonagricultural industries work 35.9 hours per week versus 41.6 hours for men.
- More men than women work in the following industries: mining, construction, transportation and utilities, farming, computer and mathematical occupations, engineering, and architecture. Men are more likely than women to be chief executives, firefighters, police and patrol officers, electricians, dentists, and surgeons.

Occupational Death

The majority of occupational deaths occur among men. In one U.S. study, 93% of deaths on the job involved men, with a death rate approximately 11 times higher than women. The industries with the highest death rates are mining, agriculture, forestry, fishing, and construction, all of which employ more men than women.

Parental Leave

Most countries require companies to grant maternity leave for working women at full pay for usually at least 12 weeks, although paternity leave is not available to the same extent. In Israel parents can use parental leave as they see fit, dividing the 12 weeks among themselves if necessary regardless of sex. In Sweden there are equal opportunities to take maternity/paternity leave. The duration is 18 months per child with 80% of full pay. Each parent must be at home minimum 60 days to qualify for the maximum pay.

Insurance

Insurance companies often charge different rates for men and women:

- Health insurance is less expensive for young and middle aged men.
- Automobile insurance companies charge more for teenage boys than their female counterparts.
- Life insurance is higher for males than for females.

Consumer Behaviour

Price discrimination can favour either men or women. For example, some night clubs offer discounts or free entry for women, while some hairdressers offer cheaper haircuts for men.

According to a 2000 report, women purchase or influence the purchase of 80% of all consumer goods and influence 80% of health-care decisions.

Education

Worldwide, men are more likely to be literate, with 100 men considered literate for every 88 women. In some countries the difference is even greater; for example, in Bangladesh only 62 women are literate for every 100 men.

In an OECD study of 43 developed countries, 15-year-old girls were ahead of boys in literacy skills and were more confident than boys about getting high-income jobs.. In the United States, girls are significantly ahead of boys in writing ability at all levels of primary and secondary education. However, boys are slightly ahead of girls in mathematics ability.

In some countries within the last generation, there has been a significant increase in women accessing tertiary education compared to men. In the United States in 2005-2006, women earned more Associate's, Bachelor's, and Master's degrees than men, but men earned more Doctorates. This is repeated in other countries; for example, women make up 58% of admissions in the UK and 60% in Iran.

Suicide

In western countries, males are much more likely to die by suicide than females (usually by a factor of 3–4:1); 69 out of 74 non-western countries found an excess male mortality from suicide.

While there are more completed male suicides than female, females are more likely to attempt suicide. One possible explanation is that males tend to use more immediately lethal methods than females, who use less violent methods while attempting suicide. Another theory is that females are more likely to use self-harm as a cry for help or attention while males are more likely to genuinely want to end their lives.

American males between the ages of 20 and 24 have a suicide rate that is seven times higher than that of women.

Crime

Men are much more likely to be incarcerated than women, although women are a fast-growing demographic group in prison. Males are more likely than females to commit murder. Men are also far more likely than women to be the victims of violent crime.

Internet Issues

In an American study in 2005, the percentage of men using the Internet was very slightly ahead of the percentage of women, although this difference reversed in those under 30. Men logged on more often, spend more time online, and are more likely to be broadband users, whereas women tended to make more use of opportunities to communicate (such as email). Men were more likely to use the Internet to pay bills, participate in auctions, and for recreation such as downloading music and videos. Men and women were equally likely to use the Internet for shopping and banking.

More recent studies indicate that in 2008, women significantly outnumbered men on most social networking sites, such as Facebook and Myspace, although the ratios varied with age. In addition, women watched more streaming content, whereas men downloaded more. In terms of blogs, men were more likely to blog in the first place; among those who blog, men were more likely to have a professional blog, whereas women were more likely to have a personal blog.

Gender-related Preferences in Web Site Design

A study was performed at the University of Maryland in 2007 which was designed to determine gender differences in preference for various aspects of web site design. Previous studies, in particular one performed at the University of Glamorgan, Key website research highlights gender bias, indicated measurable differences between men and women, with each gender tending to prefer sites designed by their own gender. Women showed a preference for pages with more color in the background and typeface, and more rounded shapes. Women also favored informal rather than posed pictures. Men responded better to dark colors and a more linear design. They also were more pleased by a three-dimensional look and images of "self-propelling" rather than stationary objects. The Maryland study sought to confirm these differences.

The subjects were given pairs of web sites to visit and were asked to fill out a short questionnaire immediately afterward. The questionnaires asked simple questions about their reaction to the colors, graphics, site organization as well as an open-ended question in which they were asked to describe their subjective impressions of the sites. Web sites were selected to present significant design dissimilarities so as to assess differences in site design preference. One pair was specifically selected because the sites themselves were targeted at male and female users respectively.

The results generally supported earlier research. Women showed a distinct preference for more color and graphics. In addition, while the object scores for the male and female-targeted sites were not significantly different, women showed a significantly higher preference for the female-targeted site. However, it is clear from the responses to the open-ended questions that site content was a significant factor in determine preference for one site over another. It is therefore suggested that in any future study real web sites not be used, but instead neutral-content sites should be designed with variations in style, to eliminate the bias introduced by the site content.

Marriage and Sexuality

Dating and marriage customs are dependent on culture and differ greatly across countries and even in subcultures within the same country. For example, many marriages in India are arranged, whereas in the Western World most people choose their own partners. In most societies, men are generally expected to play the more active role in the early stages of courtship, for example in asking the woman for a date.

Sexual Orientation

The demographics of sexual orientation in any population is difficult to establish with reasonable accuracy. However, most surveys find that a greater proportion of men than women report that they are exclusively homosexual, whereas more women than men report being bisexual.

Studies have shown that heterosexual men are only aroused by images of women. Whereas some women who claim to be heterosexual are aroused by images of both men and women. However, it's not an apples-to-apples comparison, since different methods are required to measure arousal for the anatomy of a man versus that of a woman.

Numbers of Unmarried People

In the USA, single men are greatly outnumbered by single women at a ratio of 100 single women to every 86 single men , though never-married men over age 15 outnumber women by a 5:4 ratio (33.9% to 27.3%) according to the 2006 US Census American Community Survey. This very much depends on age group, with 118 single men per 100 single women in their 20s, versus 33 single men to 100 single women over 65.

The numbers are different in other countries. For example, China has many more young men than young women, and this disparity is expected to increase. In regions with recent conflict such as Chechnya, women may greatly outnumber men.

Choosing a Partner

In a cross-cultural study by David Buss, men and women were asked to rank certain traits in order of importance in a long-term partner. Both men and women ranked "kindness" and "intelligence" as the two most important factors. Men valued beauty and youth more highly than women, while women valued financial and social status more highly than men.

Orgasm

This article may contain original research or unverified claims. Please improve the article by adding references. See the talk page for details. *(July 2008)*

- Men's orgasm is nearly essential ("nearly" as small groups of sperm can escape the penis before orgasm is reached) for reproduction, whereas female orgasm is not. The female orgasm was believed to have no obvious function other than to be pleasurable although recent evidence suggests that it may have evolved as a discriminatory advantage in regards to mate selection. Psychology Today, *The Orgasm Wars*

- According to Kinsey, for about 75% of all males, orgasm is possible to be attained within the first four minutes after initiation of sexual intercourse. For women the average time to reach orgasm is between 10 and 20 minutes. The swiftness of the male system virtually guarantees climactic orgasms for males (except for those experiencing delayed ejaculation) but is usually too quick to give the female a penetration-induced orgasm. However, the average time to female orgasm via masturbation is significantly less at four minutes (those two citations contain nothing on the average orgasm masturbation time).

- Male circumcision (removal of the foreskin) does not prevent the ability to orgasm, but female circumcision usually does. However, the two procedures are not directly comparable; in particular, the phrase "female circumcision" is used to refer to a wide variety of different practices, from minor ritual cuts to the labia (which are much less likely to impede orgasm) to complete excision of the outer clitoris.

●●

11

Ordination of Women

In general religious use, ordination is the process by which a person is consecrated (set apart for the administration of various religious rites). The ordination of women is a controversial issue in religions where either the rite of ordination, or the role that an ordained person fulfills, has traditionally been restricted to men because of cultural prohibitions or theological doctrines.

In liturgical Christianity, such as the Roman Catholic Church, Eastern and Oriental Orthodoxy, Lutheranism, and Anglicanism, ordination—distinguished from religious or consecrated life—is the means by which a person is included in one of the orders of bishops, priests, or deacons.

In many Protestant denominations ordination is understood more generally as the acceptance of a person for pastoral work. Since the mid-nineteenth century, these denominations have allowed for female office-bearers and preachers. Today, about half of all American Protestant denominations ordain women and about 30% of all seminary students (and in some seminaries over half) are female.

Orthodox Judaism does not permit women to become rabbis (instead, the women in leadership positions are often rebbetzin, wives of a rabbi), but female rabbis have begun to appear in recent decades among more liberal Jewish movements, especially the Reconstructionist, Renewal, Reform, and Humanistic denominations (see Rabbi#Women as rabbis]]).

Muslims do not formally ordain religious leaders. The imam serves as a spiritual leader and religious authority. Most strands of Islam permit women to lead female-only congregations in prayer (one of the competences of an imam), but restrict their roles in mixed-sex congregations. There is a recent movement to extend women's roles in spiritual leadership.

Within Buddhism, the legitimacy of ordaining women as bhikkhuni (nuns) has become a significant topic of discussion in some areas in recent years. It is widely accepted that the Buddha created an order of bhikkhuni, but the tradition of ordaining women has died out in some Buddhist traditions, such as Theravada Buddhism, while remaining strong in others, such as Chinese Buddhism.

Buddhism

The ordination of women is currently and historically practiced in some Buddhist regions, such as East Asia and Taiwan, and not in others, such as India and Sri Lanka.

The tradition of the ordained monastic community (sangha) began with Buddha, who established an order of Bhikkhus (monks). According to the scriptures, later, after an initial reluctance, he also established an order of Bhikkhunis (nuns). However, according to the scriptural account, not only did the Buddha lay down more rules of discipline for the bhikkhuni (311 compared to the bhikkhu's 227 in the Theravada version), he also made it more difficult for them to be ordained, and made them subordinate to monks. The historicity of this account has been questioned, sometimes to the extent of regarding nuns as a later invention. The stories, sayings and deeds of some of the distinguished Bhikkhunis of early Buddhism are recorded in many places in the Pali Canon, most notably in the Therigatha.

The tradition flourished for centuries throughout South and East Asia, but appears to have died out in the Theravada tradition of Sri Lanka in the 11th century C.E. It survived in Burma to about the 13th century, but died out there too. It was never introduced to Thailand, Laos, Cambodia or Tibet. However, the Mahayana tradition, in China, Korea, Vietnam, Taiwan and Hong Kong, has retained the practice, where nuns are called 'Bhik?u?î' (the Sanskrit equivalent of the Pali 'Bhikkhuni').

Recent Developments

The International Congress on Buddhist Women's Role in the Sangha: Bhikshuni Vinaya and Ordination Lineages took place in Germany, on *July 18–20, 2007.*

Sri Lanka

There have been some attempts in recent years to revive the tradition of women in the sangha within Theravada Buddhism in Thailand, India and Sri Lanka, with many women ordained in Sri Lanka since 1996. Some of these were carried out with the assistance of nuns from the East Asian tradition; others were carried out by Theravada monks alone. Since 2005, many have been ordained by the head of the Dambulla chapter of the Siyam nikaya in Sri Lanka.

Thailand

In 1928, the Supreme Patriarch of Thailand, responding to the attempted ordination of two women, issued an edict that monks must not ordain women. The two women were reportedly arrested and jailed briefly. In a more recent challenge to the Thai sangha's ban on women, Dhammananda Bhikkhuni, previously a professor of Buddhist philosophy known as Dr. Chatsumarn Kabilsingh, was controversially ordained as a nun in Sri Lanka in 2003. Despite some support inside the religious hierarchy, the sangha remains fiercely opposed to the ordination of women.

Burma

The governing council of Burmese Buddhism has ruled that there can be no valid ordination of women in modern times, though some Burmese monks disagree.

Tibetan Tradition

The Dalai Lama has authorized followers of the Tibetan tradition to be ordained as nuns in traditions that have such ordination.

ROMAN CATHOLIC CHURCH

Doctrinal Position and Its Supporters

The official position of the Roman Catholic Church, as expressed in the current canon law and the Catechism of the Catholic Church, is that: "Only a baptized man (In Latin, *vir*) validly receives sacred ordination." Insofar as priestly and episcopal ordination are concerned, the Church teaches that this requirement is a matter of divine law, and thus doctrinal. The requirement that only males can receive ordination to the permanent diaconate has not been promulgated as doctrinal by the Church's magisterium, though it is clearly at least a requirement according to canon law. In 1976, the Sacred Congregation for the Doctrine of the Faith discussed the issue of the ordination of women and issued a *Declaration on the Question of the Admission of Women to the Ministerial Priesthood* which concluded that for various doctrinal, theological, and historical reasons, the Church "... does not consider herself authorized to admit women to priestly ordination". The most important reasons stated were first, the Church's determination to remain faithful to its constant tradition, second, its fidelity to Christ's will, and third, the idea of male representation due to the "sacramental nature" of the priesthood. The Biblical Commission, an advisory commission that was to study the exclusion of women from the ministerial priesthood from a biblical perspective, had three opposing findings. They were, "that the New Testament does not settle in a clear way... whether women can be ordained as priests, [that] scriptural grounds alone are not enough to exclude the possibility of ordaining women, [and that] Christ's plan would not be transgressed by permitting the ordination of women." In recent years, responding to questions about the matter, the Church has issued a number of documents repeating the same position. In 1994, Pope John Paul II declared the question closed in his letter *Ordinatio Sacerdotalis,* stating: "Wherefore, in order that all doubt may be removed regarding a matter of great importance..I declare that the Church has no authority whatsoever to confer priestly ordination on women and that this judgment is to be definitively held by all the Church's faithful."

In 1995, the Congregation for the Doctrine of the Faith issued a clarification, explaining that *Ordinatio Sacerdotalis,* though "itself not infallible, witnesses to the infallibility of the teaching of a doctrine already possessed by the Church.... This doctrine belongs to the deposit of the faith of the Church. It should be emphasized that the definitive and infallible nature of this teaching of the Church did not arise with the publication of the Letter *Ordinatio Sacerdotalis*". Instead, it was "founded on the written Word of God, and from the beginning constantly preserved and applied in the tradition of the Church, it has been set forth infallibly by the ordinary and universal magisterium," and for these reasons it "requires definitive assent."

The Church teaching on the restriction of its ordination to men that masculinity was integral to the personhood of both Jesus and the men he called as apostles. The Roman Catholic Church sees maleness and femaleness as two different ways of expressing common humanity. Contrary to the common phrase "gender roles," which implies that the phenomenon of the sexes is a mere surface phenomenon, an accident, the Roman Catholic Church teaches that there is an ontological (essential) difference between humanity expressed as male humanity and humanity expressed as female humanity. While many functions are interchangeable between men and women, some are not, because maleness and femaleness are not interchangeable. Just as water is necessary for a valid baptism, and wheaten bread and grape wine are necessary for a valid Eucharist (not because of their superiority over other materials, but because they are what Jesus used or authorized), only men can be validly ordained, regardless of any issues of equality.

Pope John Paul II, in *Ordinatio Sacerdotalis,* explained the Roman Catholic understanding that the priesthood is a special role specially set out by Jesus when he chose twelve men out of his group of male and female followers. John Paul notes that Jesus chose the Twelve (cf. Mk 3:13–14; Jn 6:70) after a night in prayer (cf. Lk 6:12) and that the Apostles themselves were careful in the choice of their successors. The priesthood is "specifically and intimately associated in the mission of the Incarnate Word himself (cf. Mt 10:1, 7–8; 28:16–20; Mk 3:13–16; 16:14–15)."

Pope Paul VI, quoted by Pope John Paul II in *Ordinatio Sacerdotalis,* wrote, "[The Church] holds that it is not admissible to ordain women to the priesthood, for very fundamental reasons. These reasons include: the example recorded in the Sacred Scriptures of Christ choosing his Apostles only from among men; the constant practice of the Church, which has imitated Christ in choosing only men; and her living teaching authority which has consistently held that the exclusion of women from the priesthood is in accordance with God's plan for his Church."

Concerning the "constant practice of the Church," in antiquity the Church Fathers Irenaeus, Tertullian, Hippolytus, Epiphanius, John Chrysostom, and Augustine all wrote that the ordination of women was impossible. The Synod of

Laodicea prohibited ordaining women to the Presbyterate, although the meaning of Canon 11 has long been disputed.

The Vatican's Congregation for the Doctrine of the Faith issued and published on May 29, 2008, in the Vatican newspaper L'Osservatore Romano, a decree signed by Cardinal William Levada, on the existing ban on women priests by asserting that women 'priests' and the bishops who ordain them would be excommunicated "latae sententiae".

Deaconesses and Female Deacons

The ordination of females to the diaconate is a matter of some controversy among Roman Catholic historians and theologians. At issue are two distinct but interrelated questions: whether some women in the early Church received true sacramental ordination, or whether all were merely so called for functional or honorific purposes; and, whether the prohibition against ordaining women to the diaconate is also a matter of unchangeable divine law, or potentially changeable ecclesiastical law. If some women did receive true sacramental ordination, then the current prohibition would be ecclesiastical rather than divine law.

It can be verified that the term "deaconess" was employed in late antiquity; the word, like "deacon", comes from the Greek word *diakonos*, meaning "one who serves" (literally, "one who runs through the dust" after his master). The earlier term for women who served in the Church was *diakonos*. The term "deaconess" came to be used to refer to women who assisted the priest in receiving women into the Church for baptism by full immersion (which is still practiced by the Eastern Catholic Churches and by some parishes in the Western or Latin rite as well). These women also minstered to sick women and often served in similar positions to male deacons.

Further historical evidence points to women serving as deacons in many areas of the Church in the West as well as in the East. Monastic women deacons in the East received the stole as a symbol of their office at ordination, which took place inside the sanctuary. Hitorical-theological work by K. K. Fitzgerald, Phyllis Zagano, and Gary Macy argue for the sacramental ordination of women as deacons.

The Congregation for the Doctrine of the Faith wrote in 1977 that the possibility of ordaining women as deacons was "a question that must be taken up fully by direct study of the texts, without preconceived ideas." The opinion that women received sacramental ordination (in certain times and places) is given by Roger Gryson. In response, Aimé Georges Martimort contends they did not. Both Gryson and Martimort argue from the same historical evidence. For example, the ecumenical First Council of Nicaea (A.D. 325) stated that deaconesses: "do not receive any imposition of hands, so that they are in all respects to be numbered among the laity." However, 126 years later, the ecumenical Council of Chalcedon (A.D. 451) decreed: "A woman shall not receive the laying on of hands as a deaconess under forty years of age, and then only after searching examination." Gryson argues that the use of the verb *cheirotonein* and of the substantive *cheirothesia* clearly indicate that women deacons were ordained by the laying on of hands." Martimort argues that the "laying on of hands" refers only to a special blessing.

Until rather recently, the theologians and canonists who addressed the question almost unanimously considered the exclusion of women from ordination, including to the diaconate, as having a divine origin and therefore remaining absolute. Only in recent decades have any theologians or canonists entertained the theory that the prohibition of women from the ordained diaconate was a matter of merely ecclesiastical, rather than divine law. This renewed theological assessment was spurred on by the Second Vatican Council's revival of the permanent diaconate, which lifted the question from a purely theoretical matter to one with immensely practical consequences. Based on the theory that some deaconesses received the sacrament of Holy Orders, and based on the fact that some writers in the Middle Ages exhibited a certain hesitancy concerning the ordination of women stemming from knowledge that there had been deaconesses in antiquity, there have been modern-day proposals to ordain female permanent deacons, who would perform the same functions as male deacons and be like them in every respect.

In 2003, Father Ronald G. Roberson gave a presentation on the diaconate in the Latin Church to annual meeting of the U.S. Oriental Orthodox-Roman Catholic Consultation. He summarized the state of deaconess issue as follows: "The possibility of ordaining women to the diaconate is still an unsettled question in the Catholic Church. Latin rituals for ordaining deaconesses exist from as late as the 10th century, but the precise sacramental nature of these ordinations has not yet been determined authoritatively. There are recent indications that the Holy See intends to continue the exclusion of women from this office."

Ordination and Equality

The Roman Catholic Church states that the hierarchical structure that includes the ordained ministerial priesthood is ordered to benefit the holiness of the entire body of the faithful, and not to ensure the salvation of the ordained minister. There is no additional benefit in terms of automatic holiness that comes about through ordination. Ordination is not required for salvation, nor does it effect salvation in the one ordained. In other words, a priest can go to Hell just as easily as a layperson. Likewise, sainthood is equally open to men and women, lay or ordained. For example, the Blessed Virgin Mary is venerated as the Queen of all Saints. Furthermore, there are female Doctors of the Church.

Pope John Paul II wrote, in *Mulieris Dignitatem*: "In calling only men as his Apostles, Christ acted in a completely free and sovereign manner. In doing so, he exercised the same freedom with which, in all his behaviour, he emphasized the dignity and the vocation of women, without conforming to the prevailing customs and to the traditions sanctioned by the legislation of the time."

In *Ordinatio Sacerdotalis,* John Paul wrote: "the fact that the Blessed Virgin Mary, Mother of God and Mother of the Church, received neither the mission proper to the Apostles nor the ministerial priesthood clearly shows that the non-admission of women to priestly ordination cannot mean that women are of lesser dignity, nor can it be construed as discrimination against them. Rather, it is to be seen as the faithful observance of a plan to be ascribed to the wisdom of the Lord of the universe."

The Roman Catholic Church does not regard the priest as the only possible prayer leader, and prayer may be led by a woman. For example, outside the context of a Mass and in the absence of a priest or deacon, laypersons (both men and women) "are to be entrusted with the care of these [Sunday] celebrations." This includes leading the prayers, ministry of the word, and the giving of holy communion (previously consecrated by a priest). Also during these assemblies, in the absence of an ordained minister, a layperson may request God's blessing on the congregation, provided that the layperson does not use words proper to a priest or deacon, and omits rites that are too readily associated with the Mass.

Women are also able to live the Consecrated Life as a nun or abbess, and throughout the history of the Church it has not been uncommon for an abbess to head a dual monastery, *i.e.*, a community of men and women. Women today exercise many roles in the Church that they were previously not able to participate in. They can run catechetical programs in parishes, do spiritual direction, serve as readers and Extraordinary Ministers of Holy Communion, and teach theology. Also, in 1994, the Vatican Congregation for Divine Worship decided that women could assist at Mass as altar servers. Still many people see the Church's position on the ordination of women as a sign that women are not equal to men in the Catholic Church, though the Church rejects this inference.

Dissenting Views

The arguments for the Catholic ordination of women, include the one based on equality. Some sacramental theologians have argued that ordaining men but not women creates two classes of baptism, contradicting Saint Paul's statement that all are equal in Christ.

Another argument is based on the theological position that there is a fundamental unity between the different levels (deacon, priest, and bishop) of the sacrament of Holy Orders, as taught by the Second Vatican Council. So, if history shows that the deaconesses known to have existed in the Early Church had actually received the sacrament of ordination, then because of the fundamental unity of Holy Orders, women can also be ordained as priests and bishops. (This same argument is sometimes used in reverse, against the historical possibility that deaconesses received sacramental ordination.)

Whatever argument is used in favor of the priestly ordination of women, there is the problem of reconciling this position with *Ordinatio Sacerdotalis* (or ignoring it, if the arguer so wishes). Based on the statements from the Congregation for the Doctrine of the Faith, the official point of view is that *Ordinatio Sacerdotalis,* without itself being *ex cathedra,* authoritatively and bindingly teaches that: *(1)* the Church cannot ordain women as priests due to divine law; and that *(2)* this doctrine has been set forth infallibly by the ordinary and universal magisterium. A dissenting view is that, according to section 25 of the Second Vatican Council's Dogmatic Constitution on the Church, *Lumen Gentium,* the "ordinary and universal magisterium" is exercised by "the Pope in union with the bishops". In other words, according to the Congregation, it is an instance of the Pope 'publicising' what he and the other bishops, as the ordinary and universal magisterium' have already consistently taught through the ages.

Since the encyclical *Humani Generis,* it is well known that the Roman Pontiff can, by his own authority, settle a theological question via a fallible papal teaching that is nonetheless sufficiently authoritative to end all debate on the matter, at least under Church law. This is clearly what has occurred with *Ordinatio Sacerdotalis* in regard to point (1). Thus, theological debate on whether women can be ordained as priests is no longer seen by the Church as permitted for Catholics, and the arguments in favor of ordaining women to the priesthood in this section are termed a "dissenting position". However, several noted dogmatic theologians have questioned how this same alleged debate-ending authority can apply to point (2), which is a matter not of faith or morals, but a factual matter relative to teachings promulgated by all the bishops of the Catholic Church over her two thousand year history. These dogmatic theologians find it especially problematic that, concerning this point, *Ordinatio Sacerdotalis* gives no indication of what historical facts are sufficient to ensure infallibility by the ordinary and universal Magisterium, nor any indication of how those historical facts were verified. Because of these issues it is argued that, if it is indeed possible for the Church to ordain women to the priesthood, this would not contradict the Church's dogma regarding infallible teachings.

Some supporters of women's ordination have asserted that there have been ordained female priests and bishops in antiquity. The official Church position on this is that, although "a few heretical sects in the first centuries, especially Gnostic ones, entrusted the exercise of the priestly ministry to women: this innovation was immediately noted and condemned by the Fathers who considered it as unacceptable in the Church." In response to that position, some supporters of women's ordination take the position that those sects weren't heretical, but, rather, orthodox.

Some arguable evidence that not all ordinations in the Catholic tradition have been those of males exists. For example, the Pope Gelasius I apparently condemned the practice of women officiating at altars; inscriptions near Tropea in Calábria refer to "presbytera," which could be interpreted as a woman priest or as a wife of a male priest. Furthermore, a sarcophagus from Dalmatia is inscribed with the date 425 and records that a grave in the Salona burial-ground was bought from presbytera Flavia Vitalia: selling burial plots was at one time a duty of presbyters. There have been some 15 records so far found of women being ordained in antiquity by Christians; while the Vatican insists those are ordinations by heretical groups, the Women's Ordination Conference contends that those were orthodox Christian groups.

There is also the church of Santa Praxedis, where Theodora Episcopa—Bishop Theodora, with the word for "bishop" in feminine form—appears in an image with two female saints and Mary. That church's pastor alleges that the church was built in honor of Pope Pascal I's mother by her son, who graced her with the title "Episcopa" due to her being the mother of a Pope. However, Theodora wears a coif in the image, suggesting that she is an unmarried woman.

Setting aside these theological considerations, advocates for the ordination of women have pointed to vocations declining in Europe and North America and have made the utilitarian argument that women must be ordained in order to have enough priests to administer the Sacraments in those areas. Supporting this argument, they made public the story of a Czech woman Ludmila Javorová, who, in the 1990s, said that she and four or five other women had been ordained by the late Bishop Felix Maria Davídek in the 1970s, as priests in the underground Catholic Church in Czechoslovakia. Javorová ceased to practice as a priest at some point.

There is at least one organization that calls itself "Roman Catholic" that ordains women at the present time, Roman Catholic Womenpriests; and, several independent Catholic jurisidictions have been ordaining women in the United States since approximately the late 1990s. These organizations are independent of and unrecognised by the Roman Catholic Church. There are several others calling for the Roman Catholic Church itself to ordain women, Brothers and Sisters in Christ, Catholic Women's Ordination, and Corpus, along with others. Recently (April 19, 2009), Womenpriests elected four bishops to serve the United States: Joan Mary Clark Houk, Andrea Michele Johnson, Maria Regina Nicolosi, and Bridget Mary Meehan. The Vatican's Congregation for the Doctrine of the Faith issued a decree in 2008 clarifying that such "attempted ordinations" were invalid and that Canons 1378 and 1443 apply to those who participate in these ordinations. Edward Peters, a doctor of canon law, explains that this is a newly enacted excommunication and not just the clarification of canon law that had existed previously. In response, Womenpriests said its members are "loyal member of the church who stand in the prophetic tradition of holy disobedience to an unjust law."

Eastern Orthodoxy

The Eastern Orthodox churches follows a similar line of reasoning as the Roman Catholic Church with respect to ordination of priests.

Regarding deaconesses, Professor Evangelos Theodorou argued that female deacons were actually ordained in antiquity. K. K. Fitzgerald has followed and amplified Professor Theodorou's research. Bishop Kallistos Ware wrote::

> The order of deaconesses seems definitely to have been considered an "ordained" ministry during early centuries in at any rate the Christian East. ... Some Orthodox writers regard deaconesses as having been a "lay" ministry. There are strong reasons for rejecting this view. In the Byzantine rite the liturgical office for the laying-on of hands for the deaconess is exactly parallel to that for the deacon; and so on the principle *lex orandi, lex credendi*—the Church's worshipping practice is a sure indication of its faith—it follows that the deaconesses receives, as does the deacon, a genuine sacramental ordination.

On October 8, 2004, the Holy Synod of the Orthodox Church of Greece voted to permit the ordination of monastic women deacons, that is, women deacons to minister and assist at the liturgy within their own monasteries.

There is a strong monastic tradition, pursued by both men and women in the Orthodox churches, where monks and nuns lead identical spiritual lives. Unlike Roman Catholic religious life, which has myriad traditions, both contemplative and active (see Benedictine monks, Franciscan friars, Jesuits), that of Eastern Orthodoxy has remained exclusively ascetic and monastic.

Anglicanism

The majority of Anglican provinces ordain women as both deacons and priests. Only a few provinces, however, have consecrated women as bishops (although the number of provinces where women bishops are canonically possible is much greater). The Episcopal Church in the United States ordains women as both priests and bishops. The situation regarding women's ordination in the Anglican Communion (and churches in full communion) as of April 2008 can be seen in the following table:

Bishops (consecrated)	Aotearoa, New Zealand and Polynesia; Australia; Canada; United States, Cuba
Bishops (none yet consecrated)	Bangladesh, Brazil, Central America, Ireland, Japan, Mexico, North India, Philippines, Scotland, Southern Africa, Sudan
Priests	Burundi, England, Hong Kong, Indian Ocean, Kenya, Korea, Rwanda, South India, Uganda, Wales, West Indies, West Africa
Deacons	Southern Cone, Congo, Pakistan
No ordination of women	Central Africa, Jerusalem and the Middle East, Melanesia, Nigeria, Papua New Guinea, South East Asia, Tanzania

Anglican Communion

Some provinces within the Anglican Communion, such as the Episcopal Church in the United States of America (TEC), the Anglican Church of New Zealand, the Anglican Church of Canada, the Episcopal Church of Cuba, and, from May 2008, the Anglican Church of Australia, ordain women as deacons, priests and bishops.

Some Anglican provinces ordain women as deacons and priests but not as bishops. A number of other Anglican provinces, as noted in the table above, have removed canonical bars to women bishops but have not yet consecrated any.

The ordination of women has been a controversial issue throughout the Anglican Communion. However, by 2008, twenty-eight of the thirty eight provinces of the Anglican Communion ordain women as priests and seventeen have removed all bars to women serving as bishops.

Within provinces which permit the ordination of women, there are some individual dioceses which do not, or which ordain women only to the diaconate (such as the Diocese of Sydney in the Anglican Church of Australia).

The first woman ordained to the priesthood in the Anglican Communion was Florence Li Tim-Oi, who was ordained on 25 January 1944 by the Bishop of Hong Kong. It was thirty years before the practice became more widespread, beginning controversially in 1974, when eleven women were ordained to the priesthood in Philadelphia, Pennsylvania, by three retired Episcopal Church bishops. Four more women were ordained in 1975 in Washington D.C. These ordinations were ruled "irregular" because they had been done without the authorization of ECUSA's General Convention. Two years later, General Convention authorized the ordination of women to the priesthood and the episcopate. The Church of England authorized the ordination of woman priests in 1992 and began ordaining them in 1994. This was the premise of the television programme *The Vicar of Dibley*. The nearly simultaneous publication by the Vatican of the encyclical *Veritatis Splendor*, which argued that truth was immutable, however unpalatable, was a coincidence which was not lost on many traditionalist Anglicans who became Roman Catholics. These included women, such as Ann Widdecombe MP.

The first woman bishop in the Anglican Communion was Barbara Clementine Harris, who was ordained bishop suffragan of Massachusetts in February 1989. Later in the same year, Penelope Jamieson of the Anglican Church in New Zealand became the first female diocesan bishop when she was elected Bishop of Dunedin. The first female primate (or senior bishop of a national church) is Katharine Jefferts Schori, who was elected presiding bishop of the Episcopal Church (USA) at its 2006 General Convention, and began her nine year term as presiding bishop and primate on 3 November 2006. By April 2008 the Episcopal Church had elected 15 women as bishops.

Most Anglican provinces have taken steps to provide pastoral care and support for those who cannot in conscience accept the ministry of women as bishops. The Church of England, for example, has instituted "flying bishops" to serve parishes that do not wish to be under the supervision of bishops who have participated in the ordination of women.

There have been a number of breakaway groups established by conservative Anglicans who see the ordination of women as representative of a trend away from traditional or orthodox doctrine. The Continuing Anglican Movement was started in 1977 after women began to be ordained in the USA.

Church of England

On July 11, 2005 the General Synod of the Church of England, in York, voted to "set in train" the process of removing the legal obstacles preventing women from becoming bishops. Debate on the legislation was scheduled for February 2006. The process is currently underway but is not progressing quickly due to problems in providing appropriate mechanisms for the protection of those who cannot accept this development. On 7 July 2008 the General Synod held a more than seven hour debate on the subject, and narrowly voted for a national statutory code of practice to make provision for opponents, to be considered by the Synod in February 2009—other provisions for opponents (such as separate structures or overseeing bishops) were backed by more than opposed them but failed to win the majority required across each of the three houses (bishops, clergy and laity).

Church in Wales

On 2 April 2008, the Governing Body of the Church in Wales considered, but did not pass, a bill to enable women to be ordained as bishops. Though the bill was passed by the House of Laity (52 to 19) and the House of Bishops (unanimously), it failed by three votes (27 to 18) to secure the required minimum two-thirds majority in the House of Clerics. The Archbishop of Wales, the Most Revd Barry Morgan, expects the issue to be debated again in 2011. However the Church in Wales decisively ended the role of provincial bishop whose responsibility was to minister to opponents. In February 2009 the Church in Wales appointed the first woman Archdeacon.

Anglican Church of Australia

The Anglican Church of Australia, though its appellate tribunal, ruled on 28 September 2007 that there is nothing in the church's constitution that would prevent the consecration of a woman priest as a diocesan bishop in a diocese which by ordinance has adopted the law of the Church of England Clarification Canon 1992, which paved the way for the ordination of women as priests. Following the agreement at the April 2008 Bishops' Conference of the "Women in the Episcopate" protocol for the provision of pastoral care to those who cannot in conscience accept the ministry of a woman bishop, the first nominations of women as bishops was widely anticipated, and on 11 April 2008 the Archbishop of Perth, the Most Revd Roger Herft, announced the nomination of the Venerable Kay Goldsworthy, Archdeacon of Perth and Registrar, as a bishop in the Diocese of Perth. She was the first woman ordained as an Anglican bishop in Australia: her episcopal ordination was held on 22 May, the Feast of Corpus Christi (Thanksgiving for the Holy Communion) in St George's Cathedral, Perth. Then, on 24 April 2008, the Archbishop of Melbourne, the Most Revd Philip Frier, announced the nomination of the Revd Canon Barbara Darling, Vicar of St James' Dandenong, as an assistant bishop. Her episcopal ordination was held on 31 May 2008, the Feast of the Visitation of the Blessed Virgin Mary to Elizabeth, in St Paul's Cathedral, Melbourne.

Protestantism

A key theological doctrine for most Protestants is the priesthood of all believers. The notion of a priesthood reserved to a select few is seen as an Old Testament concept, inappropriate for Christians. Prayer belongs equally to all believing women and men.

However, most (although not all) Protestant denominations still ordain church leaders who have the task of equipping all believers in their Christian service (Ephesians 4:11–13). These leaders (variously styled *elders, pastors* or *ministers*) are seen to have a distinct role in teaching, pastoral leadership and the administration of sacraments. Traditionally these roles were male preserves, but over the last century, an increasing number of denominations have begun ordaining women.

The debate over women's eligibility for such offices normally centers around interpretation of certain Biblical passages relating to teaching and leadership roles. This is because Protestant churches usually view the Bible as the primary authority in church debates, even over established traditions (the doctrine of *sola scriptura*). Thus the Church is free to change her stance, if the change is deemed in accordance with the Bible. The main passages in this debate include Galatians 3:28, 1 Cor. 11:2–16, 1 Cor. 14:34–35 and 1 Tim. 2:11-14. Increasingly, supporters of women in ministry also make appeals to evidence from the New Testament that is taken to suggest that women did exercise ministries in the apostolic Church (*e.g.*, Acts 21:9, Acts 18:18, Romans 16:1–4, Romans 16:7; 1 Cor.16:19, and Philippians 4:2–3) and that the Biblical passages used to argue against women's ordination might be read differently when a clear understanding of the unique historical context of each passage is available.

Examples within Specific Churches

- The Apostolic Johannite Church has offered ordination to women as deacons, priests and bishops since its foundation.
- Baptist Churches
  - The Baptist Churches in Germany and Switzerland (Bund Evangelisch-Freikirchlicher Gemeinden, Bund Schweizer Baptistengemeinden) ordain women.
  - The Southern Baptist Convention does not support the ordination of women; however, some churches that are members of the SBC have ordained women.
  - Cooperative Baptist Fellowship churches actively encourage and ordain women to ministry, including as pastors.
  - Baptist groups in the United States that do ordain women include American Baptist Churches USA, North American Baptist Conference, Alliance of Baptists, Cooperative Baptist Fellowship (CBF) and Progressive National Baptist Convention.
- The Charismatic Church of God ordains women as Missionaries, Evangelists, and Pastors.
- It is believed that the Canadian Conference of Mennonite Brethren Churches does not ordain women.
- Christian Connection Church. An early relative of the Christian Church (Disciples of Christ) and the United Church of Christ, this body ordained women as early as 1810. Among them were Nancy Gove

Cram, who worked as a missionary with the Oneida Indians by 1812, and Abigail Roberts (a lay preacher and missionary), who helped establish many churches in New Jersey. Others included Ann Rexford, Sarah Hedges and Sally Thompson.

- It is believed that the Christian and Missionary Alliance does not ordain women.
- The Church of Jesus Christ of Latter-day Saints does not ordain women.
- The Church of Scotland
- Women were commissioned as deacons from 1935, and allowed to preach from 1949.
- In 1963 Mary Levison petitioned the General Assembly for ordination.
- Woman elders were introduced in 1966 and women ministers in 1968.
- The first female Moderator of the General Assembly was Dr Alison Elliot in 2004.

Ordination of Women in the Church of Scotland

- Neither the Free Church of Scotland, nor the Free Church of Scotland (Continuing) ordains women.
- The Cumberland Presbyterian Church. In 1888 Louisa Woosley was licensed to preach. She was ordained in 1889. She wrote Shall Woman Preach.
- Community of Christ. A revelation was approved at the church's 1984 World Conference which called for the ordination of women, and granted women access to all the offices of the priesthood. Although this caused many congregations to break off from the main body of the church, forming dissident

congregations and in some cases new denominations, women have been ordained in many nations since then. Currently the Council of Twelve Apostles has four female members. In addition, in 2007, Becky L. Savage became the first female member of the church's First Presidency. Following the legislative action of the 1984 World Conference, the church changed the name of one of its priesthood offices from evangelist-patriarch to evangelist, and it's associated sacrament, the patriarchal blessing, to the evangelist's blessing.

- The Evangelical Lutheran Church of Latvia reversed its earlier (1975) decision to ordain women as pastors. Since 1993, under the leadership of Archbishop Janis Vanags, it no longer does so.
- The Evangelical Lutheran Church in America ELCA is the largest Lutheran body in the USA. The church bodies that formed the ELCA in 1988 began ordaining women in 1970 when the Lutheran Church in America ordained the Rev Elizabeth Platz. The ordination of women is now non-controversial within the ELCA.
- The Independent Evangelical-Lutheran Church in Germany does not ordain women.
- The Independent Old Catholic Church of America (IOCCA), ordains women.
- The Lutheran, United and Reformed Churches in Germany (EKD) ordain women and have women as bishops.
- The Lutheran Church—Missouri Synod (LCMS), which is the second largest Lutheran body in the United States, does not ordain women.

- The Lutheran state churches in Denmark, Sweden, Finland, Norway and Iceland ordain women and these Lutheran churches in Europe have women as bishops already. However, while the Church of Sweden was the first Lutheran church to ordain female pastors in 1958, there is still considerable debate in this church as to the legitimacy of the ordination of women into the pastoral office. In fact, in 2003 the Missionsprovinsen (Mission Province) was formed within the Church of Sweden to support those who oppose the ordination of women and other developments seen as theologically problematic.

- The Lutheran Evangelical Protestant Church (GCEPC) has ordained women since its inception in the year 2000. Ordination of women is not a controversial issue in the LEPC/GCEPC. Women are ordained/consecrated at all levels including deacon,priest, and bishop in the LEPC/GCEPC.

- The Moravian Church ordains women.

- Many Old Catholic Churches within the Utrecht Union in Germany, Switzerland, Austria and Netherlands ordain women, but two churches have left the union because they do not do so. Other Old Catholic Churches do not ordain women, but accept this in other Old Catholic Churches of the Union. These are not to be confused with the Roman Catholic Church which does not ordain women (see above).

- The Pentecostal church in Germany allows ordination of women.

- The Presbyterian Church (USA). In 1893, Edith Livingston Peake was appointed Presbyterian Evangelist by First United Presbyterian of San Francisco. Between 1907 and 1920 five more women became ministers. The Presbyterian Church (USA) began ordaining women as elders in 1930, and as ministers of Word and sacrament in 1956. By 2001, the numbers of men and women holding office were almost equal.

- The Presbyterian Church in America does not ordain women. In 1997, the PCA even broke its fraternal relationship with The Christian Reformed Church over this issue.
- The Orthodox Presbyterian Church do not ordain women.
- The Reformed Churches in Switzerland and in the Netherlands ordain women.
- The Salvation Army ordains women.
- The Seventh-day Adventist Church officially does not ordain women. Recent votes at the worldwide General Conference Sessions turned down a proposal to allow ordination of women. There was a strong polarization between nations, with Western countries generally voting in support and other countries generally voting against. A further proposal to allow local choice was also turned down. In practice, there are numerous women working as ministers and in leadership positions. The most influential co-founder of the church, Ellen G. White, was a woman.
- The United Church of Canada. Divided during the 1930s by this issue inherited from the churches it brought together, the United Church ordained its first woman minister, Lydia Gruchy, in 1936.
- The United Church of Christ. Antoinette Brown was ordained as a minister by a Congregationalist Church in 1853, though this was not recognized by her denomination. She later became a Unitarian. Women's

ordination is now non-controversial in the United Church of Christ.

- The United Methodist Church does ordain women. In 1880, Anna Howard Shaw was ordained by the Methodist Protestant Church; Ella Niswonger was ordained in 1889 by the United Brethren Church. Both denominations later merged into the United Methodist Church. In 1956, the Methodist Church in America granted ordination and full clergy rights to women. Since that time, women have been ordained full elders (pastors) in the denomination, and 21 have been elevated to the episcopacy. The first woman elected and consecrated Bishop within the United Methodist Church (and, indeed, the first woman elected bishop of any mainline Christian church) was Marjorie Matthews in 1980. Leontine T. Kelly, in 1984, was the first African-American woman elevated to the episcopacy in any mainline denomination. In Germany Rosemarie Wenner is since 2005 leading bishop in the United Methodist Church.

- The United Reformed Church in the United Kingdom ordains women.

- The Unitarians ordain women. In Australia, Martha Turner was appointed minister to the Melbourne Unitarian church in 1873. Gertrude von Petzold was the first woman to be ordained as a Unitarian minister in England, in 1904.

- The Unitarian Universalist Association. The Unitarian Universalist Association has a long history of welcoming women to the ministry, reaching back to 1863 and one of its predecessors, the Universalist Church. In 1999, it became the first major religion in the US with women outnumbering men in the clergy.

- The Universalist Church. Olympia Brown became the first woman to be ordained as a minister in 1863, as an ordained Universalist minister.

Women as Bishops

Some Protestant and Anglican churches have allowed women to become their bishops:

- 1907 Church of the Nazarene—(although they do not have bishops, they have a similar office called "District Superintendent") http://www.nazarene.org they have been ordaining women for every office since their inception and more than 1/2 of their ministers were women. Today however, women are in prominent positions but less than 1% of all ordained ministers are women and women are largely relegated to subordinate roles and not given large churches. Mostly they are told to work with children, despite official claims to the contrary.
- 1929: Mariavite Church in Poland—abp. Antonina Maria Izabela Wi³ucka—Kowalska and 11 sisters.
- 1980: United Methodist Church—Marjorie Matthews
- 1989: United States—Barbara Clementine Harris
- 1989: Anglican Church of New Zealand—Penelope Ann Bansall Jamieson
- 1992: United Evangelical Lutheran Church of Germany—Maria Jepsen
- 1993: Church of Norway—Rosemarie Köhn
- 1994: Anglican Church of Canada—Victoria Matthews
- 1995: Church of Denmark—Lise-Lotte Rebel
- 1996: Church of Sweden—Christina Odenberg
- 1998: Moravian Church in America—Dr. Kay Ward

- 1998: Presbyterian Church in Guatemala
- 1999: Czechoslovak Hussite Church—Jana Šilerová
- 2000: African Methodist Episcopal Church—Vashti Murphy McKenzie
- 2003: The Lutheran Evangelical Protestant Church (GCEPC)USA—Nancy K. Drew
- 2008: Anglican Church of Australia—Kay Goldsworthy
- 2008: African Methodist Episcopal Zion Church—Mildred B. Hines
- Others: Protestant Churches in German Lutheran, Reformed and United churches (EKD), Protestant Church of the Netherlands, Evangelical Lutheran Church in Canada.

Islam

Although Muslims do not formally ordain religious leaders, the imam serves as a spiritual leader and religious authority. There is a current controversy among Muslims on the circumstances in which women may act as imams—that is, lead a congregation in salat (prayer). Three of the four Sunni schools, as well as many Shia, agree that a woman may lead a congregation consisting of women alone in prayer, although the Maliki school does not allow this. According to all currently existing traditional schools of Islam, a woman cannot lead a mixed gender congregation in salat (prayer). Some schools make exceptions for Tarawih (optional Ramadan prayers) or for a congregation consisting only of close relatives. Certain medieval scholars—including Al-Tabari (838–932), Abu Thawr (764–854), Al-Muzani (791–878), and Ibn Arabi (1165–1240)—considered the practice permissible at least for optional (nafila) prayers; however, their views are not accepted by any major surviving group.

Judaism

Jewish tradition and law does not presume that women have more or less of an aptitude or moral standing required of rabbis. However, it had been the longstanding practice that only men become rabbis. This practice continues to this day within the Orthodox and Hasidic communities but has been revised within non-Orthodox organizations. Reform Judaism created its first woman rabbi in 1972, Reconstructionist Judaism in 1974, and Conservative Judaism in 1985, and women in these movements are routinely granted semicha on an equal basis with men. The issue of allowing women to become rabbis is not under active debate within the Orthodox community, though there is widespread agreement that women may often be consulted on matters of Jewish religious law. There are reports that a small number of Orthodox yeshivas have unofficially granted *semicha* to women, but the prevailing consensus among Orthodox leaders (as well as a small number of Conservative Jewish communities) is that it is not appropriate for women to become rabbis.

The idea that women could eventually be ordained as rabbis sparks widespread opposition among the Orthodox rabbinate. Norman Lamm, one of the leaders of Modern Orthodoxy and Rosh Yeshiva of the Rabbi Isaac Elchanan Theological Seminary, totally opposes giving semicha to women. "It shakes the boundaries of tradition, and I would never allow it." (Helmreich, 1997) Writing in an article in the *Jewish Observer,* Moshe Y'chiail Friedman states that Orthodox Judaism prohibits women from being given semicha and serving as rabbis. He holds that the trend towards this goal is driven by sociology, and not halakha.

Shinto

While the priesthood was traditionally male in Shinto, ordination of women as Shinto priests has arisen after the abolition of State Shinto in the aftermath of World War II.

A partial list with the approximate dates of either the approval of female ordination in principle or the ordination of their first women clergy by Christian and Jewish faith groups appears below:

- Early 1800s: A fundamental belief of the *Society of Friends (Quakers)* has always been the existence of an element of God's spirit in every human soul. Thus all persons are considered to have inherent and equal worth, independent of their gender. This led naturally to an acceptance of female ministers. In 1660, Margaret Fell (1614–1702) published a famous pamphlet to justify equal roles for men and women in the denomination. It was titled: *"Women's Speaking Justified, Proved and Allowed of by the Scriptures, All Such as Speak by the Spirit and Power of the Lord Jesus And How Women Were the First That Preached the Tidings of the Resurrection of Jesus, and Were Sent by Christ's Own Command Before He Ascended to the Father (John 20:17).* In the U.S., in contrast with almost every other organized religion, the Society of Friends (Quakers) has allowed women to serve as ministers since the early 1800s.

- 1853: Antoinette Brown was ordained by the *Congregationalist Church.* However, her ordination was not recognized by the denomination. She quit the church and later became a Unitarian. The Congregationalists later merged with others to create the *United Church of Christ.*

- 1861: Mary A. Will was the first woman ordained in the *Wesleyan Methodist Connection* by the Illinois Conference. The Wesleyan Methodist Connection eventually became *The Wesleyan Church.*

- 1863: Olympia Brown was ordained by the *Universalist* denomination in 1863, in spite of a last-moment case of cold feet by her seminary which feared adverse publicity. After a decade and a half of service as a full-time minister, she became a part-time minister in order to devote more time to the fight for women's rights and universal suffrage. In 1961, the Universalists and Unitarians joined to form the *Unitarian Universalist Association* (UUA). The UUA became the first large denomination to have a majority of female ministers.

- *'1865:' Salvation Army* is founded, which ordained both men and women. However, there were initially rules that prohibited a woman from marrying a man who had a lower rank.
- *'1879' Church of Christ, Scientist* founded by a woman, Mary Baker Eddy.
- 1880: Anna Howard Shaw was the first woman ordained in the *Methodist Protestant Church,* which later merged with other denominations to form the *United Methodist Church.*
- 1888: Fidelia Gillette may have been the first ordained woman in Canada. She served the Universalist congregation in Bloomfield, Ontario, during 1888 and 1889. She was presumably ordained in 1888 or earlier. (or)
- '1889: The *Nolin Presbytery* of the *Cumberland Presbyterian Church* ordained Louisa Woosley.
- 1889: Ella Niswonger was the first woman ordained in the *United Brethren church,* which later merged with other denominations to form the *United Methodist Church.*
- 1892: Anna Hanscombe is believed to be the first woman ordained by the parent bodies which formed the *Church of the Nazarene* in 1919.

- 1909: The Church of God (Cleveland TN) began ordaining women in 1909.
- 1911: Ann Allebach was the first *Mennonite* woman to be ordained. This occurred at the *First Mennonite Church of Philadelphia.*
- '*1914:*' *Assemblies of God* was founded and ordained its first woman clergy
- 1917: The *Congregationalist Church (England and Wales)* ordained their first woman, Constance Coltman (nee Todd) at the King's Weigh House, London. Its successor is the *United Reformed Church (a union of the Congregational Church in England and Wales and the Presbyterian Church of England in 1972. Since then two more denominations have joined the union: The Reformed Churches of Christ (1982) and the Congregational Church of Scotland (2000). All of these denominations ordained women at the time of Union and continue to do so. The first woman to be appointed General Secretary of the United Reformed Church was Roberta Rominger in 2008.*
- 1920's: Some Baptist *denominations* start ordaining women.
- 1922: The Jewish Reform movement's *Central Conference of American Rabbis* stated that "*Woman cannot justly be denied the privilege of ordination.*" However, Reform Judaism takes a few more decades to actually ordain women.
- 1922: The Annual Conference of the Church of the Brethren granted women the right to be licensed into the ministry, but not to be ordained with the same status as men.
- 1929 Izabela Wi³ucka in Old Catholic Mariavite Church

- 1935: Regina Jonas was ordained privately by a German rabbi.
- 1936: United Church of Canada starts ordaining women.
- 1944: Anglican communion, Hong Kong. *Florence Li Tim Oi was ordained on an emergency basis.*
- 1947: Czechoslovak Hussite Church starts ordaining women.
- 1948: Evangelical Lutheran Church of Denmark starts ordaining women.
- 1949: Old Catholic Church *(in the U.S.) starts ordaining women.*
- 1956: A predecessor church of the *Presbyterian Church (USA)* ordained its first woman minister.
- 1956: Maud K. Jensen was the first woman to receive full clergy rights and conference membership in the *Methodist Church.*
- 1958: Women ministers in the *Church of the Brethren* were given full ordination with the same status as men.
- 1960: Evangelical Lutheran Church in Sweden started ordaining women.
- 1967: Presbyterian Church in Canada started ordaining women.
- *'1971:' Anglican communion, Hong Kong.* Joyce Bennett and Jane Hwang were the first regularly ordained priests.
- 1972: Reform Judaism starts ordaining women.
- 1972: Swedenborgian Church starts ordaining women.

- 1972: Sally Priesand became the first woman rabbi to be ordained by a theological seminary. She was ordained in the Reform tradition.
- *'1970's:' Evangelical Lutheran Church* in America
- *'1974:' Methodist Church* in the United Kingdom starts ordaining women.
- 1974: Sandy Eisenberg Sasso became the first woman rabbi to be ordained within the Jewish Reconstructionist movement.
- *'1976:' Episcopal Church* (11 women were ordained in Philadelphia before church laws were changed to permit ordination)
- *'1976:' Anglican Church in Canada* ordained six female priests.
- 1976: The Rev. Pamela McGee was the first female ordained to the *Lutheran ministry in Canada.*
- 1977: Anglican Church of New Zealand ordained five female priests.
- 1979: The *Reformed Church in America.* Women had been admitted to the offices of deacon and elder in 1972.
- 1983: An Anglican woman was ordained in Kenya
- 1983: Three Anglican women were ordained in Uganda.
- 1984: Community of Christ (known at the time as the *Reorganized Church of Jesus Christ of Latter Day Saints*) authorized the ordination of women. This is the second largest Latter Day Saint denomination.
- 1985: According to the New York Times for 1985-FEB-14: "After years of debate, the worldwide

governing body of Conservative Judaism has decided to admit women as rabbis. The group, the *Rabbinical Assembly,* plans to announce its decision at a news conference...at the Jewish Theological Seminary..." Amy Eilberg became the first female rabbi.

- 1985: The first women deacons were ordained by the Scottish Episcopal Church.
- 1988: Evangelical Lutheran Church of Finland starts ordaining women.
- 1988: Episcopal Church chooses Barbara Harris as first female bishop.
- 1990: Anglican women are ordained in *Ireland.*
- 1992: The Church of England passes a measure to allow women to be ordained priests.
- 1992: Anglican Church of South Africa starts ordaining women.
- 1994: The first women priests were ordained by the Scottish Episcopal Church.
- 1994: The first women priests were ordained by the Church of England.
- *'1995:' Seventh-day Adventists.* Sligo Seventh-day Adventist Church in Takoma Park, MD ordained three women in violation of the denomination's rules.
- 1995: The *Christian Reformed Church* voted to allow women ministers, elders, and evangelists. In 1998-NOV, the *North American Presbyterian and Reformed Council* (NAPARC) suspended the CRC's membership because of this decision.
- 1998: General Assembly of the Nippon Sei Ko Kai (Anglican Church in Japan) starts ordaining women.

- 1998: Guatemalan Presbyterian Synod starts ordaining women.
- 1998: Old Catholic Church in the Netherlands starts ordaining women.
- 1998: Some Orthodox Jewish congregations started to employ female "congregational interns." Although these 'interns' do not lead worship services, they perform some tasks usually reserved for rabbis, such as preaching, teaching, and consulting on Jewish legal matters.
- *'1999:' Independent Presbyterian Church of Brazil* (ordination as either clergy or elders)
- 2000: The *Baptist Union of Scotland* voted to allow their churches to either allow or prohibit the ordination of women.
- 2000: The Mombasa diocese of the *Anglican Church of Kenya.*
- 2000: The *Church of Pakistan* ordained its first women deacons.
- 2005 The Lutheran Evangelical Protestant Church, (LEPC)(GCEPC) in the USA elects Nancy Kinard Drew first female Presiding Bishop.
- 2006: The Episcopal Church elects Katharine Jefferts Schori first woman Presiding Bishop, or Primate.

●●

12

Women Status in Society

With the break-through in science, emergence of reform movements and philosophers and thinkers propagating concepts like equality and freedom a questioning to the position of women, her role and status in society also started. The 20th century in particular promoted the cause of gender justice by internationalising struggles for equality by women and other oppressed people. Women's struggles against their subordination were intertwined in varying degrees with ideologies and movements based on the values of freedom, self-determination, equality, democracy and justice. Confined earlier by local or limited foci, these now found expression through movements against imperialism, for national liberation and social transformation. As a result the biological basis of sex role stereotypes, economic and social base of women's status, power relations and other related gender issues have become not only subjects of study but also for movements for change, assertion and justice. These came to Indian also first as a part of national movement and then as issues in development after independence. In last two decades or so these have become significant both in tenns of studies and women's development and movements.

Anthropological studies in various parts of the world point out to a wide variation in male and female roles across cultures and demonstrate the possibility of change in these sex determined roles. There is little physical determinism about which gender performs which role apart from pregnancy and child birth. In this context status and position of women in India, has also not been same always.

The relationship between the sexes during the earliest period of our history—the Vedic Age (before 1000 BC)—was characterised by a reciprocity in which the right and obligations of each were nearly equivalenced. Sex norms were liberal and marriages though valued was not obligatory. Neither the Rig Veda nor the Brihya Sutras enjoined any kind of binding obedience of the wife to her husband. She was free to participate in all religious practices and sacrifices and was 'entitled to all the samskaras' or religious sacraments like men; and not only were religious prayers and sacrifices jointly offered by the husband and the wife, but the wife alone could offer them in the absence of her husband.

During Aryan consolidation from 1000 BC onwards, particularly in north India several drastic changes took place in Hindu society which led to the curtailment of the freedom of women. With the consolidation of Aryan power a vast majority of subjects were non-Aryan people. The Aryans married the non-Aryans women. But non-Aryan women were prohibited from participating in religious rituals. Gradually all women, Aryan as well as non-Aryan became ineligible for Vedic studies and religious duties. The code of Manu combined with the Shrutikaras and Smritikars. Nath Upnishad and Shankaracharya launched the sexual apartheid in Indian society. The Muslim conquest of India in 900 AD introduced the Purdah system and further pushed women deep into domesticity. During the Muslim rule the percentage of literacy among women went down rapidly. *Sati* also became prevalent along with religious ban on the widow remarriage.

In general the Indian society like a number of "classical" societies was patriarchal. Patriarchal values regulating sexuality, reproduction and social production prevailed and were expressed through specific cultural **metaphors.** Overt rules prohibiting women from specific activities and denying certain rights did exist. But more subtle expression of patriarchy was through symbolism giving messages of inferiority of women through legends highlighting the self-sacrificing, self-effacing pure image of women and through the ritual practices which day in and day out emphasised the dominant role of a women as a faithful wife and devout mother. The basic rules for women's behaviour as expressed in the Laws of Manu insist that a women must constantly worship her husband as a God, even though he is destitute of virtue or a womaniser. Women should be kept in dependency by her husband because by nature they are passionate and disloyal.

The contradictions introduced into Hinduism also gave rise to disenchantments and periodic protects and revolts. Thus, Buddhism, Jainism, the Bhagati Movement, Islam, Veerasaivism, Sikhism, Christianity—all testify to the need felt by large sections of the Indian society for more satisfactory alternative to the existing socio-religious orders of the day. In each of these religions, except perhaps Islam, the position of women marginally improved. But it was not until the impact of western liberalism had made itself felt through English education that reform movements really launched their crusades.

It was during the British colonial period after coming into contact with the English education and in some cases as a reaction to British rule there sprang up many reformist movements in India. Brahmo Samaj, Arya Samaj, Prartha Samaj and many other movements took up the cause of injustice against women. As a well known the early reformist Raja Ram Mohan Roy denounced child marriage, and sati and worked for the emancipation of women in general. The nineteenth century also saw for the first time the enactment of social legislation by the government which included abolition of Sati (1829), Widow Remarriage Act (1856), Civil

Marriage Act (1872). Another significant feature of the nineteenth century is the attempts towards girls education.

In Nationalist movement also the Indian women's immense hidden potential found a forum for its release. Gandhiji called on women to give up Purdah and participate in Politics. In 1917 a women's delegation met the Secretary of State for India to demand franchise for women. In 1927 was launched All India Women's Conference for the welfare and development of women.

While as a result of social reforms and nationalist movement there emerged awareness about women's plight and consciousness for their upliftment in general there was not much change in the social attitude towards women, particularly in rural areas. Also inspite of some significant social legislature, property, inheritance and such laws remained against women.

Legal Equality for Women

The National Movement leaders had not only called upon the women to participate in the freedom struggle as equals but have also committed themselves to the ideology of gender equality. In the Fundamental Rights Resolution of the Indian National Congress adopted in 1931. It was postulated "freedom, justice, dignity and equality for women was essential for nation-building". The framers of the Constitution of India, therefore, tried to give proper place to the women in the social structure of the country. In the Preamble of the Constitutional the solemn resolve of the founding fathers contain two specific objectives which have a direct bearing on the status of women:

(a) Justice.... Social, economic and political for all.

(b) Equality.... of status and opportunity for all.

Parts III and IV of the Constitution dealing with Fundamental Rights and Directive Principles elaborate these declarations in concrete forms. In chapter on Fundamental Rights, Article 14 envisages that the State shall not deny to any person equality before the law or equal protection of law. Article 15 specifically prohibits discrimination on grounds such as caste, religion and sex. Article 16 provides for the equality of opportunity in matters relating to public employment. The Constitution at the same time gives power to the state to make special provisions for women and children. The inclusion of this provision makes it possible for the state to enact legislature for the welfare of women even if that violates Fundamental Rights in general.

The chapter on Directive Principles apart from directing the state to work for the socio-economic betterment of society provides four women-specific directives:

(i) Men and women equality have the right to an adequate means of livelihood. (Article 39a)

(ii) There is equal pay for equal work for both men and women. (Article 39cd)

(iii) The health and strength of workers men and women and the tender age of children are not abused and that citizens are not forced by econotnic necessity to enter avocations unsuited to their age or strength. (Article 39e)

(iv) Make provision for just and humane conditions of work and maternity relief.

Apart from these negative and positive obligations on the state the Constitution also (after the 42nd Amendment 1976) imposes a fundamental duty on all citizens. "to renounce practices derogatory to the dignity of women" (Article 51A). As mentioned earlier the Constitution of India has also granted universal franchise. Thus women has equality both in right to vote and contest elections.

Besides providing a formal structure of equality through the Constitution. the Government has also been using law as a major instrument for change and development. Right from the time of achievement of Independence, Jawaharlal Nehru in particular, initiated legislature with a view to remove disparities with regard to women. Thus various Acts like Special Marriage Act 1954, the Hindu Marriage Act 1955, the Hindu Minority and Guardianship Act, 1956 the Hindu Adoption and Maintenance Act 1956, Suppression of Immoral Traffic in Women Act 1956 and Dowry Prohibition Act 1961 were enacted.

A major initiative in legislature field was taken in 1970s and 1980s particularly after the submission of report by the Committee on the status of women in India (1975) and emergence of women's movements and organisations.

Some of the important enactments in this regard include the Medical Termination of Pregnancy Act 1971, the Equal Remuneration Act 1976, the Child Marriage Restraint (Amendment) Act 1978 and the Criminal law (Amendment) Act 1983, the Family Courts Act, 1984, The Criminal Law (Second Amendment Act) 1985, The Dowry Prohibition (Amendment) Act 1984. Through these acts the discrimination against women on the grounds of sex in the matter of employment has been removed, the age for marriage for girls has been raised to 18 years, the onus of proof in cases of rape has been shifted to offender and punishment for rape has been made stringent, cruelty to a women by her husband or in-laws has been made punishable. In addition to enactment of laws by the legislature the Judiciary also has been interpreting some existing laws in more favourable ways for women. In a landmark judgement in November 1995 the Supreme Court gave the widow and daughter of a deceased equal right to property left by him. Earlier in two other cases the Supreme Court granted a divorced Hindu Women the right to sell, use for income or dispose in any way she likes land given to her in lieu of maintenance, and gave the widow full ownership rights on the residence given to her as part of maintenance.

Welfare Programmes

The efforts towards women's development and gender justice have not been limited to enactment and favourable interpretation of laws. It has also been recognised and realised that women need access to inputs like education, skill development, management, training and gender sensitisation. For this efforts have been made by the government for inclusion of women's development in Five Year Plans. The approach to women's development in First Plan was included in Community Development Programme. The Third and Fourth Five Year Plans accorded a high priority to education and welfare of women. The Fifth Plan shifted approach from welfare of women to the development of women. In the Sixth Five Year Plan there was a major thrust on health, education and employment of women. A separate department of women and child development was set up at the centre in 1985 to give a distinct identity and provide a nodal point on matters relating to women's development. The Seventh Five Year Plan emphasised on the need to open new avenues of work for women and perceived them as a crucial resources for the development of the country. The Eighth Plan marks a further shift in its approach from Development to Empowerment of Women. Later in the ninth, tenth and eleventh plan the government take bold steps for the improvement regarding empowerment of women in many ways.

The Government of India in 1953 also established a Central Social Welfare Board with a nation-wide programme of grants-in-aid, for promoting welfare and development services for women, children and under privileged groups. The Board has its state counterparts. This programme of the government on the one hand encouraged growth of a large number of women's organisations and on the other hand provided status and activity to many of the erstwhile active women social or political workers. Proliferation of Mahila Mandals is a striking phenomenon of this. Many State governments have also made provisions for free education for girls upto secondary or in some cases even university education. Family planning and welfare programmes are also targeted towards improvement of women.

Inspite of freedom and equality granted to women in terms of participation and contest of elections women's share in elected decision making bodies had remained not only low but in many cases negligible. For this an initiative was taken in 1988 for reservation of seats for women in local self government bodies. 73rd and 74th Constitutional Amendments passed in 1992 have provided for 33 per cent reservation of seats at various levels of Panchayati Raj bodies and Municipalities. Same is now proposed for Parliament and State Legislatures.

India has also been participant in programmes for women's development undertaken at international level and has also signed covenants and declarations at these for it may be pointed here that in the post second world war period there had been consistent efforts in this direction at various international fora, important of these are mentioned below.

In 1945 United Nations adopted Article 8 of the character pledging non-discrimination against women; "in any capacity and under conditions of equality" in all UN bodies. In 1946 was established the Commission on the status of women. This commission has drafted declarations and conventions, monitored and highlighted issues on a spectrum of issues and served as secretariat for major conferences on women issues. In 1967 the Declaration on the Elimination of All Forms of Discrimination Against Women was adopted. It called for recognition of equality for women in fact as well as in law. In 1972 UN General Assembly designated 1975 as the International Women's year to focus on women's issue and in the international Women's year at the first conference on women at Mexico was adopted "World Plan of Action" and also proclaimed first decade for women with the themes of equality, development and peace. The General Assembly in 1976 established voluntary fund for women. In 1985 this was broadened to become UN Development Fund for Women. The second conference on women was held in Copenhagen in 1980 and the Third in Nairobi in 1985. This Conference adopted the forward looking strategies for the Advancement of women to the year 2000. The UN Conference on Environment and Development held in 1992 recognised that women were not only the most adversely affected victims of environmental devastation and social change but also the most potent agents for change. The world conference on Human Rights held in Vienna in 1993 integrated violence against women and other women's human rights issues into the overall UN human rights agenda. m 1994, the international Conference on Population and Development for the first time recognised that gender equity and the empowerment of women through education, health and nutrition were linked to traditional population issues such as family planning. The Fourth World Conference on women in Beijing held in 1995, reviewed and debated 12 critical areas of concern and adopted a new "Platform For Action."? In June 2000 was held Beijing plus five at UN headquarters at New York to stake stock of the progress since Beijing India is a party to all these.

Status of Women

The term status denotes position of an individual in a social system; it also encompass in itself the notions of rights and obligations, of superiority and inferiority, in terms of power authority and grading. In the context of women, status implies :What is her position in a particular sub-system? What are her rights and privileges? How are they determined? Does she have access to power, authority and privileges?

How does her status compare with that of men? How has her position been changed?

In this context Centre for Women's Development studies brings out the evidence of growing inequalities and vulnerabilities of women in all sectors—economic, social demographic, health, nutrition, etc. The process of development, instead of reducing inequalities based on divisions like caste, class, gender "religion and ethnicity have at time strengthened these. Some of these forces have their roots in old obscurantist traditions which are trying to reassert themselves like widow burning, while some represent new sociopolitical forces which seek to avert sectional identities at the cost of women's rights and constitutional goals. The centre brings out the status of women on the basis of four indicators—demographic, literacy, economic and social.

(1) Demographic Declining Sex-ratio. Normal demographic distribution in most countries demonstrates a slightly higher number of women. In India, however, the sex-ratio (number of women per 1000 men) kept declining for well over hundred years with no change in the trend till 1981. According to 1991 census the sex ration was 927 women per 1000 men but the recent survey (2007) showed decline in the lower ration of 880.

Sex ratio is an indicators of health, nutrition and survival status of women and girl children. Several factors contribute to this imbalance.

(a) Bias and discrimination against the girl child and preference for the male child leading to higher female infant mortality due to neglect, malnutrition and inadequate access to health care.

(b) Preference for sons, leading to misuse of amniocentesis (sex determination tests) and selective abortion of female foetuses. Female infanticide is reported to be on the increase in some areas. There

is an expression of systematic bias against girls and misuse of scientific knowledge and tools.

(*c*) Over work and malnutrition and repeated pregnancies among women in poor households leading to higher maternal mortality, morbidity and low expectancy.

(2) Literacy Rates. One of the major changes which has occurred during this century is the importance given to education of women. But inspite of various plans, schemes and programmes education for girls has not showed the desired results. The female literacy rate in 1991 was 39.29 as against 64.13 for males. The literacy rate among men has gone up from 24.95 in 1951 to 64.13 in 1991. While for women it has increased from 7.9 to 39.29 in the same period. The latest female literacy rate in 2002 increased upto 9 percent approximately and the recent trends of government shows another 5 percent increase in the literacy rate. The literacy rates are uniformly low among women in rural areas and particularly among Scheduled Castes and Scheduled Tribes. While the overall literacy rates have improved paradoxically, the number of illiterate women has also increased over the decades due to population growth, non-enrolment of girls and drop-outs from the formal system of education. In absolute terms the number of illiterate women has increased from 153.7 million to 241.7 million. Besides literacy, even if one looks at the progress of education at various levels, not only the rate of progress is very slow, but there is a wide gap between the education of boys and girls at all stages. In school education the enrolment of girls has been increasing, but due to various socio-economic factors the drop-out rate is schooling. As per a Union Education Ministry report, 74 per cent of the girls in the 6-14 age groups quit school before completion of education.

Illiteracy and lack of education among women limits their achievements in the field of employment, training and utilisation of health facilities. It is also negatively related with fertility rates and infant and child mortality rates. According to National Family Health Survey 1992-93 the age of marriage increases sharply with the education of women. Among women age 25-29 the medium age at marriages rises from 15.3 years for illiterate women to 21.7 years for women who have completed high school.

(3) Economy and Employment. Constitutional rights, expansion of economy, industrialisation and urbanisation have all opened various opportunities for women's employment and sectoral balances. The census evidence, however, shows that there are marginal changes in the employment of women by economic sectors. Even these marginal changes suggest that women when compared to men, are lumped into low paying or unpaid work. The number of women employed in the organised sector has increased from 13.7 lakhs in 1962 to 35.7 lakhs in 1989. This represents an increase in the women's share in employment in the organised sector from 1.3 per cent to 13.7 per cent in 1989, which is substantial.

Both National Sample Survey and the Census data show that women make up about 44 per cent of the agricultural wage workers. It has also been observed that almost all rural women are involved to some extent in agriculture. The nature and extent of their involvement varies widely and is also strongly influenced by the economic status, caste and ethnic background of the family. Female agricultural labourers are indeed among the poorest in India, with the lowest wage level and highest unemployment. 61 per cent of them are below poverty line.

Estimates of the average hours of unpaid work done by women outside their homes vary from 6.1 to 7.5 hours per day, with some women working upto 10 hours and more. This, work, though productive, is just not recognised. In the unorganised sector women almost universally get lower wages than men. In the organised sector almost 90 per cent or more are engaged in unskilled or semi-skilled jobs and on that pretext are paid lower wages.

As far as employment rates they are higher for women than for men. It is also found that under employment is also higher amongst women compared to men. The estimated back log of unemployment among women in the year 1990 was 3.96 million. There are about 30 per cent rural households headed by women who bear all the burden of earning and caring for the families and suffer on account of lack of access to land and other property. Yet, the trend of increase in the incidence of open unemployment is stronger in the case of women than men.

It has also been observed that processes of modernisation and economic liberalisation have affected the job opportunities for women. These on the one hand have reduced the jobs and on the other have created necessity of technical and skill qualifications for various jobs which are just not available to most women, more in rural areas.

(4) Social Indicators. The Indian Constitution guarantees legal and social equality to women. There had also been enacted various laws to make the equality in fact. Yet if a close scrutiny of the existing legislation is made, it would be abundantly clear that in social sphere the rights of women are still inferior to those of men. What is more important in practice social behaviour towards women in full of biases.

The old notions of Hindu law of inheritance which discriminate against women, still persist. Only in November 1995 Supreme Court has given a new interpretation to these laws which strengthens the position of women. The Matrimonial law in India varies with every community, there being no uniform civil code. Religion based personal laws in almost all the communities are discriminatory against women in one form or other.

At social behaviour level the attitude and outlook towards women's place and role in society remains almost medieval. The rising incidence of crime and violence against women are manifestations of a deep rooted social malaise and an expansion of a gender ideology which systematically discriminates and oppresses women. The challenges posed by cultural, caste, ethnic, religious and revivalist forces are part of today's social and political reality jeopardising women's right to survival with dignity. Threat and/or use of violence against women has been increasing over the years despite legislative enactments. There is a rising trend in reported rape cases against Scheduled Castes and Scheduled Tribes women. Problems of escalating dowry and violence against women negate the gains from women's participation in the freedom struggle.

The wave of fundamentalist xenophobic upsurges sweeping across the world is also threatening the women's movement as a whole. In India, these have adopted aggressive postures, showing scant regard for the Indian Constitution or the fundamental rights its guarantees. All religious, ethnic or cultural fundamentalists are basically hostile to gender equality whatever the rhetoric they profess. Indu Agnihotri and Venna Muzumdar point out that the fundamentalist/communalist organisations, aware of the ferment in women's minds, are today making a bid to chanelise/harness, the nascent consciousness about women's rights for their own purpose. Taking advantage of women's deep attachment to religion they are today floating new organisations and fronts such as the Hindu Mahila Sammelan and the Durga Vahini, wherein women's role as mothers, progenitors and defenders of the faith etc. are highlighted along with their role in the family.

In matters of property inspite of recent laws and judicial decisions giving women's equal share in the family property very often justice is denied to women by their families. In many instances, the women concerned are illiterate and, therefore, are duped into signing away their legal rights to property. If they are aware of their rights, they are either coerced or emotionally blackmailed into giving up their share in the interests of maintaining harmonious relations with their families. Women are also hampered in their quest for justice by the fact that necessary documents related to inherited land are either not available or withheld from them by local administration or village panchyats.

Thus, in actual practice, inspite of visible improvement in conditions of women in various middle classes, and constitutional guarantees of equality and freedom, the oppression of women and their unequal status within the family continues. In fact, even in the case of middle class working women, employment has not really changed the role and status of women in India. It has only meant adding to the existing roles of women without a corresponding redefinition of the roles of other with whom they interact. The increasing use of birth control and the growth of the small family norm have helped in emancipating women somewhat in this strata though this trend is by no means unambiguous, for nuclear families have made child rearing more onerous and anxiety provoking for the young mother. Various women's organisation participating in the "Global Women's March 2000 Against Poverty and Violence" highlighted the following points were regard to women's position.

- Women to two-thirds of the work, earn one-third of the income, own one-hundredth of the property.
- Hundred per cent of women income goes for family survival as compared to partial contributions of male incomes.
- The percentage of women has never crossed 10 per cent in the Lok Sabha or in State Assemblies. The affirmative action to rectify this in the shape of the Women's Reservation Bill is still pending.

- Violence against women and children is growing as minor girls constitute almost thirty per cent of all victims of sexual assault cases. Conviction rates are below ten per cent in all cases of atrocities against women.

- Female illiteracy is one-third more than male illiteracy. Girl drop-out rates are higher.

As already mentioned, in the twentieth century there had been growing a consistent concern about the women's status and gender justice. One important aspect of this during that period had been emergence of women's studies. These studies have tried to locate the causes for the existing status of women and failures in developmental programmes. The Government of India setup a Committee on the Status of Women (CSW) in 1971. This committee in its report offered some explanations for regressions from the norms of development. Many researchers have also pointed out several reasons for that. Important of these are discussed below.

1. Socialisation. The process of socialisation both of male and female, children makes them grow with the future acceptance of their roles. According to Leela Dube the first importance aspect of socialisation of females in the family, is the preference shown to male children as the permanent members of the family and inheritors of the family name. Even if female children are given affection and made to feel wanted, the message is that daughter's stay in the paternal home is limited. The son is seen as a source of support and often in middle class households, strapped for resources, more is spont on the son's education. Girls are encouraged to play with dolls and house and kitchen games emphasising their nurturant and domestic role. Girls are also taught the notion of service of "sea"—eating left overs, withstanding pain and deprivation and developing tolerance and selfrestraint. Women are so trained for domestic work and repeatedly told that it represents the best that life can offer them that many of them become vigorous advocates of their home and family destiny.

2. Patriarchy. The notion of patriarchy was deep rooted in Indian society through religious commends. Patriarchal values and normative structure established more than two thousand years ago still persist though in a different garb. The hierarchical relations arising out of it are concentrated in the family. An illustration of the importance of the family as the social location of patriarchy in the Indian case is provided by the fact that while the political and economic emancipation of women was never opposed and in fact pursued as an important objective by the Indian national movement, efforts at emancipation in the family sphere were met with bitter opposition.

3. Lack of Funds. There has been an inadequate and lopsided investment in the social service sector of education, health and welfare services, the only development policies of which women were supposed to a target. Neglect of the critical issues of universal elementary education, universal preventive health care and adequate outreach of welfare services had left women as the major victims of planned development. In the process of structural changes as part of globalisation. social order expenditures by government are being further cut. This effects women more.

4. Biased Planning. Urban middle class male bias of planners has lead to neglect of or exclusion of women from the scope of policies and programmes for agricultural, industrial and economic development.

5. Bureaucratic Apathy. The nature of bureaucracy and law enforcing agencies, especially policy continue to be moulded in traditional social and colonial administrative framework. They are thus incapable to design or deliver appropriate programmes for development, especially at grass-roots level. In fact in implementing policies or taking action they express, though not always open, in-built bias against women's emancipation, more so empowerment.

The above shows that in the male dominated family structure, caste and kinship based society, lopsided development and planning designed and implemented by ruling mentality bureaucracy and inadequate resource allocation, the change of treatment of women has been quite inadequate. This non-fulfilment of expectations on the one hand and realisation of limitations of state action by itself has given rise to women's movement for assertion of their identity, acquisition of power and achievement of justice.

Women's Movements

It has already been pointed out that one of the striking developments of the 20th century in many parts of the world is the emergence of women's movement, wherein women have started raising their voice against inequality, patriarchal values and inequalitarian social structure.

In India the social reformers of the nineteenth century was the pioneers in raising discussion on women's issues like child marriage, prohibition of widow remarriage, Purdah, denial of education to women etc. The growth of nationalist movement, particularly the direction, strength and inspiration provided by Gandhiji created a space for women in public life. Combined with the social reform movement created a climate of acceptability for improving women's social status, while the nationalist movement provided an opportunity for women to take part in extra familial and non-caste activity and a new sense of power and self-image.

In terms of feminist movement Pandita Rama Bai, a great Sanskrit scholar can be said to be the founder. Author of the first book on feminism. "The High Caste Hindu Women" she was treated as a notorious outcaste since she married outside her caste. Rama Bai wrote and worked for the emancipation of women. She also established "Seva Sadan's" for women in prisons.

Quite a few women's organisation were started in 1880s. Many of them were dominated by benevolent men reformers and concentrated mainly on providing education and organised debate on social reform topics. With the formation of the All India Women's Conference (AIWC) in 1927, a new trend set up. A production of nationalist ferment, AIWC was inspired, formed and dominated by women. It began with a modest objective of promoting education for women and creating awareness about evil social customs. From the 1930s the AIWC talked in terms of equality between the sexes as a necessary condition of social development. It also played a very important role in creating a favourable climate for new social legislation. During the pre-independence phase various state-level and local organisations were also founded, some by different castes and communities.

A very important aspect of these women's organisations was that its leaders served as role models for women who wanted to take part in activities outside the home. Though women's organisations were not direct wings of political parties, some of the women were members of political parties and took part in political activities.

Women's Movements in Independent India

After independene there was a general expectation that the new government with national movements heritage will bring social justice. Introduction of planning and emphasis on development gave credit to this hope. Most of the women leaders got accommodation into official positions. Nation-building imperative took priority over other debates. All this, to begin with led to fragmentation of women's movement and women's question faded from the public arena. The mainstream women's organisations got engaged in cultural activities, craft classes, beauty shows and philanthropic programnmtes. However, left parties were organising the poor women. They particularly in 1960s, participating actively in anti-price rise movements, the trade union movement, the students movements and various peasant movements.

Soon these activist women started realising that there was a contradiction between their activism on general issues and their passivity in the face of subjugation as women, in both their personal and public life. Also there was growing awareness among a new generation of women that all was not well and Indian women, despite independence, the Constitution, some social and legal reforms, despite increased access to education for women of middle and upper income groups, despite the country's then woman-headed government. Thus in 1970s the women's movement started getting a new shape and rejuvenation. The year 1975, in particular gave impetus to this.

The year 1975 heralded two or three crucial events. It was in the early part of the year that the Committee on Status of Women in India (CSWI) presented a document entitled "Towards Equality" which pointed out some of the glaring inequalities and worsening position of women in Indian society. 1975 was the International Women's year, which was later extended to decade. The decade not only provided an opportunity for drawing attention to women's issues but it also stimulated the growth of new women's groups. Finally it was the year when the Indian Government declared an emergency, when for nearly two years, dissenting women's organisations were unable to function. It is worthwhile to remember that it was during this year for the first time, March 8th was celebrated us International Women's Day, when a huge united left conference of women of left scholars and activists in Trivendrum was convened. There were indications of a new style of women's organisations. During last two decades a number of new autonomous women's groups have emerged.

These groups and organisations provide an alternate pattern of working for women's course. In contrast to earlier, established women's organisations the new groups are ready to protest militantly against injustice in the streets if need be. There autonomous groups have taken up a wide range of issues: rape, alcoholism linked of wife beatings, dowry, violence in the family, the problems of working women, traffic in women, devadasi system, superstition and witch hunting, the torture and harassment of women undertrials and prisoners, women's health, personal laws, the socio-economic and cultural oppression of tribal women.

Of course there are differences in women's group both in terms of ideology and interest and style of functioning. On the basis of ideology the movements and organisations can be said to representing liberal Feminism, Radical Feminism and Socialist Feminism. In terms of interests and style of functioning women's organisations according to Neera Desai can be divided into six categories.

1. Agitational propagandist, consciousness raising groups which may be termed autonomous groups.
2. Grass-roots or mass based organisations like trade unions, agricultural labours organisations, democratic rights groups, tribal organisations etc.
3. Groups that concentrate on providing services, shelter homes etc. to needy women.
4. Women's wings or fronts of the political parties.
5. Professional women's organisations such as doctors, lawyers, scientists, researchers, journalists etc. that seek to agitate against discrimination more often create alternate channels for professional activity.

●●

Index

I

J

K

L

M

N

O

P